ISBN-13: 978-1-59311-246-2
ISBN-10: 1-59311-246-7

Printed in the United States of America

originally published by

MILKEN FAMILY FOUNDATION

LIBRARY OF CONGRESS CATALOG

CARD NUMBER: 98-66845

©1998 LEWIS C. SOLMON

$45.99

contents

list of tables and figures   a

foreword   a2

preface   a6

acknowledgments   a14

chapter1
TECHNOLOGY FOR AMERICAN SCHOOLS   1

chapter2
CAN A FEW PCS MAKE SOCIALISM WORK?   20
Case Study: A Lesson from the Private Sector   35
Case Study: Lessons from the Past: The Television Experiment in Education   38

chapter3
ECONOMIC BENEFITS OF EDUCATION TECHNOLOGY   50
Case Study: GI Joe and the Post-World War II Economy   58

chapter4
THE COST OF EDUCATION TECHNOLOGY   62

chapter5
THE IMPERATIVE OF TEACHER TRAINING   76
Case Study: Phantom Lake Elementary School   87

chapter6
CAN THE PRIVATE SECTOR SOLVE THE PROBLEM?   96

chapter7
CAN THE FEDERAL GOVERNMENT TAKE ON THIS TASK?   120
Telecommunications Act of 1996: A Background and Chronology of Events   127
Case Study: The Interstate Highway System   150

chapter8
STATE FUNDING FOR TECHNOLOGY   162
Case Study: California Education Technology   166
Case Study: Debt Financing in Arizona   171

chapter9
ALLOCATION AND IMPLEMENTATION ISSUES   180

chapter10
CONCLUSION   198
Top 10 Reasons *Not* to Put Technology in the Schools, But...   207
Case Study: When Voices for Education were Heard: Special Education   210

appendix
THE MODEL TO ESTIMATE GAINS IN LABOR MARKET PRODUCTIVITY   224

bibliography   236

endnotes   246

about the authors   266

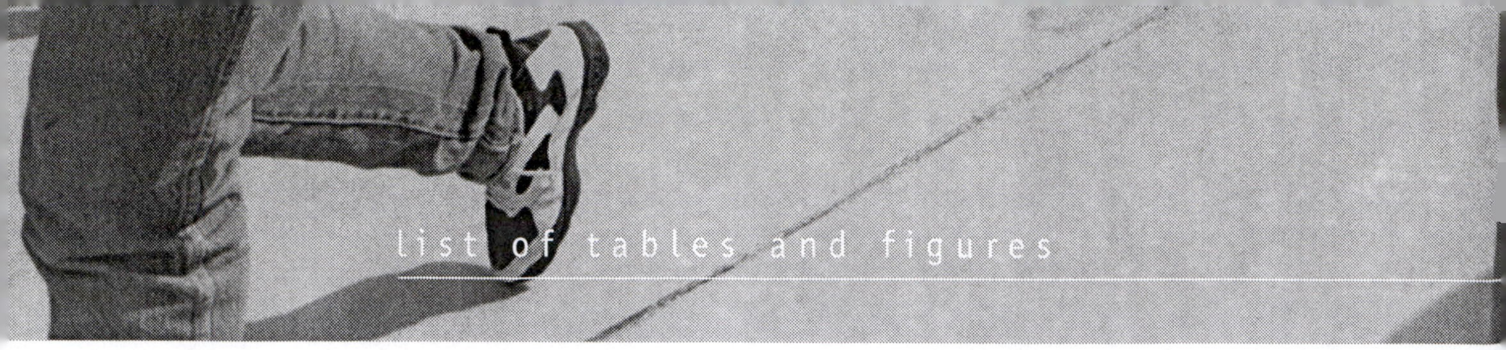

list of tables and figures

Table 1-1
INTERNATIONAL LITERACY RATES 4

Table 1-2
AVERAGE EXPENDITURE PER STUDENT IN THE UNITED STATES, 1950-1996 7

Table 4-1
FULL MODEL: TOTAL FOUR-YEAR PLAN COST 64

Table 4-2
REDUCED COST MODEL 66

Table 4-3
ADJUSTED FULL-MODEL AND ADJUSTED REDUCED COST MODEL 68

Table 4-4
PAST, CURRENT, AND PROPOSED EXPENDITURES ON K-12 EDUCATION TECHNOLOGY 70

Chapter Appendix 4-1
COST ELEMENTS 73

Figure 5-1
CURRICULUM GUIDELINES FOR ACCREDITATION OF EDUCATIONAL COMPUTING AND TECHNOLOGY PROGRAMS 82

Table 6-1
EMPLOYMENT IN HIGH-TECHNOLOGY MANUFACTURING INDUSTRIES 98

Table 6-2
SHARE OF EMPLOYMENT IN HIGH TECHNOLOGY FIRMS RELATIVE TO TOTAL MANUFACTURING 99

Table 7-1
ALLOCATING $4 BILLION FROM A FEDERAL EXCISE TAX TO THE STATES 137

Table 7-2
PUBLIC'S REACTION TO SPENDING $50 BILLION ON TECHNOLOGY 147

Table 7-3
FEDERAL TAXES 147

Table 7-4
STRONGLY FAVORED TAXES 148

Table 7-5
FEDERAL AND STATE MOTOR-FUEL TAX RATES BY YEARS, 1932-1994 160

Figure 7-1
FEDERAL GAS TAX RATE COMPARED TO FEDERAL DEFICIT   161

Table 8-1
POLITICAL AFFILIATIONS   165

Table 8-2
CALCULATION OF TRUE PRINCIPAL FROM ARIZONA BOND PAYMENT SCHEDULE 173

Table 8-3
LOTTERY FUNDS FOR EDUCATION   176

Table 8-4
WHAT ARE YOUR FUNDING PRIORITIES?   178

Table 8-5
PUBLIC FUNDS ALLOCATED TO STADIUMS AND ARENAS   179

Table 10-1
EXPENDITURES FOR SPECIAL EDUCATION   222

Figure 10-1
ESTIMATED TOTAL SPECIAL EDUCATION EXPENDITURES IN 96 $ 223

Figure 10-2
FEDERAL ON-BUDGET FUNDS FOR SPECIAL EDUCATION (1996=100)   223

Table A-1
DISTRIBUTION OF EDUCATIONAL ATTAINMENT BY AGE   229

Table A-2
EDUCATIONAL ATTAINMENT OF CURRENT 0-YEAR-OLDS FROM 16 TO 65   230

Table A-3
EXPECTED MAXIMUM EDUCATIONAL ATTAINMENT (BY AGE 31) OF CURRENT
POPULATION (000) AGED 0-14   231

Table A-4
ESTIMATED AVERAGE ANNUAL LABOR INCOME (96 $) BY AGE AND
EDUCATIONAL ATTAINMENT FOR PEOPLE CURRENTLY 0-14 YEARS OLD   231

Table A-5
AVERAGE ANNUAL LABOR INCOME PREMIUM (96 $) FROM SCHOOLING
USING TECHNOLOGY BY AGE AND EDUCATIONAL ATTAINMENT   233

Table A-6
NET PRESENT VALUE OF LIFETIME EARNINGS PREMIUM FROM COMPUTER
USE FOR THE 1996 POPULATION AGED 0-14 BY MAXIMUM LEVEL OF
EDUCATIONAL ATTAINMENT (96 $000)   234

f o r e w o r d

For the last several years, the Milken Family Foundation has been studying the significant impact education technology can have on student learning. The use of modern information and communications technology properly employed should be commonplace in the life of every school, teacher and student. Needless to say, however, this is not the case. Indeed, the K-12 education industry is the only "knowledge business" still debating the utility of technology. While in 1995, 75 percent of all Fortune 500 companies already were completely networked, by 1997 we estimate that about 10 percent of all instructional rooms even had Internet access. (I might add that in 1996, 80 percent of Fortune 500 companies had Web sites, but in the same year fewer than 4 percent of schools had a Web site.) We shall learn in this book that America's public schools are less than one-third of the way to achieving their technology implementation goals.

That is unfortunate because education technology offers much of the assistance that schools need in order to serve children fairly and well. This is not a hunch. It's what we've observed in schools from coast to coast, and it's what we've concluded from extensive research and personal involvement. It is clear to us that in schools where educators have laid a solid groundwork, technology works well. High standards, linked to assessment and accountability, are essential to that groundwork and, indeed, are unlikely to be realized without the kind of support that telecommunications, multimedia databases and computers supply.

The effective implementation of education technology systems requires: a school-wide plan to integrate these systems across the disciplines, anchored in course content and reflecting the diverse needs of teachers and students; appropriate hardware and software that create the connectivity that links the classroom to the world; the technological curiosity and fluency of the educator; and rigorous professional development and technical support that allow teachers to master technology and harness it to the potential of education.

The Milken Exchange on Education Technology, established by the Foundation in 1997, has identified seven progress indicators that point out the conditions necessary for learning in a digital age. Teacher and learner access to contemporary technologies, communications networks, productivity tools, on-line services, media-based instructional materials, and primary sources of data are all important. So is professional competency in using technology, which requires pre-service or in-service training. Although appropriate learning environment, student attitudes, external support, system capacity and accountability systems are all necessary for the success of a technology plan, let us be clear: Adequate funding is one of the irreducible elements required for technology to be provided and used effectively in schools.

That is why I suggested to Lew Solmon three years ago that he try to determine how much it would cost to fully fund learning technology for all America's public schools, and then, how that money might be found. Lew accepted the challenge as he mobilized the resources of the Milken Institute and Milken Family Foundation to undertake the extensive research and analysis that are reflected in this volume.

The Foundation believes the analysis by Lew Solmon and Kalyani Chirra represents an important advancement in the discussion of the funding, a critical issue of education technology policy. While the Milken Family Foundation does not take formal positions on such specific policy proposals, we want to make valuable research and analysis available to a broad audience.

The authors' comparisons of the potential benefits from school technology to those of the interstate highways and the G.I. Bill lend support for their suggestion for public funding of school technology. Whether or not any opportunity exists for a targeted national sales tax to fund school technology, the idea is provocative and likely to spawn ideas for alternative funding mechanisms. Indeed, the reactions to the authors' tax proposal already have led to an enlightening discussion of the role of business in the efforts to fund education technology.

Education technology is—right now—at that point in its rapid evolution where it still can be designed and directed for the good of children. Information and communications technology properly employed by talented educators has the potential to help restore rigor to children's learning.

Our purpose in publishing The Last Silver Bullet? is to introduce ideas, methods, and people from the world of education technology that we believe will be of real assistance to all those who will utilize learning technology in teaching and learning, and especially to those whose responsibility it is to put in place the policies necessary to make that happen. We intend to help develop an understanding of what education technology is, and of the role educators, business, policymakers, and the public can play in its creative, responsible development.

Lowell Milken

President

Milken Family Foundation

May 20, 1998

Technology is the new literacy.

It should not be considered an advanced

skill, but one of the basics.

preface

Originally this book was meant only to recommend a way to pay for placing modern technology into all of our country's public schools. As we began to formulate that financing plan, however, we realized the task was not as straightforward as we had thought. We were struck by the vehement opposition to our basic premise—the importance of using technology in education—voiced by most relevant constituencies: educators, taxpayers, and especially many businesses.

As we began to talk and write about school technology and how to pay for it, we were invited to present our ideas to various groups interested in education. We were also asked to help some of these groups actually implement technology-funding programs, particularly in California and Nevada.

It's one thing to sit in the ivory tower of academe or a think tank and pontificate about what should be done. It's quite another to actually try to put these pontifications to practical use to get something done. The process of moving from an academic to an advocacy perspective was in itself an education. It's interesting to see how your perspective changes when you read "research" that is less academic and more advocacy or adversarial—how you realize that you can "prove" almost anything with the right anecdotes and selective use of data. You learn a lot about people playing roles, too—believing one thing but forced by their position to say just the opposite.

This book has become much more than a funding plan. It's also now something of a story, or a series of stories, about how technology has or has not progressed in our schools, and why. It is advocacy, sort of a debate with one seat empty. Our belief in the value of modern technology properly implemented in the schools has not wavered—we just realize it's a more complicated case to make than it might seem at first blush. Our original funding plan is still the most logical and our favorite, *but we recognize that logic alone will not make it happen. We have provided the rationale for its use, but we have also suggested alternatives, fallback positions in case our plan never sees the light of day, and ways to supplement the funds our plan could garner.*

This is also a book about interest groups and about people, most of them well meaning, even if not always well informed. They are mostly self-interested groups and individuals—which isn't necessarily bad, especially when their interests coincide with the public good.

We were advised not to call this book The Last Silver Bullet? *because such a title promises too much; we've also been reprimanded for being too pessimistic. We have been urged to hurry to complete the book because it has important things to say; we have also been advised that no one will read it. These contrary reactions typify, in a nutshell, the state of public education in our country today.*

Many proposals for reforming K-12 schools have already been put forward, and since those that have been tried have rarely shown significant positive impacts, reformers have become wary of over-promising. This reluctance is underlined in the case of technology because of K-12's history of failed efforts with earlier technologies and the paucity of scientific evidence (as opposed to anecdotes) about successful introductions of computers in the schools. Our optimism is based upon the clear and significant positive impacts we have seen when modern technology has been properly integrated into the K-12 curriculum, even though this has been accomplished only in a few places so far. The key descriptor here is "properly integrated," which means putting computers into regular classrooms and not just labs, making sure the computers are multimedia ones hooked to the Internet, providing teachers with the proper training and technical support, and supplying teachers and students with state-of-the-art software relevant to the basic skills and advanced content of the academic curriculum. We are optimistic because we know that technology facilitates teaching and learning approaches such as individualized instruction, self-paced learning, cooperative learning, and active involvement of students, all of which enhance students' ability to learn. Finally, we know that the teacher is the sine qua non *of a successful learning experience and that technology not only facilitates teacher professional development, but also frees teachers from the mundane clerical tasks that take away from their time with students.*

So why are we pessimistic? We are not. Rather, we are realistic in recognizing the great expense of implementing school technology properly—at least $50 billion is probably still required. Although over a four-year period that represents only about 5 percent of what schools are currently spending in total each year, no one seems able to find the money. In Nevada, where we estimate the total bill for school technology will be $300 million, $27.5 million was won from the legislature after a major campaign by the governor. In California, over $6 billion is still required, and although the governor there has proposed a $1 billion five-year program to get technology into the state's high schools, for a while finding even the first $100 million was highly problematic. Finally, a program to provide $100 million from state funds for 200 high schools, which must match their grant, was adopted as part of the 1998 budget. In total this amount is $600 per student. The cable industry and most of the computer companies supported the program, but Apple Computers held out in favor of a program for grades 1-6 rather than for high schools. Business claims it will help, but spends more money on "summits" than on school technology—about 6-10 percent of spending for school technology to date has come from the private sector. Public money is shrinking these days and there are many claimants to what is available.

We recognize that funding school technology is a complicated task and will require commitment and participation from virtually all segments of our society: educators, parents, business, and government. They all must understand the urgency of improving our schools, and the role of technology in doing so. They also must understand the benefits that will result from a successful campaign for school technology, not just in the workplace, not just because students will learn more, but for society as a whole. And they must recognize that when society benefits, society should pay. Even Chicago economists (like one of the authors) understand that, despite a general reluctance to have government interfere with our institutions and our lives, some things do call for government involvement. School technology is one of those.

We are not pessimistic, but we recognize that our goal is a difficult one. We have a large funding challenge, and to meet it we have a great responsibility to educate every citizen about our objectives and why they are so important. That is why we have written this book. In fact, a draft was completed a year ago and we have spent the past year updating it, adding new experiences, and working to make it accessible to a broader audience.

In every opinion poll the public expresses despair about the state of our nation's schools. Why, then, don't they want to read about how to help the schools improve? Have they given up on the public schools? Unlikely, since about 90 percent of kids are still attending public schools. Have the changing demographics of our nation caused us to be less concerned with institutions that serve the young? Perhaps, but schools are the source of our future labor force. Perhaps people think that because they attended schools themselves, they don't need to read books to learn what's wrong with schools or how to fix them.

Perhaps the general public is skeptical about being able to have any impact on K-12 education, given the power of the teachers' unions and entrenched bureaucracies, and the seeming indifference of their political representatives. If so, they are very wrong. Today we are in an era of policy making by public opinion poll. If politicians see that voters want technology for the schools, they will advocate it. If voters understand the benefits of technology in the schools, and therefore are willing to pay for it, it can be achieved.

In the chapters that follow, we analogize school technology to earlier massive national efforts to build America's infrastructure—physical capital such as the Interstate Highway System or human capital through the GI Bill. In these efforts, we knew the goals were achievable. We knew how to build highways and how to expand higher education. Before the fact, however, we could only speculate about the magnitude of benefits compared to the very high costs. In the case of our space program, not only were we unable to predict the benefits, we were not even certain that we could land a man on the moon, among other goals, before we actually did it. But we tried, and we succeeded.

In these and other cases, had we waited for conclusive benefit-cost analyses before embarking on the projects, they would never have been started and they would never have paid off. Rather, as a nation we speculated, hoped, and accepted the challenges. We thought "outside the box," as it were.

Let's take another example of thinking creatively and taking seemingly irrational risks. If Bill Gates had been "rational," he would have stayed at Harvard and then taken a job at IBM. Who would pay for a home computer, other than a few nerds who liked to write programs? How in the world could a computer be designed for the nonscientist, the person who had no interest in computers per se?

Compare the benefits of working for IBM to what Gates did from a 1970s perspective. Once considered crazy, Gates is now the richest man in America!

Yet today even those in the technology business, those who know the power of technology and understand its potential, look at the schools and do "inside the box" benefit-cost analyses. Sure, they donate a few computers to the schools—but they look at the business market, the household demand, and the interest in computer games and entertainment, and conclude that the education market is not worth their time. They look at purchasing regulations and textbook-adoption requirements, segmented markets, and the education bureaucracy in general and conclude that a new version of Windows with a few more bells and whistles or a better search engine for the Internet will be more profitable than getting technology for the schools.

Perhaps this book can be viewed as a challenge to the hardware and software titans and to the futurists, all of whom know the potential of technology for the schools and for the students and teachers in them, and for the economy and society that will receive their graduates. Stop being rational economic men like Bill Gates is today. Think outside the box and forget classical benefit-cost analysis, which gives extra weight to certainty and present value.

Let's be like the Bill Gates of the 1970s. Ask what paradigm shift is possible (and how I can help make it a reality) to propel our schools into the 21st century? If hardware costs are the issue, what hardware can we make that will be both affordable and effective for schools? If software is the bottleneck, what is the analogy of Windows 95 for the schools? Let's figure that out and develop it. What must be done to raise the expertise and enthusiasm of educators as we did for families? Everybody talks about school technology, but few do much about it. It would be a costly and risky undertaking—but so was the personal computer.

This book attempts to bridge the gap between understanding and advocacy, between belief and action. It is intended to tell voters, business leaders, and politicians, as well as those educators who remain skeptical, that technology will work, that technology is expensive, that the funds must be found, and that everyone must play a part in reaching these goals.

Our schools are the last holdouts from the modern technology that pervades every other aspect of our lives. Our public schools are also the only institution in our society that serves every child, rich or poor, more or less able, black, brown, yellow, or white. Our schools produce tomorrow's workers and voters. Today's voters must understand the perils of our schools and their clients, and what they can do to help.

Those are the purposes of this book, and the reasons for our optimism.

a c k n o w l e d g m e n t s

This book has been years in the making, and so, has benefited from the contributions of many past and current employees of the Milken Family Foundation and the Milken Institute. Tamara Schiff wrote parts of several chapters, and always has been helpful and supportive. Sang Han helped design and execute the model to estimate labor force productivity increases if students were to use technology in school. Kristen Droege and Cheryl Fagnano allowed us to borrow many of their ideas and experiences. Hollis Harman managed the whole process of pulling various drafts together, finding references, and making everything consistent and understandable, while contributing her own substantive ideas along the way. Librarians Karen Hsiao and Allison DeCamara provided valuable and expert reference services. Research assistance came from Judith Wiederhorn and Noah Hochman. Tim Wolfe made significant contributions after he officially left the Institute, including some significant rewriting. Editorial support came from Beverly Werber and Ron Lewton. The Production Department (Alena St. James, Pamela Cohn, Karen Slobod, Paul Bliese, Della Davidson, and Brenda Koplin) at the Milken Family Foundation designed the book and, under the direction of Lawrence Lesser, saw it through to publication.

We are very fortunate to have had the opportunity to develop our ideas on school technology under the auspices of the foundations of the Milken families. The Milken Family Foundation National Educator Awards program works closely with chief state school officers, and that enabled us to develop close relationships with many of them. Detailed interviews with State Superintendent of Schools Dr. Henry Marockie of West Virginia, and former Commissioner of Education in Kentucky Dr. Thomas Boysen added richness to our analysis. We are fortunate now to have Tom Boysen as a colleague at the Foundation. State Superintendent Delaine Eastin of California invited Lew Solmon to serve on her California Education Technology Task Force where Kalyani Chirra provided some staff support, and that greatly informed us both about the process of and the hazards faced by those trying to effect good policy.

The Foundation's relationships at the gubernatorial level led us to Gaston Caperton when he was governor of West Virginia. Governor Caperton was a pioneer in advocating school technology and he was an early supporter of and contributor to our thinking. Governor Bob Miller invited us to help with school technology planning in Nevada and this taught us a great deal about policy making as well. We are grateful to Richard Whitmore and Joe Rodota of California, Catherine Cunningham of Nevada, and Brenda Williams of West Virginia who have helped us learn about how to work in their states. Richard Gordon, formerly of Indiana Governor Evan Bayh's staff, also gave us valuable insights.

The Foundation is deeply involved with educational practitioners in many states. These involvements helped us meet and learn from Principal Sylvia Hayden, in Phantom Lake. The Milken Institute involves business leaders in all its programs, and one of the most active business participants in recent years has been Bert Roberts, chairman and CEO of MCI. During the National Educator Awards conference in 1996, Lew Solmon argued for a national sales tax to pay for school technology in a debate with Mr. Roberts who wanted to let the private sector try to meet the need. Although there was no clear winner of the debate, we learned a great deal during that and subsequent discussions with Mr. Roberts.

Finally, we would like to thank Lowell Milken for initially asking us to think about how much school technology might cost and how we as a nation could pay for it, and for supporting our wanderings beyond those specific questions. Lowell has added immensely to our thinking about the topics of this book, because as he has pressed forward with his own education about school technology, he has insisted that those around him keep up with him, which is never an easy task. Lowell's clear and original thinking have added to our own understanding.

We are indebted to all those we mentioned, and to many others at the Milken Family Foundation and Milken Institute, but of course none of them should be held responsible for the views that appear in what follows. The views expressed are our own.

—LCS

—KRC

chapter 1

technology for America's schools

> "This 'telephone' has too many shortcomings to be seriously considered as a means of communication. The device is inherently of no value to us."
>
> — WESTERN UNION INTERNAL MEMO, 1876

Over one hundred and twenty years later, Western Union's memo seems myopic to say the least. In the information age, the telephone has become not just essential, but downright pedestrian. Cheap and simple communication is everywhere—except in classrooms—and it's ever adapting to our fast-paced and technological world. More than a decade ago, telephony was augmented by fax machines, voice mail, and e-mail—technologies that are not dependent on two parties having concurrent free time. Thanks to these innovations, even time and schedule constraints, to say nothing of geographical ones, are becoming less important. We can maintain continuous productive exchanges with virtually anyone—except maybe public school teachers.

Our age is remarkable not in its development and application of new technologies, but in the way change, per se, has been integrated into our thinking. The rate of change has been increasing over time, and has produced a culture in which sweeping change is both abundant and expected. Computer power is expected to double every eighteen months, while the number of sites and users on the World Wide Web is expected to double several times each year. We can observe the democratization of data on the Internet, the birth of narrowcasting and the growing income gap between the technologically savvy and the technologically challenged. In short, the writing is on the wall—or on the screen!

Computers will increasingly become our communication tools of choice and the communications we have with each other will become more visual, more information rich, and more interactive. Information will become even more central to our activities and the cyber world will increasingly become the place to get it. Using it will be the focus of many kinds of work and the computer will be *the* information tool. Yet, as powerful and compelling as the changes sweeping society are, there are those in high places who look at computers and the Internet like Western Union executives looked at the telephone.

Academics, policy makers, and business leaders continue to debate whether our schools are in decline or if they are the same as they always were. Although it is important to discuss the various methods of measuring scholastic progress, much of this debate misses the point. Our children are being prepared for life in the information age using a communication system based on "scraping soft white rocks against a hard black rock." The real question is are children learning the skills that they will need to function in our society, find jobs, and meet the needs of our businesses? Education is more important than it has ever been, and the kind of education that is needed is different. If you cannot read well enough to follow instructions, or reason well enough to work with modern equipment, you will not be able to find a decent job. In earlier times those lacking basic education skills could earn a living through physical labor, but such jobs are already becoming scarce and may not exist in the future.

Along with the greater need for basic education, technological skills are also becoming a necessity. Technology is the new literacy. It should not be considered an advanced skill, but one of the basics. Ten years ago, only computer programmers needed to list computer skills on their résumés. Today, "computer skills" is a standard category on the résumés of people applying for jobs from receptionist to accountant. Our entire culture is moving toward technology. Computers and other modern technology are prevalent in homes, offices, and stores, even at the local gas station. Our K-12 schools are probably the only place where technology is not commonplace. Children should be given access to technology when they are young, during the years that learning comes easily.

Technology is the new literacy. It should not be considered an advanced skill, but one of the basics.

As our economy becomes more high-tech, our students, the workforce of our future, need to be better prepared than in the past if we are going to be able to compete globally. Manufacturing and service jobs require more than physical labor. Jerry Jasinowski, president of the National Association of Manufacturers, described today's factories as "Star Wars" sets with skilled employees working together in teams. If you cannot read, perform basic mathematical calculations, think flexibly, and use modern technology, you will not be able to find a job.

Education technology is the tool that schools need to prepare students for the next century. It is not a replacement for fundamental reforms or sweeping overhaul, but unlike other plans debated in ivory towers, this one is viable. Computers and communication technologies have the almost magical power to excite young minds, stimulate ideas, and shake up tired institutions. Technology will let us transform schools from within. We need to provide our students with modern education technology. This book is about why we need it, and how we can get it.

In 1998, more than a decade after the "Nation at Risk" report heralded the onset of the latest public school reform movement, our public schools are still in disarray. The product of that disarray is visible everywhere. Walk into a fast-food restaurant when the computers are down and watch the young clerk try to make change; take note of the composition skills evident in the newspapers and magazines you read; listen to the level of discourse on most radio or television talk shows. By virtually every practical observation, our students are learning less than in the past—and less than we expect of them.

The story is much the same when you look at measures of student achievement. In the mathematics portion of the Third International Mathematics and Science Study (TIMSS), U.S. fourth graders scored above-average in math and science when compared to children in 26 other nations. Unfortunately, students in the U.S. make less progress between the fourth and eighth grades in either science or math than do their counterparts in those 26 other nations—so much so that by eighth grade, we have reverted to a mediocre standing. U.S. eighth graders scored significantly below their counterparts in Singapore, Korea, Japan, the former Soviet Union, and Israel.[1] These results are similar to those of the 1991 International Assessment of Educational Progress. In that test, only in reading did our students perform adequately—on average. Even here we must look deeper than final numbers. The high performance of our nine-year-olds was diminished by that of our fourteen-year-olds. In that age group, U.S. students slipped behind six other countries (Finland, France, Sweden, New Zealand, Hungary, and Hong Kong).[2]

In October 1995, the U.S. Department of Education released the findings of a test of world geography (a part of the National Assessment of Educational Progress); three in ten U.S. students failed to reach the "basic" competency level regarding the world's places and peoples. Fewer than a quarter of the students were deemed "proficient" in the subject, and only 2-4 percent (depending upon grade level) scored in the "advanced" range.[3]

Meanwhile, employers tell us that today's high school graduates are unprepared for the work force. When Trans World Bank recently advertised for six entry-level jobs, it received some 100 responses. However, only one of these many applicants was hired; most applicants lacked basic skills in reading, writing, and arithmetic. Peter Steinfman, a senior vice president of the bank, is quoted as saying, "It's the product of our schools. This is an ongoing concern that many employers have."[4] In 1996, businesses spent $58 billion to train employees. Of that, $6 billion was spent on providing training in basic skills that used to be taught in high school or earlier. Clearly, schools are not producing the workers that businesses need.

Colleges are also finding that their entering freshmen are unprepared. Nearly 90 percent of four-year colleges offered remedial instruction in the 1993-94 academic year, up from 81.4 percent eight years earlier.[5] Even more disturbing, the California State University system, which admits only the top third of the state's high school graduates, recently reported that nearly half of the entering students were not ready to take college-level English and mathematics.[6] What must be the abilities of the middle third or the bottom third of California's high school graduates? Experts have found that many of the remedial students have passed high school math and English classes without gaining a real understanding of the subject matter. In other words, they have failed to attain the basic education required to complete high school, yet their report cards reflect passing grades. Both corporations and colleges are now teaching young adults what they should have learned in grades K-12.

The rate of illiteracy is another indicator that our schools are performing inadequately. The U.S. is not at the top of the literacy rankings of countries (Table 1-1). We are now facing a gradual increase in adult illiteracy. A 1992 survey by the Department of Education estimated that 40-44 million Americans over the age of 16 had only elementary reading and writing skills. This means that one out of every four adults in this country demonstrates skills only at the lowest level of proficiency measured by prose and quantitative proficiencies. In 1992, 90 million adults, about 47 percent of the U.S. population, performed at the two lowest levels of literacy on a national survey.[7] We should be particularly concerned that we are producing students even less prepared than students before them. The literacy proficiencies of young adults assessed in 1992 were somewhat lower, on average, than the proficiencies of young adults who participated in a 1985 literacy survey.[8]

Table 1-1 International Literacy Rates

COUNTRY	1994 GDP PER CAPITA ($)	LITERACY RATE (%)
Luxembourg	29,454	100
Australia	18,646	100
New Zealand	16,248	99
United Kingdom	17,650	99
France	19,201	99
Germany	19,675	99
Japan	20,765	99
Italy	18,681	97
Canada	20,210	97
United States	25,512	97
Spain	13,581	96
Mexico	7,239	90

Source: *Statistical Abstract of the United States,* 1996, Bureau of the Census
World Factbook, 1996, Central Intelligence Agency
(Literacy rates are estimates based on most recent data available for each country.)

Moreover, we see enough irresponsible behavior by our youths, including crime, drug use, and teenage pregnancy, to convince most people that the schools have not moved successfully from the goal of inculcating students with knowledge to the purpose of providing them with the ability to conduct their lives in pro-social ways.

Moreover, we see enough irresponsible behavior by our youths, including crime, drug use, and teenage pregnancy, to convince most people that the schools have not moved successfully from the goal of inculcating students with knowledge to the purpose of providing them with the ability to conduct their lives in pro-social ways.

Education professionals rebut these findings using four main arguments:

1. Test scores are not in fact declining; recent efforts have yielded a slight but steady increase in test scores from 1991 to 1995.
2. America is an egalitarian nation with all students (not just the elite) encouraged to attain the highest educational opportunities, hence our averages are lower when compared to other nations where only the elite are being tested.
3. Schools can't attain their goals because they lack sufficient money.
4. Schools are failing because their resources must often be directed to nonacademic duties; they must now provide all manner of social services, from day care for the children of students to physical protection from weapons and gang warfare.

However, these arguments may not represent the entire picture, as demonstrated individually below.

Are Test Scores on an Upswing?

Many educators contend that test scores indeed are improving. In 1995, the National Center for Education Statistics reported that between 1982 and 1995, the *average* scores on the National Assessment of Educational Progress (NAEP) increased slightly in both mathematics proficiency and in science, while reading scores remained roughly the same.[9]

We believe the slight upswing in, for example, SAT averages may be merely an indication that our students and teachers are becoming more sophisticated in test-taking preparation, not more proficient in skills such as synthesis, analysis, verbal communication, and creative problem-solving skills that are more illustrative of substantive learning and that translate into real-life job proficiency. A typical high school junior sitting down to the SAT has taken fill-in-the-bubble type standardized tests at least every other year since she was in the third grade. In addition, her parents may also have had the wherewithal to enroll her in a three-month Stanley Kaplan SAT Preparation Course.

More important, tests such as the SAT may address and measure only a minute portion of the education necessary for a productive career in the 21st century. High scores on the SAT might indicate that a high school graduate could be an expert at Trivial Pursuit or Jeopardy or that he may be likely to gain a seat on his academic college bowl team. They do not indicate that he has the insight to perceive problems in the workplace, the communications skills to share that insight with superiors, the problem-solving skills to compile a list of possible solutions, the analytical skills to select the most efficient solution, or the organizational skills to carry out the plan and ultimately solve the problem. No SAT score makes such predictions.

Does Education for All Mean Success for Some?
It is also argued that declines in SAT scores are due to the fact that more American children have gained access to more education, and thus we cannot expect the same level of achievement as when only the financially and intellectually elite participated. However, in a letter to our office, David Reisman of Harvard University's Department of Sociology made an interesting observation. He wrote, "The larger number of people taking the SAT (for example) does not explain the decline in test scores at the top. The sharpest decline is in women's verbal scores, where they once were higher than those of the men and are now slightly or (in some cases) considerably lower." The fact that we educate all children in the United States does not mean that we have merely added more students to the bottom tier.

It's Not That We Haven't Tried Buying Better Schools
Another line of thinking blames school failure on profligate waste of resources by the public schools. Certainly, throwing money at public education has not helped it improve. Since 1950, average expenditures per student have increased from $1,747 to $7,371 in 1994 dollars, but no one will claim that this fourfold increase has resulted in a commensurate improvement in student achievement (see Table 1-2). Bureaucracies eat up huge amounts of funds before they are ever seen as directly benefiting students. Educational decisions are made at the federal or, more frequently, the state level, and so are unable to take account of the particular needs of individual schools, classrooms, or students. Money spent on pregnancy counseling, driver education, nutrition, condoms, and cultural diversity curricula is money not spent teaching students basic and advanced academic skills. Special education spending (which is most of the new money since the 1970s) is money not spent on regular or gifted children.

Table 1-2   Average Total Expenditure per Student in Average Daily Attendance in the United States 1950-1997

School Year	Unadjusted Dollars Expenditure ($)	1996-97 Dollars Expenditure ($)
1949-50	260	1,747
1951-52	314	1,901
1953-54	351	2,074
1955-56	387	2,288
1957-58	447	2,490
1959-60	471	2,547
1961-62	517	2,734
1963-64	559	2,879
1965-66	654	3,256
1967-68	786	3,675
1969-70	955	4,017
1970-71	1,049	4,198
1971-72	1,128	4,355
1972-73	1,211	4,494
1973-74	1,364	4,648
1974-75	1,545	4,740
1975-76	1,697	4,863
1976-77	1,816	4,917
1977-78	2,002	5,080
1978-79	2,210	5,127
1979-80	2,491	5,098
1980-81	2,742	5,031
1981-82	2,973	5,021
1982-83	3,203	5,186
1983-84	3,471	5,419
1984-85	3,722	5,592
1985-86	4,020	5,870
1986-87	4,308	6,154
1987-88	4,654	6,384
1988-89	5,109	6,699
1989-90	5,550	6,946
1990-91	5,885	6,983
1991-92	6,075	6,984
1992-93	6,281	7,003
1993-94	6,492	7,055
1994-95*	6,724	7,104
1995-96*	7,024	7,224
1996-97*	7,371	7,371

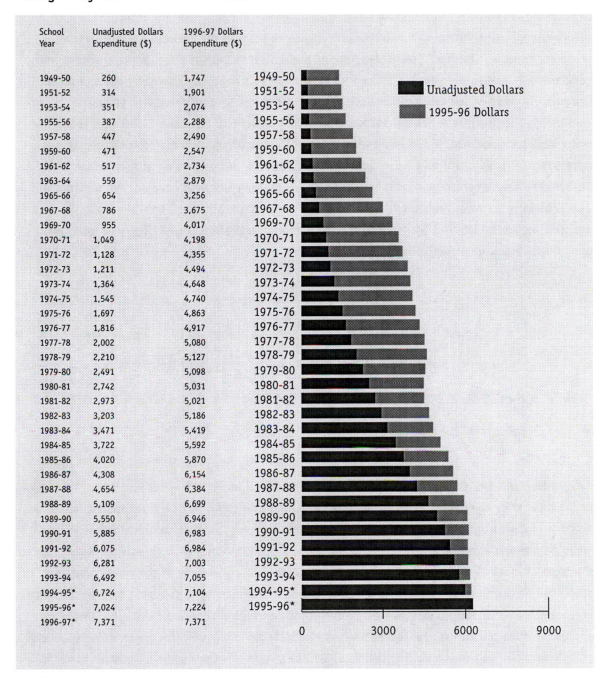

Legend: Unadjusted Dollars; 1995-96 Dollars

* Estimated

Source: U.S. Department of Education, National Center for Education Statistics, Statistics of State School Systems; Revenues and Expenditures for Public Elementary and Secondary Education; Common Core of Data surveys

Teacher and administrator salaries rise unrelated to the demonstrated competency or accomplishments of the recipients. If teachers were paid more, would we attract a higher quality of individuals to teaching, and would those already teaching work harder and stay longer? Or would we just reduce the incentive for the least competent teachers, who have the poorest alternative job prospects to leave teaching? Clearly, teaching is a relatively low-paying occupation—unless you compare days worked per year by teachers to time spent on the job by other workers and unless you add the value of job security (tenure). Yet, even if public sentiment were to support a 25 percent across-the-board raise for all teachers, this would amount to less than $9,000 per teacher—and would cost over $20 billion every year. If, as in this paradigm, average salaries were to rise from $35,934 to $44,918, how many future doctors, lawyers, or business executives would then be attracted to teaching? Occupations that pay more highly than teaching have a wider variance in earnings, with the most productive individuals earning substantially more than the least. In teaching, salaries are determined by years on the job and advanced education credits, with teachers going unrewarded for effectiveness

If teachers were paid more, would we attract a higher quality of individuals to teaching, and would those already teaching work harder and stay longer?...Until we see the establishment of merit pay and the elimination of tenure, teaching will continue to be a tough sell to the best and the brightest.

We question whether simply increasing teachers' salaries will improve America's schools. The decline in the number of competent students selecting teaching as a career is directly proportional to the opening of career opportunities for women. Years ago, we joked that a bright competent woman could be either a nurse or a teacher—and the schools of education got the ones who couldn't stand the sight of blood. The women's movement has enabled greater numbers of the most competent career-oriented women to move from selecting teaching and nursing to selecting business, science, law, medicine, or other professions—professions that pay more and reward merit. Teaching remains a largely female profession, yet the number of women in the profession has grown only by a factor of four over the past 50 years (860,000 to 3,401,848). Although the numbers are much lower in other professions, their rates of increase have been staggering: The number of women employed as physicians increased nearly 20-fold (6,825 to 121,246), while the number of women serving as lawyers and judges increased an amazing 56-fold (3,385 to 190,145).[10] By updating the figures to compare the share of women in the professions, we can see that this long-term trend has continued during the most recent period for which data are available. Between 1983 and 1995, the share of women K-12 teachers rose from 70.9 percent to 74.7 percent, an increase of 3.8 percentage points. However, the share of women lawyers and judges rose from 15.8 percent to 26.2 percent, the share of women professors rose from 36.3 percent to 45.2 percent, and the share of women physicians rose from 15.8 percent to 24.4 percent. Although women are less prevalent in these other fields, the growth in their representation is higher in them than in teaching.[11] The fact is that most self-confident entrepreneurial professionals are attracted more by the potential reward for performance than by job security. Until we see the establishment of merit pay and the elimination of tenure, teaching will continue to be a tough sell to the best and the brightest. Given the power of teachers' unions, these changes are highly unlikely.[12]

More money to schools can also mean smaller class sizes. Will this increase the effectiveness of education? Common sense tells us that very small classes (five or fewer students) are probably more effective than classes with more than 50 students, but very small and very large classes are neither feasible nor realistic. Research indicates that in or around the affordable range (an average of 20 to a high of 40 students), there is little instructional benefit to smaller classes.[13] (Only in one Tennessee experiment did students learn more in classes of 15 than they did in classes of 25.[14]) In the meantime, decreasing class size from the average of 25 to, say, 15 students per class, would cost between $28 and $40 billion more, and these additional costs would accrue every year.

In 1996, the state of California made available $971 million to reduce class size in K-3 classes to 20 students per teacher starting in the 1996-97 academic year. Although it is too early to assess the impact of this policy on student learning, the difficulties in implementing the program were quickly apparent. The required 20,000 new teachers were not immediately available, so many of those hired were given emergency credentials (i.e., permission to teach without formal teacher training) even though the bulk of them had no training in how to teach. Once the staff was hired, many schools had no place to put them as classroom space was at a premium, particularly in inner cities. In some cases libraries and cafeterias were converted, or portable facilities were set up on playgrounds. A huge backlog developed in orders for portable classrooms. Despite all the problems, parents and teachers love the program that enables unprepared teachers to do the same old thing, albeit with smaller groups of kids.

It's Only School. Do We Ask Too Much?
We believe, indeed, that we are asking too much of our schools. Today, the school is expected to do the work formerly handled by religious institutions, recreation facilities, health centers, social service providers, community support networks, and even families themselves.

For example, we know of schools that have decided they must:
- provide before- and after-school child care (sometimes making for 12-14-hour days)

- have their fifth-graders carry around "pretend babies" to help introduce roles and responsibilities of teenage parenting
- translate all "sent-home materials" into four or five different languages so that parents might read them

The cost and energy required to fulfill these "noncognitive" needs sap the entire system. Moreover, schools have not made children generally healthier, less crime prone, more sexually responsible, or—we could argue—even academically proficient. In short, the school cannot replace all social structures.

Admittedly, we cannot change social reality. We now have more single-parent households, more families in which both parents work full time, more students who are themselves parents, and many other societal changes. Perhaps the prime argument for improving education through information technology is that increasing the employability of students moving through the system may be the only way to tackle our social ills.

Has Anything Worked So Far?

Despite all noble attempts, the decade-long reform movement has not been successful. We have tried, somewhere, just about everything that can be tried in a classroom: new curricula, new methods of student assessment, new ways to train teachers, teacher empowerment, site-based management, charter schools, schools within schools, limited "choice" schools, business partnerships, smaller classes, higher expectations for low-achieving students (accelerated learning), higher standards, and much, much more. Those schools that do implement positive changes must contend with a system resistant to any substantive change. Yet, even with isolated success, none of these methods seems to have had a systemic impact. Sadly, there has been little independent evaluation of most experimental efforts in public schools, even within those that have been funded most generously.[15]

What Will Turn Our Schools Around?

Massive systemic changes offering some potential for solving the problems discussed—abolishing teachers' unions, instituting merit pay, putting an end to tenure, and school choice—carry so much political baggage that they surely will not be tried in our lifetimes and possibly not in the lifetimes of our grandchildren. What *will* work? Is there a solution that can be implemented within the current framework that (a) does not threaten teachers and/or destroy public schools and (b) can have a significant positive systemic impact? After several years of reviewing and analyzing school reform, we conclude that America's schools should follow in the footsteps of our businesses and our culture. Technology has brought dramatic changes to the way we live and the way we work. It should now be used to modernize the way we teach and learn.

We propose a massive, national effort—similar to the interstate highway initiative—to bring information technology into every public classroom. We propose catapulting every one of our children into the 21st century. We call our plan "Technology for America's Schools."

First—What Do We Mean by Information Technology?

Information technology is often thought of as computer hardware when, in fact, the concept is much more inclusive. It involves elements that help student learning, the professional development of teachers, and the actual systems management process necessary for a school to function. It can include:

- computers and wiring classrooms to the Internet and to research databases
- fax machines, modems, satellite television, CD-ROMs, laser disks, and the broad use of traditional telephones
- teacher training, the development of appropriate software, and the integration of technology into school curricula
- continued maintenance of all such systems

It's Just Another Tool

Those of us who have not grown up with information technology (and that includes a majority of present-day teachers) sometimes fear the unknown. Computers, databases, and the Internet can seem like alien territory—even worse, the stuff of mere games and entertainment. Lew Solmon himself will admit that he was once resistant to changing his personal work habits. He espoused the concept and theory of new science, but keep his own daily calendar on a computer? Toss out his favorite graph paper and calculator when working on statistics? No way! He learned to get over it, however, and his productivity improved. All of us need to think of information technology as simply another tool, albeit a very powerful one. When Lew was working on his dissertation, he spent months making tedious calculations about the costs of schooling in all 50 states in the 19th century on a Monroe calculator (the old adding machine contraption with a handle and rows of digit keys). Halfway through the process, he accepted a position at Purdue University, where he was given access to a mainframe computer. He finished the second half of his work in a few weeks. If he had had a present-day spreadsheet program, he could have done the whole project in a few days. Today his work probably would not even be considered adequate for a doctoral dissertation— even though it won awards in its own day.

Certainly computer technology offers access and flexibility (and in Lew's case, computing power) to an education profession and an education establishment that has never had either. If Lew could have surfed the Internet and used electronic library catalogues to assist in the literature review for his dissertation, the review would have been both more complete and accomplished in much less time. Such access to people and ideas is accentuated with an immediacy unlike anything education bureaucracies and tradition-bound institutions have ever known. The result is flexibility to think about issues and then to act upon them quickly or over time. Most important, information technology is technology in service to education—opening up the broadest possible horizons in every individual classroom and for every individual student. If you thought typing was an important skill in previous generations, tomorrow's workers will need to have capabilities with computers that are much more than word processing alone.

The Real Benefits of Information Technology

In rural McFadden, Wyoming, Jim House's one-room school has a bell tower that works and a totem pole in the front yard. It appears to be a picturesque throwback to the 1890s—except for the satellite dish out back and the seven computers inside for his five elementary students. The students in this small school check the Internet first thing every morning for word from their "keypals" in Romania and Japan. Later in the typical day, these rural scholars may take an electronic field trip to Gettysburg and watch reenactments of the old battle scene via satellite, while quizzing Civil War experts on the Internet. Some may make an electronic museum visit to the Louvre, or check in with NASA's space link. Sometimes, they even join the ongoing "cyber-exchange" with Mayan researchers in Central America.

A geometry class can use a computer to create enhanced visual representations of three-dimensional objects. Science students can replicate the movement of waves or travel to all points on the globe.

In the hands of a gifted or motivated teacher, information technology becomes a powerful instrument for real learning. For example, a geometry class can use a computer to create enhanced visual representations of three-dimensional objects. Science students can replicate the movement of waves or travel to all points on the globe and interact with peers, scientists, artists, and scholars from every culture. The whole of human experience is available simply by tapping into computerized research databases. Through the use of computer modems, a teacher can edit and critique a student's essay while both student (and parents) observe and respond. Computer Assisted Instruction (CAI) can be used for rote learning—individualizing the difficulty of the task for a student—and at the next desk, it can present another student with complex problem-solving tasks. Sophisticated learning software, often similar to computer games, can motivate and maintain a student's interest for hours while presenting educational material. Thus the amount of time students spend on-task is increased, and this leads to greater learning.[16]

CD-ROM and laser disks add to the computer's capacity to store information and provide expanded resources for both the teacher and the student. Increased verbalization, discussion, and collaborative learning are also outcomes of the environment created by such interactive technology, thus motivating students to communicate in order to complete group projects.[17]

Even the more traditional forms of audiovisual equipment are presently unavailable in many classrooms. Films, videotapes, audiocassettes, video cameras, and tape recorders allow expanded exposure to resources and materials—and exposure through a medium better suited to some individual learners. In addition, students with access to cameras and recorders are able to *contribute* to the store of knowledge, record their own work and progress for assessment purposes, and demonstrate their capabilities to a larger and more meaningful audience.

At Alexandria Avenue Elementary School in Los Angeles, the *Puma Press* is the school newspaper. It's written, edited, printed, sold, and distributed by the students. Grade school children with an idea for an article, a regular column, or a piece of creative fiction submit their work to the faculty sponsor via the school's local area network (LAN). Student photographers scan in their photos for inclusion in the newspaper, and other students keep database records of subscriptions. Danielle, a fourth-grader, writes a regular "Star Trek" column, updating readers on trivia and information about the series and the many offshoot shows. Her wide audience makes her even more conscientious about the quality of her work.

Finally, network technology (the Internet) provides access to otherwise inaccessible materials and people, reduces teacher isolation in the classroom, exposes children to a wider variety of perspectives, and allows for communication outside the confines of time and distance. Students demonstrate increased interest in learning and greater motivation when allowed to use the modern technology and thus connect with an adult workplace. For example, access to real-world information such as weather data and real-time pictures from the Hubble telescope cuts down on questions such as, "What's the use of doing this?"

Alda Hanna teaches fifth grade in one of the poorest districts in Pennsylvania. Driven by the belief that her students "are just as talented, bright, and valuable as anyone else's," Hanna has acquired a wealth of technology through her own efforts at grant writing. Through their computers, her students access information from all over the world. Because of their curiosities at what they were finding, she has completely reworked her curriculum to focus on the sciences. Amidst her exhausting work to provide her students with knowledge and tools to enable them to compete with students from more affluent schools, Hanna has taught these children to be excited about education. In her words, "We dance almost every day, and we just have a lot of fun learning."

Technology offers solutions to education reform that money alone simply cannot and will not supply. It can give teachers the means to reach multiple goals, including more expert pedagogy, greater professionalism, higher incomes, and greater job satisfaction. We all understand that computers can greatly simplify tasks such as attendance and grade keeping, but these detailed journals also validate the grade by providing immediate and ongoing feedback to the students.

Technology can empower creative teachers, offering them many new opportunities to reach a broader range of students. For example, one experienced Spanish teacher at Blackstock Junior High, Oxnard, California, almost left the profession when he faced dragging out flashcards one more time for his Spanish 1 vocabulary review. Then he discovered a way to use technology to spice up his classroom drudgery. He designed his own CD-ROM and even rented a helicopter to fly over the town taking pictures of objects in the vocabulary that related to the community. His "creation" was so successful at teaching basic vocabulary that school administrators decided to produce and market the software to other schools.

Alda Hanna teaches fifth grade in one of the poorest districts in Pennsylvania. Driven by the belief that her students "are just as talented, bright, and valuable as anyone else's," Hanna has acquired a wealth of technology through her own efforts at grant writing. Through their computers, her students access information from all over the world.

Studies reveal that student attitudes, creativity, and learning can accelerate when technology is placed in a classroom. For example, one fifth-grade class in Minnesota theorized about probability while playing a coin-toss game; but in order to test their ideas they needed results from hundreds of thousands of tosses. They put instructions for their game on an Internet bulletin board called a Web page, and asked everyone reading it to play the game and send them the results. Not only did they receive information to further test their mathematical theories but they also were introduced to students and adults from New York City; Flagstaff, Arizona; Miami, Florida; St. Louis, Missouri; Portland, Oregon; and other cities around the country.

Technology also has the capacity to support all the changes presently endorsed within the education reform movement, including ideas such as:
- cooperative learning experiences
- heterogeneous grouping of students
- long-term, cross-curricular projects related to real-life events
- opportunities for students to work concurrently with professional experts struggling with similar problems

Technology allows teachers to be more stimulated on the job, and in its capacity as a versatile tool, it promises greater career mobility. Technology-related job skills increase teachers' professional status and self-respect.

Finally, and perhaps most important, technology can expedite a shift in the role of the teacher, making him or her a partner in student learning.

Teachers as Learning Partners

In the hands of educators lacking basic skills, knowledge, and motivation to inspire learning, the tools of information technology can do no more to solve the problems of education than can books, pencils, and chalkboards. Used properly, they can facilitate an active partnership between teacher and student. This learning partnership still requires that teachers come to class with basic job skills, including:

- complex working knowledge of the cognitive and social development of children
- appreciation for how these developmental needs translate into classroom behavior and practice
- skill in classroom management
- ability to function within the school environment
- expertise in the subject being taught, coupled with ability to communicate that knowledge

However, once the basics are in place, information technology allows the teacher to expand beyond the traditional roles of lecturer, classroom manager, activity coordinator, helper, and friend. In this way, technology allows the teacher to evolve from a *bestower of knowledge* to a *facilitator of learning*. It allows him or her to teach concepts and thinking skills while providing one-on-one interaction with every student. The teacher becomes a coach—showing students "how to learn" rather than merely holding them responsible for "receiving information."

A third-grade class at the Alexandria Avenue Elementary School was conducting a class project at the Los Angeles city zoo. Each student first researched an individual animal with the use of CD-ROM encyclopedias, a *National Geographic* laser disc collection, a network connection with the local public library system, and the Internet. In the next phase of the project, students studied the physical facilities of the zoo; and then, using the space and budgetary confines of the facility, they created a clay model for the ideal environment for each animal. No teacher, short of Joan Embry, could provide these students with the necessary information about all 32 species within the facility —no school librarian could retrieve that many books on so many different animals; however, with the most basic technological research tools, these nine-year-olds can conduct their own research. The teacher is then free to teach organizational skills, cooperative work techniques, synthesis and analysis, and all the higher-order thinking skills required for this complex task.

In this role of facilitator of learning, teachers must have access to a much wider variety of resources than is currently available to them. The curriculum can then expand beyond the time and space boundaries inherent in assigned textbooks. As students begin to do work reflecting their own interests and ideas, lesson plans expand into even wider areas, and so having access to libraries, museums, universities, individuals within other cultures, and so forth, becomes essential.

Teaching has always been an isolated occupation. Teachers spend six to eight hours a day in a room with children and, generally, no other adults. Network technology can enhance communication and collaboration, allowing teachers to form relationships with peers outside the classroom for reflective discussion or social support. Just as technology presents opportunities for interaction, it also allows for professional development—either through on-line in-service training courses or through contact with experts and professionals in other fields.

Jake Chaput in Poughkeepsie, New York, teaches fifth grade during the day but at night, in the comfort of his own home, he is taking an on-line university-level education course. He can log on and talk with other teachers throughout the country who have taught the same lesson that day in their own classrooms. With the assistance of the university professor who monitors the exchange, teachers share tips and techniques that help each to become better instructors. Best of all, Jake and his classmates receive this professional development without the hassle of driving to the university once a week or without sacrificing their Saturday afternoons with their own families.

Most teachers are drawn to teaching because of its inherent and deep emotional rewards. Although this element remains extremely important, it is not enough to keep a bright and capable mind from considering the exciting possibilities available in other fields. The resultant "burnout" is an all too common problem for teachers—and for our entire system of education. Technology offers a means for infusing some challenge and excitement into the job. It can affect teachers in much the same way it affects students: making the work more intellectually stimulating and more professional.

Pamela Burish teaches third grade at the Eakin School, in Nashville, Tennessee. Burish developed a unit for her classroom titled, "Hobo Geography—The World on a Stick," during which her students explore the geography, cultures, and ecology of the continents through hands-on activities. Students use CD-ROM programs and other computer-based resources, as well as books and artifacts, to research various world communities. "The old paradigm of 'sage of the stage' didn't work effectively with technology," says Burish. "My students taught me to be a 'guide at their side' and to learn just as much from them as they were learning from me...There is never a dull moment in my classroom."

The availability of technology will separate teachers who are willing to accept change (and grow with it) from those who are not willing to do so. To the extent that the system seeks to reward innovation by teachers, creative use of technology could be an important measuring rod of such innovation.

When the teacher embraces information technology, the school day becomes one filled with independent learning, problem solving, and active participation. Key to this classroom revolution is ongoing technology staff development. In Chapter 5 we will explore teacher training in more depth, but it's important to note here that this element of the technological revolution will probably cost more than buying, maintaining, and upgrading equipment and software.

Teaching is one of the few professions in which there are few income-supplementing consulting opportunities. As the examples above demonstrate, technology enables creative teachers to package their ideas and disseminate them to colleagues around the world. Thus, there evolve subtle opportunities for teachers who use technology most effectively to sell their new products and be paid for their creativity. It is merit pay through the back door.

Students as Active Participants
As the teacher's role changes, the role of the student changes also. Information technology can create learning experiences that require students to be active, rather than passive, learners. In the technology-rich classroom, students have opportunities to contribute to the learning experiences of others, share ideas, explore possibilities, ask "Why?" and "What if?" more often, and contribute their observations and conclusions. More dramatic, perhaps, is that with on-line databases, students can access information—not just when the school library is open, but at any time and using any database around the world. Technology literally extends the school day and the learning partnership far beyond its current parameters.

Access to more sources helps students develop skills in discovering and processing information. And rather than all students in a class having access to the same, limited information, each can bring different perspectives to classroom discussions. Finally, since an integral goal of the school experience is to enable students to form respectful and warm emotional ties with capable high-functioning adults, network technology expands the opportunities for such communication.

How Can Technology Help the Very Young Child?
Sometimes it's difficult to imagine how very young children and their teachers can take advantage of informational technology. Here, too, however, the possibilities seem limitless. For example, among the many concepts five-year-olds learn in kindergarten is prereading skills. These skills include an understanding of the concept of symbolic language—the idea that letters on paper (or

computer screen) are "written talk" and available in many languages. One CD-ROM program by Broderbund, called "Just Grandma and Me," allows children to take part in an interactive story book. The pages from a book are brought to life on the computer, for when a child clicks on various parts of the picture, he brings the book to life, expanding the details of the story and illustration. Each child controls the turning of pages, so he can go back to the beginning to review something, or can go straight through the entire story. This child receives many of the benefits of being read a story, but does not require the individual time and attention of the classroom teacher.

In another activity, kindergartners can learn to recognize the shapes and sounds of the letters of the alphabet. Young children learn best when they utilize a variety of senses to experience material in a concrete manner. This becomes difficult when introducing the abstract notion of symbolic language. With a multimedia alphabet curriculum, children are introduced to a letter per week in a variety of ways. During the week of the letter "A," for example, the program includes a video cartoon of the letter "A" teaching children a song about "Adam the anteater eating apples in the attic," so that children hear and sing the short "a" sound. A large, inflatable letter "A" is set out in the room for the children to play with, climb on, and manipulate so that they learn the shape of the letter by touch. A computer program allows the children to participate in five different activities that help differentiate the letter "A" from other letters and reinforce the sound of "A" in words through songs, rhymes, and games. Then, the classroom teacher supplies apples, avocados, and apricots for a cooking activity that allows children to use their senses of smell and taste in conjunction with the lesson. With this simple curriculum, the teacher knows that each child can be involved in the learning of letters throughout the day, and across many different activities, rather than isolating the learning experience to "circle time" and desk work.

Computer and video technology is integral to the daily lives of both younger and older students' experiences outside the classroom; and, as illustrated earlier in this chapter, when schools utilize this same technology in the classroom, students perceive the process as being more relevant. In this way, school is more likely to capture a student's attention and imagination, sparking his enthusiasm for learning. In one such example, a sixth grader in Minnesota, using the Internet for a report about World War II, made contact with a woman who had lived in Germany during the Holocaust. She gave him a firsthand account of her family's experiences. This moment in history became real and alive to a child who was otherwise removed from it by both space and time.

Finally, technology can expand the intellectual, emotional, and developmental horizons for children with special learning problems and those who come from deprived home environments. Because technology cannot distinguish among students based on gender, race, ability, experience, or reputation, it can function free of bias and provide all children with objective feedback, information, and evaluation. Moreover, students with physical disabilities may have a difficult time holding a book, turning pages, or writing with a pencil. Computers, which often require just the touch of a button to advance through text, write, or operate a laser disk, can accommodate many such students. Thus, providing information technology for every schoolchild would truly fulfill our national goal of equal educational opportunity.

Parents as Learning Partners

Technology also offers the potential for connecting the school with the student's home. In the most literal sense, teacher-parent communication can be enhanced. Parents can attend "electronic" teacher-parent conferences at any convenient time, even if they are not available during working hours. Through electronic communication (e-mail), they also can be kept up to date regarding their children's assignments and curriculum, thus involving them more thoroughly in the work of the school. The fact that greater parental involvement leads to more positive student outcomes is a point upon which every educator can agree. We will address specific ways in which parents can become involved in this partnership in several subsequent chapters.

Benefits to Our National Economy

There can be no equivocation of the following statement: Technology will be a part of the job market challenging every student in school today. If these students are taught in technology-rich classrooms, the transition to employment will be more efficient and more successful than if these same students must be retrained by business and industry. This concept is the focus of Chapter 3, "Economic Benefits of Education Technology," a hypothetical benefit-cost analysis comparing the value gained from the increased productivity of a technology-wise labor force to the cost of putting technology in our nation's public schools. As you will see, we believe the returns of doing so are an astonishing 400-plus percent.

The United States was the first and only country to espouse and facilitate the education of its citizens. We've taken pride in an accomplishment never seen before in human history. This first chapter should awaken us to the fact that we've slipped—and continue to slip—from preeminence, but this is not a book about the failure of our endeavor. In the chapters that follow, you will find detailed, practical ways we can put information technology in every classroom and thus restore our position of educational and economic leadership.

can a
few pcs
make
socialism
work?

"If I had thought about it, I wouldn't have done the experiment. The literature was full of examples that said you can't do this."

— SPENCER SILVER ON THE WORK THAT LED TO THE UNIQUE ADHESIVES FOR 3M "POST-IT" NOTEPADS

Since the early seventies, it has been clear that the computer has a rare power to fire a child's imagination. Somehow, this tool can captivate a young mind in a way usually associated with another magical box—television. In front of a computer, however, children are less likely to be eating, and more likely to be sitting at rapt attention, pondering strategies, formulating plans, or considering the relationship between objects. In short, thinking—and usually quite fast.

You might ask, however, are we talking about games or learning? Well, both! One of the authors was first exposed to computer learning in the early 1980s, watching five children sitting around an Atari 800 home computer. One boy sat typing commands into a text-based game called "Adventure," which confronted the kids with one puzzle after another as they explored an imaginary world. The four children who were not typing read along as the computer printed information across the screen. In fact, they seemed to naturally take turns reading aloud. As they played, they would shout out ideas, and debate possible courses of action. One would suggest, "Pick up the bottle and drink." Another would admonish, "No! Look in it first." At one point the small band of imaginary travelers was attacked by "chiggers." None of the kids knew what a chigger was, but this was only a minor problem, because they were already in the habit of consulting a dictionary every few moves. Half an hour later, as the party entered a tomb, I watched a proud little girl sound out "sarcophagus" before any of the other kids could decipher the word.

Were they playing a game? Sure. Were they learning? Unquestionably! It's unfortunate that many of us feel a need to draw a line between playing and learning. Play, we have been taught, is something children do voluntarily because it's fun, whereas learning is something compulsory, even unpleasant. There is no more false or regrettable dichotomy in education. Unfortunate also is the inclination to interpret these words as a call to turn education into entertainment. As a syntactic matter the word "entertainment" is far too passive and we will try to avoid it. A teacher with flair and glitzy presentations is great but not necessarily more interactive than any other talking head. Conceiving of education technology as nothing but glitz is a dangerous pitfall. What it's really about is interaction. Computers do not simply offer amusing presentations, they demand active participation.

All children are explorers and investigators. Yet too often we fail to build on children's natural curiosity. At an early age, children are demoted from the position of principal investigator to the objects of instruction. Adults spend less time facilitating learning and more time directing, confining, and controlling it. "Younger children," says Seymour Papert, "are more completely engrossed in a world within the range of immediate exploration."[18] At a later age, unless, as too often happens, the spirit of inquiry has been extinguished, they will be able to explore beyond touch and sight. Papert contends that it is technology which will allow us to smooth the transition between the exploring of childhood and the more formal learning of adulthood—perhaps even to blur the distinction between the two. The computer can offer children an "extended immediacy"—a chance to personally explore the world.

Play, we have been taught, is something children do voluntarily because it's fun, whereas learning is something compulsory, even unpleasant.

One of us taught a four-year-old boy named Nick how to search the Internet, using the Yahoo Search Engine, soon after his parents purchased a computer. Nick had mastered the alphabet, but could not yet read. The next day he asked his mother how to spell "blackbird," so he could search the Internet for information on the supersonic aircraft. When Nick found the site, he found a few great pictures and a whole lot of words he couldn't read. Before the experience learning to read was a low priority, but afterward Nick was determined. The computer presented to Nick the opportunity to explore and get answers to his questions without having information filtered through an adult. Nick began reading soon after this discovery—and enjoying reading because it was a way to satisfy his curiosity. This same curiosity is so common to preschool children but often fades as they grow older. Soon after this, it was a globe that caught Nick's attention. He noticed a seam across the middle labeled "The Equator." His fingers felt the large bump labeled "Mt. Everest." As the Earth's features piqued Nick's curiosity, he typed their names into his new window on the world. This time he didn't have to ask an adult how to spell "Mt. Everest." Within minutes he was sharing with his mom all his new insights into the tallest mountain in the world. A few days later Nick's kindergarten teacher asked if anyone knew what the equator was. Nick not only answered the question but also shared his personal experience examining pictures of equatorial jungles and reading about the hot, humid climate.

It's fair, of course, to ask whether Nick's experience with the computer is necessarily a story about technology. Wouldn't a good encyclopedia have provided him with a wealth of information and pictures? An alphabetical index is at least as intuitive as a search engine on the Worldwide Web. Indeed, it is easy to find innumerable success stories in education that have nothing at all to do with high tech hardware.

Our response to skeptics is that it is true: Nick could have found a great deal of information in an encyclopedia. But he did not! Though academic investigation is just beginning to document the educational value of technology, years of less formal observation support the conclusion that kids are drawn to technology. Mastering and controlling the computer has its own appeal to children, quite independent of the problems the machine is being used to address. Somehow, young children simply do not find the prospect of mastering a shelf full of books as compelling as the interactivity of a computer. Interacting with the machine provides a sense of power and control that other educational tools lack.

One of the advantages of a connected computer is the sheer vastness of the world it opens up. No encyclopedia can offer the depth of hundreds of thousands of server computers around the world acting in concert. In five minutes on the Internet, we were able to find several dozen pictures of Mt. Everest. We found views of camps, satellite images, and expedition maps from base camp at 17,700 feet past the Khumbu Icefall and on to the 29,028-foot summit. There were records of all attempts at the summit, death tolls, pictures of the climbers, videos from recent expeditions, discussions of the physiological effects of the thin air, inventories of the gear, descriptions of climbers' clothing, and on and on. In fact, the Everest Expedition of 1997 was cybercast in real-time. Our encyclopedia, by contrast, follows a rather dry blurb on Everest with a discussion of the Everglades, and doesn't even offer us a chance to e-mail questions to the climbers, or to cut and paste pictures into a word processor. This flexible nonlinear quality also contributes to the magic of the computer.

As a child explores on a computer, she is truly exploring. A discussion of Mt. Everest can logically lead to other mountains, life in Tibet, the agony of frostbite, or to density of the atmosphere. Furthermore, the Internet is not about what happened in the past; it's about what's happening right now. If a child watches the Pathfinder landing on Mars and then runs to his encyclopedia, he is unlikely to find anything more recent than Viking II's 1976 mission. We suspect, however, that it is more than the vastness of the Internet or the currency of the information available in the cyber-world that accounts for the computer's appeal. It is the thrill of controlling a powerful machine or hundreds of machines around the world. It's the power to blaze a new and entirely personal trail. The computer rewards creativity and imagination as much as formal learning, and thus puts children on a much more even footing with adults. Even before the Internet, we could see the computer as a powerful equalizer. The computer is a place for students to show their discoveries, not just to teachers, but to peers. Computers afford children the rare opportunity to teach the teacher and, perhaps more important, the opportunity to win peer approval for intellectual excellence.

Indeed the computer world is such a meritocracy, and is so well tuned to the talents of a young mind that children who master the machine frequently find themselves interacting with adults as peers. Computer experience not only cultivates the real skills children will need in the working world, but also teaches kids that learning and being smart will reap rewards, not just in the distant future but in the present.

Children know that the computer is theirs—part of their future—and they know when school is old-think and out-of-touch. They know that the computer arena is one in which the young have an advantage over the old and that companies like Microsoft, Apple, and Netscape were the products of brash young kids. It should hardly surprise us that young people are often unresponsive to traditional education—that children of the 1990s are more difficult to impress than children of the 1890s. Nor is it just that high tech entertainment has dulled kids' senses. Growing up in the information age has given today's children a well-honed sense of the anachronistic. It may be difficult to swallow, but the next time a smartaleck youngster declares the card catalog a stupid waste of time, we might all do well to consider his point.

So where does this all get us? Kids like computers, smartalecks hate the card catalog and, given the right situation, most human beings enjoy learning, but does this somehow solve the nation's educational ills? In a word, no! The worth of a classroom computer depends critically on its implementation. No reform can be considered independent of the larger educational system and no innovation can be evaluated until we know what it is meant to achieve. In our view the enthusiasm for education technology is dulled by a mismatch between popular hype and the reality of implementation and evaluation.

Consider a 1995 *Los Angeles Times* article that begins, "Picture a large, comfortable room where teachers enthusiastically discuss the Los Angeles River as a real-world laboratory for lessons in biology, botany, and the environment. Students are there too, sharing data they've gathered on the river's plants and animals. Now think of all this taking place in cyberspace, a few keystrokes away from the computer screens of hundreds or even thousands of teachers, students, and parents."[19] In his book, *The Road Ahead,* billionaire Bill Gates asks us to "Think of a high school art teacher using a digital white board to display a high quality digital reproduction of Seurat's *Bathing at Asnières,* which shows young men relaxing on the bank of the Seine River in the 1800s..."[20] He goes on to explain that the white board will pronounce the name of the painting in French and display a map of the area around Paris. From there, the teacher can transition into topics as diverse as Impressionism, the Industrial Revolution, or color theory. In a similar spirit, a Microsoft press release recounts the tail of Jacobo, a Harlem fifth-grader who was not interested in school and didn't do his homework. "Then," says the article, "Jacobo got a laptop computer to use...Now [he] does all of his homework and classwork, loves working in groups, and goes out of his way to be helpful to other students."[21] Or, recall our story of Nick's personal journey along the steamy equator.

Computers can be exciting, and the press doesn't want us to forget it. Indeed, they may very well be one of the great forces in the rebirth and reinvigoration of education. Too often, however, the public and the policy makers get so wrapped up in gee-whiz musings that all successes seem pale and unsatisfying. Frequently, the education establishment is underwhelmed as well, but for a different reason. The bureaucracy evaluates innovations, not in terms of their potential to recast traditional pedagogy, but in terms of their ability to bolster traditional pedagogy. The result is that the education technology movement is cursed with a severe mismatch between its promises, expectations, and evaluation methodology.

One of the advantages of a connected computer is the sheer vastness of the world it opens up. No encyclopedia can offer the depth of hundreds of thousands of server computers around the world acting in concert.

Though we clearly favor technology as an element in the larger transformation of education, as a practical matter we think most implementation will be incremental. In the long term, one of the keys to the successful wiring of our schools is keeping our expectations in context and realizing that some teachers and some schools will adopt technology slowly and in small ways, while others will adopt it in bold and daring ways. Many teachers will be interested but will need training, others may never make technology an integral part of their teaching styles. None of this concerns us as much as the idea that traditional schools and traditional researchers will continue to evaluate technology's performance by very traditional standards. As a result, they often fail to apprehend the full significance of truly innovative programs. If we were to test Nick a few months after learning to navigate the Internet, would we find that his basic math skills had improved? Probably not. Would we find improved writing skills? Very probably. But whether we found improvement by these traditional measures or not, we'd likely miss much of the impact of his improved grasp of geography, comfort with information technology, his new passion for learning, or the pleasure he takes in being able to teach his parents and teacher new things. For this reason much of the research that has been done to date only gets at a small aspect of education technology's benefits. Several studies support the conclusion that even very commonplace implementations result in improved basic skills. They even support the idea that computers contribute to a more positive attitude toward school and classwork. But the majority of studies have been poorly designed and only show technology's more sweeping benefits. Let us review the research.

Research Findings

It is instructive to note that education technology has been a focus of study by academic researchers for nearly 90 years and has an established history of exploring the impact of passive media.[22] The experts we refer to in this section are all highly regarded scholars from academe or research organizations. Early research focused primarily on the behavioral changes that might occur in students when exposed to media in the classroom. Researchers believed that media instruction allowed for control of learning behaviors.[23] This "behavioral" research stemmed from social-psychological perspectives that concentrated on the effects of mass media on audiences.[24] It was known as "communication effects" research and examined the changes in behavior that occurred after the transmission of a media message.

During the late 1950s and into the 1960s the preponderance of education technology research was conducted to evaluate the influence of television and radio on learning. Much of this research continued to fall under the behavioral model. Additional early research compared the influence of other media, such as motion pictures, slides and stereographs, on education. We might call this the heyday of the entertainment paradigm. The communications effect researchers were chiefly interested in technology for its potential as an attention grabber. Computer technology was still too young, and the PC too many years away for these researchers to fathom the interactive potential of education technology. Furthermore, the notion that technology might become a force for educational diversity and individualism was also quite foreign. More often than not, television was praised for its power to standardize—its potential to control educational content.

Current review of early media studies has found that researchers tended to ask inappropriate questions. Studies focused on which medium most impacted students without regard to other confounding influences such as the teaching methods being used.[25] As a result, early media research is problematic.[26] By the beginning of the 1970s, media research shifted from the behavior-theory model to a cognitive-based paradigm.[27] Within this new model, learning is defined as "a process in which the learner is actively engaged integrating new knowledge with old knowledge."[28] This new paradigm provided a more appropriate method of evaluating the benefits for "interaction" with technology.

During the 1980s, the computer produced more excitement in elementary and secondary education than any other instructional medium.[29] However, acceptance of this new technology has in part been slowed by a narrow notion of technology's role. Research has also been slow to focus on technology's full potential. Since the 1960s, research into the educational use of computers has focused primarily on computer-assisted instruction (CAI). This type of instruction is also referred to as computer-based learning (CBL) or computer-based instruction (CBI). Two categories of CAI studies have been conducted, each with its own set of results. First, the research that looked at CAI as a replacement for traditional classroom instruction found that there was little or no significant difference in student achievement between the CAI classroom and the conventional learning environment.[30] The second group of studies looked at CAI as a supplement to the teacher. In general, these studies found positive effects (though often small) of CAI on student learning. It is our opinion that this research bears little weight in terms of the ways schools currently use technology or the ways they will use it in the future.

In 1976, Gene Glass introduced a new statistical means ("meta-analyses") that allowed results across studies to be aggregated into one summary result. Since then, many researchers in the education community have embraced meta-analysis as a method of analyzing results across education technology studies.[31,32,33] A number of landmark meta-analyses were conducted in the 1980s, reviewing early education technology research. We review them here to provide context and background for our discussions. Kulik, Bangert, and Williams reviewed over 50 studies conducted on secondary students.[34] They found that secondary school students who used CAI outperformed their counterparts and had a very positive attitude toward both the computer and their academic courses. CAI appears to have an even greater influence on elementary school students and for younger, disadvantaged, and low ability students.[35,36] CAI was also found to have a stronger effect for boys than for girls.[37]

Some have been critical of the results of these early meta-analyses. Clark reexamined samples of CAI studies from earlier meta-analyses and found that effect sizes were much smaller when the same teacher provided instruction in both the treatment and comparison groups.[38] That is, when teacher quality is accounted for, the effects of CAI are reduced. Further, Clark found that effects of CAI were larger in shorter-term studies.[39] These findings support the novelty theory, suggesting that the newness of the technology boosts immediate performance.

According to Roblyer, Castine, and King (1988), most studies of computer-based instruction from 1975 to 1987 and the meta-analyses from 1980 to 1987 focused on basic skills in mathematics and reading. Further, about half of the research was conducted on the elementary grades. Roblyer and her associates found that almost no studies showed that computer applications were effective as a total replacement of traditional methods. However, they did find a significant positive effect of computer-based learning on attitudes toward school and content area. Further, they noted that attitudes toward learning were studied more frequently than was actual student achievement.

In recent years, the notion of technology as an instrument for controlling curricula has largely fallen from favor, with experts realizing the broader potential of education technology. In fact, to the disappointment of some, the trend has been more in the direction of studies that inquire into students' problem-solving skills, ability to work cooperatively, attitudes, attendance, and retention rates. We have even seen studies begin to downplay the importance of tests of basic skills. After all, can a basic skills test measure creative thinking or the ability to locate, gather, and organize information? Those may seem less rigorous, but we believe it is a positive development in keeping with computer technology's potential for broad, sweeping impacts. The introduction of multimedia and connected computers has highlighted the transition from passive education technology to interactive. Studies looking at the broader effects of these new technologies have found substantial impacts.

Fletcher conducted a meta-analysis of 47 studies that compared computer-controlled interactive videodisk (IVD) instruction with conventional instruction in military training, industrial training, and higher education.[40] He found that, on average, the achievement scores of those students who were taught with IVD were higher than those who learned in a conventional setting.

In another study, reading and writing skills were enhanced by the use of an interactive on-line "newswire" service.[41] This service provided students with the experience of editing each other's writing. This study accentuates the power of connected computing to provide an authentic audience and thereby motivate students to perform at higher levels. The researchers found that this editorial experience produces more improvement than does practice in correcting one's own mistakes. Students who utilized this technology showed an improvement of more than one grade level in their reading and writing skills.[42] Similarly, secondary students who wrote essays with an interactive computer tool that provides guidance regarding writing wrote better essays.[43] These students also showed evidence of having internalized the guidance when writing without the computer tool.

Research on hypermedia—a combination of several different technologies[44]—has found that there are some positive relationships between using hypermedia in the classroom and student achievement.[45] Learning theorists have stressed the fact that when forced to interact and participate with content, people process information at a deeper level. This translates to greater understanding of the material. Unlike previous passive forms of technology, hypermedia has this ability to demand more thoughtful interaction. Lehrer, Erickson, and Connell studied the use of hypermedia in teaching students about the Civil War.[46] They found that students using hypermedia recalled more facts about the Civil War, grasped more elaborate concepts, and had a better understanding of the role of the historian.[47]

Students using hypermedia recalled more facts about the Civil War, grasped more elaborate concepts, and had a better understanding of the role of the historian.

The concept of constructivist learning is based on the idea that children learn by constructing knowledge through their own discovery and exploration. Constructivism sees the role of the teacher as coach in the child's own exploration, rather than as a director. Based on this philosophy, researchers at Vanderbilt University[48] examined the influence of interactive video-based hypermedia instruction on student learning. They found that this technology-rich method of instruction allowed students to learn new information in the context of meaningful activities. They also found that recognition and writing skills improved significantly after the use of interactive video-based instruction in comparison to students who were taught with traditional instructional methods. The impact of interactive videodisks on attitudes toward mathematics, mathematics concepts, and ability to plan problem solving were examined through the use of an instructional program called the "Adventures of Jasper Woodbury."[49] They found that classrooms using the Jasper videodisks showed significant advantages over control-group classrooms in terms of student attitudes on the measures being tested.

Having looked at the studies that have been done, we should ask, "What are the best ways to assess the impacts of education technology?" Ideally, we would like to see "controlled experiments" wherein there are two identical groups of students with one group subjected to the policy in question (e.g., technology integrated into the curriculum) and the other group not, although treated identically in every other way. In such a case, we could attribute differences in student outcomes to the policy because that would be the only thing different between the two groups.

There are a number of reasons why controlled experiments are difficult in education. First, it is virtually impossible to be certain that two groups of students are exactly alike. Second, if a policy such as providing students with technology is viewed by parents as a benefit, most will not accept putting their child in the control group rather than the group using technology. Third, the students using the technology may feel special, and so, work harder and achieve more. But their higher achievement may have much to do with the attention they are getting and little to do with the technology itself. Finally, it is very difficult to ensure equal treatment of both groups of students, except for the technology. Every teacher is an individual and it is highly unlikely that any two are identical. Since teachers are complementary to the technology provided and to other resources available to the control group, it will always be difficult to attribute all the differences in students' changes to the technology alone.

Given the problems with "treatment/control" experiments, we are more likely to use the results of pilot projects to test the efficacy of education technology. Here a group of students (in a classroom, school, or district) is exposed to technology, and by looking at academic achievement, attitudes, and behavior before and after such exposure, we might infer that changes can be attributed to technology, if we assume that nothing else has changed. Of course, this requires testing the students before and after their experience with technology. Even though the same teacher may be with the same students before and after technology is introduced, it is hard to believe that nothing else has changed; the students are older, teaching methods are likely to have been modified to take advantage of the technology, and so on. If the test becomes one of comparing this year's first-grade class with last year's, even though ages of students are similar, it is unlikely that two different groups of students are identical in regard to other factors that affect achievement.

Additional problems arise because technology is constantly changing and improving. Moreover, although some of the benefits we expect from introducing education technology should be observed quite soon after implementation (e.g., increased student engagement, improved attendance), other impacts will be seen much later. Improvement in grades and test scores might be seen after a school year is completed, but job-related benefits await graduation. Thus, by the time the introduction of technology is evaluated fully, circumstances will have changed so that the technology evaluated is outdated. Short-term evaluations that look at only a limited number of outcomes are incomplete and may not reveal significant impacts. Longer-term studies, even those with positive results, will be irrelevant to the cutting-edge technology then available. And negative findings can always be countered by claiming that the newer technology will be more effective.

Given the problems with "treatment/control" experiments, we are more likely to use the results of pilot projects to test the efficacy of education technology.

After considering the issues above, we must ask what we can expect in regard to evaluating the benefits of technology, if they exist. It is likely that what we will get are case studies wherein learning technology is introduced in a classroom, school, or district and evidence will be gathered on how students have changed after using that technology. We will not be able to control for all possible intervening factors. We will not be able to observe long-term effects. However, if test scores rise, dropout rates fall, attendance improves, attention spans are longer, and so on, we can be confident that technology is playing a positive role.

Even in these cases, however, we still must be cautious. We cannot argue that if better trained, more able teachers dealt with the same students, their grades would not have improved even without technology. We cannot say that better teaching methods would not have caused the same improvements. We can only ask whether these other changes would occur or would not occur in the absence of technology. Nor can we say from such evidence that we are anticipating that the costs of technology are warranted by the benefits to students.

On the other hand, how much of an impact would be significant? We have made a rough calculation of the economic value of reducing the high school dropout rate of those currently 5-17 years of age by 10 percent from its current level of 11.7 percent. Based upon the difference in earnings of high school dropouts and graduates and the number of people currently 5-17, we could increase the total earnings over their work life of those influenced by technology *not* to drop out of high school by an amount whose present value is over $30 billion. This says nothing about increased labor market productivity of all students exposed to technology-rich education. That will be discussed in the next chapter.

The point here is that if technology is shown to have limited effects on a relatively small number of students, the benefits still could be immense once all students are exposed to it. Thus, when interpreting the results of pilot technology programs on students, we must keep in mind that even modest impacts will yield very large benefits once technology is implemented nationally.

Though we've seen technology implementations evolve to encompass a broader notion of technology's salutary effects, a common weakness in all the studies described to this point is a short-term focus. As we've discussed, this leaves them open to the criticism that their effects stem chiefly from the novelty factor. In 1986, however, Apple Computers inaugurated a rather daring experiment to test the educational potential of computers as never before. The Apple Classroom of Tomorrow (ACOT) began with seven classrooms, and eventually expanded to dozens. Each participating student and teacher was given a computer for both school and home use. The goal of the project was to examine how having constant access to computers effects changes in the classroom and in the relationship between students and teachers. Researchers under contract to Apple have characterized the resulting classroom evolution as a five-stage process of entry, adoption, adaptation, appropriation, and invention.[50] The first element in this development was the introduction of a huge number of machines into the classroom—a rather dramatic transformation of the traditional environment. In the beginning, however, sweeping environmental changes were not accompanied by similarly sweeping changes in instruction. Indeed, the *entry* period can be confusing and frustrating. Even after the tribulations of redesigning the classroom are overcome, first-year ACOT teachers are noticeably boxed in by tradition, state requirements, and standardized testing. Thus, the *adoption* phase involves computers in classroom activities but witnesses only limited reengineering of classroom activities. Drill and kill exercises are popular during this phase, but there is no significant pattern of change in test scores. However, better motivation and reduced discipline problems appear to be a universal benefit of the new environment.

The *adaptation* phase is generally characterized by improving educational "output" and hints of new ways of doing things. For example, Apple's synopsis of the program notes that before ACOT and the introduction of ubiquitous word processing, students would rarely revise papers. Handwritten work simply does not facilitate an iterative system of feedback and modification. The new technology, say the Apple researchers, "led to a need for new strategies for instruction, feedback, and evaluation."

All ACOT sites entered the *appropriation* phase during the second year of the program. That is to say the integration of computer technology became more natural while significant evolution was evident in the structure of pedagogy and interaction. This was marked by a wholesale shift toward a constructivist paradigm. Students showed increased motivation and enthusiasm while teachers became comfortable with more self-directed and work-group level learning. As natural outgrowth of this system, some students develop specific expertise and assume responsibility for helping peers and influencing the direction of curricula.

The most striking results of the program can be seen in the substantially reduced dropout rates and greatly increased college enrollment rates.

Apple largely leaves the final phase, *invention*, to the future and the imagination, although this is hardly the end of the ACOT story. The most striking results of the program can be seen in the substantially reduced dropout rates and greatly increased college enrollment rates of ACOT students. West High School, serving students in a blue-collar neighborhood in Columbus, Ohio, is an example. Twenty-one freshman students were selected at random to participate in the ACOT study at their school. These students remained in the ACOT program until they graduated. At the end of their senior year, all 21 graduated. This is compared to a 30 percent dropout rate for the student body as a whole! Even more impressive, while only 15 percent of the general student body went on to college, 90 percent of the ACOT students became college students. Seven of the ACOT students were even offered full scholarships. Most important, however, is the positive difference in the way ACOT students worked. ACOT students demonstrated the type of skills and behavior that reformers are advocating—collaboration, creative problem solving, and the ability to explore and synthesize information. Moreover, ACOT students were noted for being independent learners and self-starters.

By its long-term longitudinal implementation, its flexible concepts of instruction, and uniquely massive infusion of hardware, ACOT stands apart as the most instructive experiment to date. It stresses several points that are critical to understanding technology's role in education reform. Number one among these is the point that technology is a real instrument for reform. It has the power not just to improve education in incremental ways, but to recast our entire conception of school and the dynamics between students and teachers. Second, it stresses the importance of considering the wide range of impacts technology can have on learning and development. This is missed by research that narrowly focuses on standardized test scores. Third, although the ACOT project illuminated many of the changes that technology can unleash, it also showed that large-scale benefits are not immediate. The adaptation and appropriation of technology are incremental, and their pace depends on factors such as the capabilities of teachers and the amount of hardware available. Along the path to broad-based integration of technology, there are numerous smaller benefits such as better attendance and enthusiasm.

Even with strong funding, then, our schools will not get immediate access to the gee whiz classrooms of the future. In the short term, our triumphs may be a little more mundane. We will see teachers take attendance more easily and schools will get better drill and kill systems—maybe even better word processing. Studies will even find that students seem to be doing a little better on standardized tests, but we still find this underwhelming because taunting us in the background will be the hype about the technology revolution in our schools. The truth, however, is that it will be more of an evolution and, in the end, this will achieve far more than any frontal assault on the bureaucracy.

We have a colleague (an economist) who periodically pokes fun at our thesis with the question, "Do you guys really believe a few PCs can make socialism work?" By which he means to say that the problem with education is a structural one that will not be remedied without a complete overhaul of its centralized bureaucratic foundations. We're quite prepared to concede that he has a point—to a degree. We (and many others) would be tickled to see the comprehensive reinvention of education. However, the genuine reinvention of anything is not something politics does particularly well. Computer technology, however, does have a rather illustrious career as a real-world force for change. As we've seen, the secret is in its side effects. Computers empower students, and thus put pressure on teachers to create an environment that allows more personal learning and autonomy. When enough teachers move in this direction, it becomes a significant challenge to the system's centrally prescribed curricula. A few computers won't make socialism work, but they may subvert the powers that be. Put more simply, computer culture empowers individuals, democratizes information, and upsets hierarchies. Perhaps that's why children love it and dictators do not.

CONCLUSION

Learning technology works in schools when it is properly integrated into the curriculum, when teachers are trained to use it, and when good software and technical support are provided. We know this from research studies, and we can verify it by looking at specific cases of successful implementation by classrooms, schools, districts, and even states.

We also have theoretical support for our conclusion about technology's value to student learning. A number of teaching methods have been shown to have positive impacts on children, including cooperative learning, individualized instruction, and active learning, among others. And it has been shown that when students are engaged, are not threatened, and do not feel they are being singled out or embarrassed, they learn more. Technology enables all the above to occur. Because all these educational approaches have been shown to be effective across many groups, for long periods of time, we can say that because technology enables methods and attitudes that increase student learning and result in other positive effects on students, technology itself enhances these positive outcomes. That is, if technology causes teaching to take a certain form that causes positive student outcomes, then we can say technology causes positive student outcomes.

We conclude that the case that technology leads to positive student outcomes is iron clad. But how do we respond to the skeptic who will not be convinced until the "perfect" educational research study is completed, or to the opponent of spending what is required for school technology who tries to stonewall all proposals to do so by claiming the evidence to justify it is not yet in? First, in education there never are absolutely unequivocal research results. There could always be some unidentified factor causing an observed change. Second, the rapid improvements in the available technology means we are always studying what has been, rather than what can be. Third, where technology has been done properly in schools, the results are positive to a very acceptable level of statistical certainty. Fourth, theoretical evidence supports these positive findings. Finally, technology, as we envision it, has rarely been tried. Just as there was no proof that we could land a man on the moon before we actually did it, although there was theoretical reason to believe we could, we will never *prove* technology's effectiveness in schools until we do it better, more extensively and, yes, more expensively than we have done so far. Just as the experts had confidence before the fact that we could land a man on the moon, it is fair to say that most people who have looked into education technology are highly confident that the benefits of doing so would be immense.

A LESSON FROM THE PRIVATE SECTOR

Twelve years ago, the May 26, 1986, cover of *Fortune* magazine decried "The Puny Payoff from Office Computers...Business has spent billions, but white-collar productivity hasn't budged." Today it is difficult to imagine any business not using computer technology. Indeed, try to even buy an IBM Selectric or to get one repaired, to say nothing of finding an accountant under the age of 60 who will do your taxes by hand without using a computer program.

Although schools today may be a decade behind business in installing and utilizing modern technology, a decade from now schools will have had to catch up. Hence, we can learn from what was being said about the failure, or lack of results, from business technology over a decade ago. Let us consider what the *Fortune* cover story said.

"Getting large productivity benefits from computer systems usually requires a learning process. Often management has to change work flow to realize the benefits of automation. Sometimes computers have been set to doing the wrong tasks, or simply have sat idle. Most of the productivity payoff from computers now in place may still lie ahead." Just as was the case with business a decade ago, schools and teachers require a learning process to understand how to make best use of computers in the classrooms. Computers in labs have been

doing the wrong things, and some have sat idle. The benefits of education technology lie ahead.

In business, according to *Fortune*, "In some instances computers may have been pushing white-collar productivity while other influences have been pulling it down." Hence, overall productivity has stayed constant. Similarly, even if early implementations of school technology have not shown large achievement gains for students, without technology achievement might have fallen due to other factors that are negatively affecting student achievement.

"Underuse represents a possible contributing reason for failure of computers to improve productivity. Many personal computers...sit idle much of the time." Clearly this has been the case in schools when teachers are not trained to use the technology. "Some computers are used in ways that partly wipe out their efficiencies." The article cites electronic junk mail, excessive e-mailing, and too many revisions of letters and reports, which are much easier to revise on a computer than on a typewriter. The school analogy might be game playing, improper use of the Internet, or uncreative drill and kill exercises, along with the points made regarding business. It is important to understand ways in which school technology enhances effectiveness of teachers most, and to use technology in those ways.

The article notes that "Ideally, you should change the way work is done before you put in new equipment...If people are doing the wrong things when you automate, you get them to do the wrong things faster." In schools, we cannot expect technology to turn bad teachers into good ones. If our goal is to improve the quality of the teaching force, that must be done prior to and independent of technology.

and without interruptions. By the end of 1985, productivity had doubled from the level of precomputer days, but if the program had been evaluated at the end of the first year, it would have been terminated.

Productivity can increase by increasing output for a given level of inputs (staff) or by getting the same output with fewer staff. The latter was the case regarding Allied Stores. In education, productivity will increase with technology, *not* by cutting staff

Schools and teachers require a learning process to understand how to make best use of computers in the classrooms.

"One thing that everybody who has been through it agrees on is that you do not get the benefits just by plugging in the equipment, even if it is the right equipment. The learning process often takes years." So is the case in schools where we must allow time for technology to show its worth. At Allied Stores, a big retailer in New York, the collection department bought computers in 1982. For the first three months, the productivity gain was "zilch." By the end of the first year, the staff in collections had decreased by 25 percent, but changes in the structure of work were required. Clerks were hired to retrieve hard copy files to supplement the information available on the computer screen so callers could work more quickly

(indeed more staff will be required as teachers will need technical support) since no one advocates increasing class size. Rather, achievement and other positive student outcomes will rise for a given (or larger) staff.

PPG Industries, a manufacturer of glass, paint, and chemicals, achieved cost savings by consolidating accounts-payable invoices and simplifying credit checks. Its director of management information systems was quoted as follows. "We recognize that automating what you're doing isn't enough. There are some savings in the game in that regard, but the larger savings come from automating what you're doing and then doing it better." Again, some teachers will have to change what they do in the classroom in order to maximize benefits from technology.

The article also points out that "To get vivid results, you need a leader, a manager who pulls the process along instead of waiting to get pulled." Leadership and support are also required in schools, especially from principals. Without their support, technology is likely to fail.

The *Fortune* article concludes by reiterating "some of the disappointment with productivity payoff comes from expecting results too soon. Learning lags have occurred before in the annals of technology. For a while after typewriters came along, businesses used the machines to prepare drafts of a document, then had a final version copied by hand for sending out. When it comes to using computers, many managers are still at the stage of redoing letters in longhand." That was business a decade ago—and perhaps our schools today. This "history lesson" should provide both hope and caution as we begin implementing modern technology in our schools.

LESSONS FROM THE PAST: THE TELEVISION EXPERIMENT IN EDUCATION

Having heard the claims that technology would revolutionize education through the introduction of both radio and instructional television, and then having witnessed their failures, it is not surprising that the public and educators are skeptical of this latest technological panacea. Instructional television was introduced with claims that it would provide effective lessons at low cost, solve such problems as teacher shortages and overcrowded classrooms, motivate and excite children about learning, and dramatically improve the quality of education in the United States.[51] Despite the enthusiasm and rather generous funding for instructional television, these goals were not realized. By examining the history of instructional television, we can identify factors that contributed to its failure, and apply those lessons to our current efforts to utilize more modern technology in the schools.

A Brief History of Educational Television

During the early 1950s, concern grew over the quality of education in the United States. A dramatic increase in the number of postwar children resulted in overcrowded schools and a shortage of qualified teachers. Under these circumstances, the improvement of American schools became a national priority. Supported by educational administrators, public officials, state superintendents of schools, private foundations, university presidents, deans, and professors, instructional television was given its chance in 1952 when the FCC reserved 242 channels for noncommercial educational television.

Financing for the initial use of instructional television came from the Ford Foundation and its Fund for the Advancement of Education. From 1955 to 1965, the Fund invested over $70 million in schools and colleges around the country. A subsequent source of funding that was crucial to the development of instructional television came after the Soviet launch of Sputnik in 1957. Congress reacted to this intimidating event by passing the National Defense Education Act, which made funds available for educational television stations. In 1962, the passage of the Communications Act provided $32 million for the development of classroom television. By 1971, public and private funding for instructional television totaled over $100 million (or over $366 million in 1994 dollars).[52]

Throughout the country, courses began to be offered exclusively over television. In 1955, ninth-grade students in St. Louis public schools received televised English grammar and composition classes for 30 minutes a day, five days a week. The Midwest Program of Airborne Television Instruction used airplanes circling over Indiana to transmit videotaped lessons to an estimated 400,000 students from 1961 until 1968.[53] Hagerstown,

Maryland, became the site of an ambitious closed-circuit television project that eventually provided lessons in 39 different subjects to nearly every public school in the county. In 1964, American Samoa began to use instructional television as the core of its entire curriculum, which was perhaps the boldest venture in instructional television.

Each of these projects varied in its structure and use of instructional television. Most commonly, instructional television was used as a teaching aid to supplement classroom lectures. The pattern of combining daily television lessons with supplementary classroom lessons, although used less frequently, was given the most attention. Using instructional television for presentation of the entire curriculum was often discussed, yet this usage existed only in American Samoa.[54] Despite these differences, a pattern of similar problems existed across most instructional television projects. Before discussing these problems, we examine the often cited Hagerstown project to discover under what circumstances instructional television was advocated, implemented, and ultimately utilized. Though Hagerstown followed a pattern of utilization (supplemented television learning) that was relatively uncommon, it is still instructive to review its history.

Hagerstown

In 1956, Hagerstown, Maryland, was faced with a serious shortage of adequately prepared teachers and a rapidly growing student population. Out of 352 elementary school teachers, 97 had no bachelor's degrees and 75 had only emergency teaching certificates. Given that these teachers were inadequately trained, it is not surprising that areas such as mathematics, science, and the arts were neglected. To remedy this situation, the county board of education planned to install television receivers in new schools. A different future was in store for Hagerstown, though. Hagerstown was chosen by the Fund for the Advancement of Education as the site for a school district experiment using closed-circuit television.[55] According to the Ford Foundation's philosophy, "a good teacher on television can be much more effective in stimulating learning than a mediocre teacher in the intimate environment of a classroom." [56] Thus, it was thought that television lectures by more qualified and experienced teachers would compensate for the shortcomings of many of Hagerstown's classroom teachers.

The experiment attempted to determine whether instructional television could provide a better and more cost-effective education than traditional methods. The district was provided with over $1.5 million in subsidies by 1959. This came in the form of $774,000 from the Ford Foundation, $250,000 in equipment from the Electronics Industry Association, and an estimated $500,000 in equipment and cable installation from the telephone company.[57] Six studios, equipped with vidicon cameras, film-projection facilities, and a videotape recorder, were provided for the production of programs. Initially 23 of the district's schools were linked to the studios by coaxial cables. By 1963, nearly every school in the district was connected to the studios.[58]

Hagerstown's closed-circuit instructional television was controlled completely by educational administrators. Television lessons were written, produced, and presented by 26 classroom teachers, selected from the regular teaching staff. The television stations were staffed with individuals who were familiar with, but had little experience in producing television programs. Additionally, the television stations were not fully equipped. There was no means of broadcasting outdoors and there was no equipment for shooting or editing films. No dramatizations were used in the Hagerstown productions.[59] As a result of these personnel and technical limitations, television lessons were generally in the form of "lecture and the talking head"[60] and did not exploit the full potential of classroom television.

At no time was it intended that television lessons be used as the primary source of instruction. The bulk of instruction was still to come from the classroom teacher. In general, television was not used for more than half an hour each day. A team-teaching approach was envisioned between television teachers and classroom teachers. The time before televised lectures was to be spent preparing and going over problems with the previous homework. Following the lecture, classroom teachers were to guide students in a follow-up lesson that would clarify and expand on ideas presented in the television lecture.[61]

As an experiment, Hagerstown proved successful. Students in wired schools made improvements in standardized test scores for arithmetic, science, reading, advanced math, and other subjects, as compared to students in unwired schools. This comparison is somewhat questionable, however, given that the unwired schools were mostly in rural areas and not an ideal control group. Regardless, Hagerstown students' scores showed improvement compared to national norms.[62]

In 1963, five years after the experiment had expired, the Ford Foundation's Fund for the Advancement of Education withdrew its support. Other private funds and telephone subsidies were also withdrawn. Eventually, instructional television in Hagerstown was greatly downsized and focused on providing music and art lessons that would otherwise require the hiring of itinerant teachers. Though it had proven to be a success, and had saved money for the district, this success was tempered by the fact that instructional television in Hagerstown struggled to maintain itself through local funding. The support of the Ford Foundation made it possible to demonstrate instructional television's value, but the true test of its effectiveness came only after the Foundation's withdrawal. Henry Cassirer explains that

> ... foundations are not part of the normal administration of education. They may be able to induce the educational establishment to accept their funds and their approach, but their efforts are limited in scope and time. The final test of their effectiveness lies in the acceptance of their pioneering work by tax-financed educational systems, by the educators and by the people at large, when they are convinced that television makes a valuable contribution. Otherwise the initial effort comes to a halt when the flow of outside funds is stopped.[63]

The success of the Hagerstown experiment, and Hagerstown's subsequent struggle to finance its instructional television program, illustrate that instructional television of itself was a useful tool, but its effectiveness and viability in the natural school district environment was questionable.

Extent of Teacher Use

To ask if instructional television is an effective method of teaching children is quite different from asking if instructional television has had an impact on our teaching system. A device's effectiveness can be determined by controlled studies in a relatively static context. Its impact, however, is affected by the dynamic relationship between device and environment, and is determined by the extent to which it has an effect on that environment. In the early 1960s, researchers were concerned with instructional television's effectiveness as a medium. Today it is important to ask if instructional television has had an impact on the way we teach. To answer this question, we shall look at surveys that examine the way teachers used instructional television and the extent to which they used it.

Studies based on self-reports of Minneapolis, West Virginia, and Maryland teachers between 1970 and 1981 indicated that those teachers who used television used it between 2 and 4 percent of the weekly instructional time. This small percentage is no more than one hour a week. For the 1981 school year, 13 percent of the elementary, 43 percent of the junior high, and 60 percent of the high school teachers in Maryland indicated that they did not use television at all.[64]

The most comprehensive study of the use of instructional television since the 1950s was conducted by Peter Dirr and Ronald Pedone in 1976-77.[65] Using a stratified sample of 3,700 classroom teachers, they found a similar pattern of greater use in the lower grades and diminishing use in the higher grades. Elementary teachers reported using instructional television 66 minutes a week, while junior high school teachers reported use for only 45 minutes a week. In a typical five-hour instructional day, this is no more than 4 percent of the instructional week.[66] Though it is estimated by Dirr and Pedone that 15 million children used instructional television regularly, the extent of this use appears to be minimal.

Larry Cuban[67] offers another source of data on teachers' use of instructional television. His reports are based on notes from personal observations while he was superintendent in Arlington, Virginia. These were schools where television use was encouraged by administrators, and televisions and in-service workshops were provided. During the week of the study, seven of the thirteen teachers signed up for use of a television set. Television use ranged from 4 to 15 percent of the instructional time per week, in those classes where it was used at all. Teachers also reported that they generally used television programs in the afternoon, while the morning hours were used to teach core subjects such as math and reading.

At the second school a similar pattern was found. County surveys indicated that of the twelve teachers on staff, only six to seven teachers reported themselves as regular users. From discussions with three of these regular users, Cuban estimates that they were using instructional television from 2 to 6 percent of the instructional week. The pattern of using television lessons in the afternoon also occurred in this school. From conversations with these teachers, it was Cuban's judgment that television was used as a diversion in the afternoon, so that teachers could have some relief time and the students could have a change of pace.[68] This observation is supported by research on the "ThinkAbout" instructional television series. In a survey of six suburban elementary classrooms in the Midwest and the West, it was found that in all but one classroom "ThinkAbout" programs were shown in the afternoon. These teachers thought of the programs as a filler activity, a break from the heavy morning schedule of core subjects.[69]

From these studies and observations, it becomes apparent that teachers' use of instructional television has been minimal. Some teachers did not use it at all, and those that did, used it for a very small percentage of the total instructional time. Use in the elementary schools appears to be greater than use in secondary schools. Additionally, television is most frequently used in the afternoons, not in the morning when core subjects are taught. From this we can conclude that *instructional television, though it may be an effective teaching tool, is used minimally and has had little impact on the way children are taught.*

What Went Wrong?

As we mentioned, the impact of instructional television was not determined by its effectiveness in a vacuum, but by its effectiveness in a specific context. This context was largely shaped by the social and political currents of the time, those that controlled funding for instructional television and those that used it. The following historical view describes some of the factors that shaped the way instructional television was implemented and used, and how those factors contributed to its failure.

American education from the early 1900s to the early 1950s was dominated by the practical life curriculum. This curriculum hoped to eliminate elitist education and stress the preparation of children for "a practical job, worthy home living, and appropriate leisure."[70] By the mid-1950s, however, this curriculum was being attacked as anti-intellectual as well as elitist. The failure to stress the education of academic skills was considered anti-intellectual. Tracking students into either academic or vocational programs was considered elitist. It resulted in disparities in education for different children. As a result of this criticism, education in the mid-1950s shifted toward a "back to basics" curriculum, emphasizing academics.

In 1957, while this change in the curriculum was occurring, the Soviets launched Sputnik.[71] This event augmented criticism of the practical life curriculum. Practical life, it was argued, had not prepared our children adequately in science and mathematics, and therefore put them in danger of falling behind their Soviet peers. Significantly, it was educators and instructional technologists who were blamed for the existence of the practical life curriculum. Education professors took the blame for the dismal state of the national curriculum. As a result, professors of education were not sought out in the subsequent development of a new curriculum that included instructional television.[72]

As we have seen, there were social and political factors that shaped the nature of instructional television. Criticism of the practical life curriculum contributed to the exclusion of educators and instructional technologists in the formation of the new curriculum. The Cold War climate of the 1950s led the government to focus on American technological strength and emphasize math, science, and foreign languages. The benefactors of instructional television also contributed to the context that surrounded its development and use. The two primary benefactors of instructional television, the Ford Foundation and the federal government each had specific agendas for American education. The Ford Foundation sought to "automatize" the classroom and limit the control of classroom teachers, while the government pursued a congressional mandate to maintain our technological strength. These factors all contributed to a pattern of control that was predominantly top-down.

Through its various agencies, the Ford Foundation provided the bulk of funding for instructional television and guided the form it took. From 1952 to 1957, it is estimated that $24 million was spent on instructional television, $20 million coming from various agencies of the Ford Foundation.[73] The Foundation executives did not simply grant funds; they had their own vision for American education. They viewed instructional television as the automaton that would replace classroom teachers. Classrooms of 150 students, all learning from television, were envisioned by the Foundation. Guided by this philosophy, the Foundation did not attempt to include teachers or education faculty in the creation of instructional television programs. Instead, letters and science college and university professors, excluding education faculty, were sought out to formulate their program.[74] The federal government also was another key player in the development of curriculum and instructional television. Like the Ford Foundation, the government had a specific agenda for American education. During the post-war 1950s, and particularly after the Soviet launch of Sputnik, the government's concerns were our competitiveness and technological strength. In 1958, the National Defense Education Act (NDEA) appropriated $160 million for education. It allocated half of the funds specifically for mathematics, science, and modern foreign languages, and mandated the purchase of audiovisual equipment for the teaching of these subjects.[75] NDEA funds were also available at the university level for the development of instructional technology. It was made clear, however, that these funds were earmarked for the development of materials for math, science, and modern foreign languages.

Implementation

Instructional television was pushed primarily by "educational administrators, foundations, government officials, equipment manufacturers and public-spirited citizens rather than by the practitioners of education."[76] Foundations may fund a new technology, and administrators may decide to implement it, but it is the teachers who must ultimately use it. Teachers control if, how, and when technology will be used in the classroom. Questions of the technology's impact hinge on teachers' use of the technology. Despite this obvious fact, most teachers were not involved in the implementation of instructional television until the very end of the process. Teachers were not part of the original impetus for instructional technology, yet they were expected to use it and make it work. Their resistance to instructional television is not surprising in light of these facts and must be considered essential to understanding any future implementation issues involving educational technology.

Top-down implementation was not unique to instructional television. It was common practice in districts to impose changes upon principals and for principals, in turn, to impose those changes upon teachers. This pattern of implementation avoids lengthy discussions of advantages, disadvantages, and other concerns of teachers and principals. This was probably not the most prudent method, but it was the most expeditious. In response to such mandates, teachers will exercise control in the only manner available to them, the actual use or nonuse of the technology. According to Larry Cuban, "compliance with authority is expected in organizations. To those mandates that awkwardly fit the contours of a work setting or are inconsistent with the beliefs of the implementers, token compliance is a common response. Embracing the barest minimum that is necessary to convince supervisors that the mandate has been executed is common in those organizations where orders trickle down

to the lower levels of the organization."[77] Consequently, top-down implementation contributed to instructional television's failure by creating an environment where it was to teachers' benefit to engage in only token compliance.

Teachers' use or nonuse of instructional technology is not entirely explained by the direction of implementation. "Teachers are prone to teach the way they have been taught."[78] Teachers learn to teach from their own experience as students, from one another and, to a lesser extent, from their formal training. Most do not have a model of teaching that includes technology. Additionally, most students of teaching receive minimal, if any, training in the use of instructional technology (see Chapter 5). As a result, the nature of teaching has remained remarkably consistent decade after decade. In his history of teachers and machines, Larry Cuban points out that the tools that teachers have added to their routine "have been simple, durable, flexible, and responsive to teacher-defined problems in meeting the demands of daily instruction."[79] Chalkboards and textbooks are given as examples of tools that meet these criteria. The chalkboard aids the teacher in communicating lessons to students. Anything can be written on it at any time. It is easy to use, with no setup required. Textbooks are also flexible and fit easily into the way teachers teach. Students can be assigned the same lesson, or different groups can be assigned different lessons. Textbooks can travel with the teacher and the student, and like the chalkboard, do not require additional setup. The failed technologies—radio, film, and television—did not meet the above criteria. None of these technologies fit simply or flexibly into different classroom environments. As we shall see, there were several hardware and software problems that made instructional television neither simple, durable, nor flexible.[80] Computers, networks, CD-ROMs will all have to have these traits in order to gain acceptance.

Hardware

Educators' problems with television hardware began at the point of purchase. With the availability of funds from the National Defense Education Act and Title I, educators set out to purchase television equipment. Unfortunately, the states did not provide any guidance as to what type of equipment to buy. As a result, educators were at the mercy of aggressive television equipment salesmen. After purchasing equipment, educators often realized that equipment from one manufacturer was incompatible with equipment from other manufacturers. The lack of guidance from the states and the inexperience of educators also led to the purchase of equipment that was not always suitable for the purpose envisioned. For example, schools often purchased 17-inch sets, not realizing that this

size was inadequate for classroom viewing. Some states added to these problems by requiring that districts purchase equipment from the lowest bidder regardless of the quality of the equipment. Schools were left with a mountain of television equipment, much of which was incompatible with other equipment, not suitable for the school's purposes, and of poor quality.[81] This is one of the strongest arguments for implementing technology all at once.

The breakdown of equipment further contributed to schools' problems with modern electronic technology. Most schools stretched their budgets to purchase television equipment. As a result, there was little money left to repair or maintain it.[82] In a study of teachers' use of instructional television, 34 percent of the teachers responded that equipment was not available and not in good repair when needed.[83] Consequently, many teachers were unable to take advantage of available television programming. The same study also found that over 56,000 teachers who had instructional television available did not have TV available to them.[84] This combination of a limited amount of equipment and the breakdown of the available equipment kept many teachers from using instructional television.

Going back to Cuban's criteria for technology that teachers will accept, we can see where hardware factors alone failed to meet these criteria. Was it simple? Television equipment was not always simple to use. Incompatibility of components was probably the source of much frustration for many teachers. Was it durable? Television equipment also failed to hold up adequately. Poor-quality equipment and insufficient funds for maintenance and repair meant that equipment was not always available or functioning reliably. Even if teachers intended to view an instructional television program, the limited availability and unreliability of equipment probably discouraged them from doing so. Additionally, there was probably a feeling that they could not count on the equipment and, as a result, television took on more of a supplementary role. Each of these hardware factors—incompatibility of components, poor quality, insufficient numbers, and breakdown of existing equipment—point to the failure of instructional television to meet the criteria of simplicity and durability.

Software

Software, in television terms, is the programming available through television. Instructional programming came in the form of television broadcasts and, in some places, recorded programs. The problems common to both of these formats were poor quality and limited quantity and variety. Broadcast lessons were further limited by the inflexibility of broadcasting schedules. Taped lessons suffered from the compatibility and reliabili-

ty problems we have already discussed. All of these difficulties have been cited by teachers as reasons for their infrequent use of instructional television.[85]

Programming for instructional television was generally uninspiring. Lessons were in the format of a teacher standing and lecturing in the traditional fashion. (Control over the production of programs was in the hands of Foundation executives and university professors, outside of education and outside the experienced television media.) The choice of this format was unfortunate. These individuals outside of education had limited knowledge of the effectiveness of different teaching methods. Their talking-head format was too long, passive, and did not take advantage of television's versatility. Like education faculty, educational film makers, consisting of educators, instructional technologists, and Hollywood people, were excluded from the development of instructional television programs. The input of these professionals along with the expertise of commercial television producers might have served to make instructional television programs more effective and entertaining.[86]

Other factors that contributed to the poor quality of programs were more technical in nature. Programs that were broadcast were often fuzzy because of weak signals. When combined with small television monitors and inadequate antennae, instructional television programs were considerably less effective than they could have been. This unengaging instruction presented to students in the form of small, blurry images fell far short of television's potential.[87] The clean images provided by hookup to cable systems were not yet available.

Two other problems with instructional television programming address the issue of its flexibility. The first has to do with the limited number and variety of programs. There were not enough programs available to meet existing curriculum needs. Nearly 38 percent of teachers in Dirr and Pedone's study said that this factor was a hindrance in their use of instructional television.[88] A class might be studying Abe Lincoln but find that the only programs on presidents are about George Washington. Granted, the number of programs that are available would increase with time, but the very nature of television broadcasting limits the variety of programs that are available on any given day. Recorded tapes offer an alternative, but this too requires foresight and planning on the part of the teacher, plus the availability of functioning tape players. These factors all contribute to the *inflexibility* of instructional television.

For programs that were available only through broadcasting, another problem came up. Teachers were unable to control the time of broadcast and therefore had to shuffle the class schedule in order to watch a particular program (remember that at this time, VCRs did not exist).[89] This can be complicated when various classroom activities must be coordinated with programs and their schedules. In the Dirr and Pedone study, 45 percent of the teachers said that inconvenient broadcast schedules hindered their use of instructional television.[90] In elementary schools the necessary schedule shuffling is accomplished more easily because teachers have more control over the entire instructional day. In secondary schools, however, with their 50-minute periods, this can be nearly impossible. This scheduling difficulty might partially account for the greater pattern of use in elementary schools than in secondary schools previously mentioned. Again, the inconvenience of broadcast schedules points to the inflexibility of instructional television. Combined with hardware features that fail to meet the simplicity and durability criteria, this inflexibility sheds considerable light on why teachers did not embrace instructional television.

Additional Problems

Problems mentioned so far have been related to instructional television as a technology. Hardware and software issues have little to do with education per se. There are other problems with the use of technology in schools that are more fundamental in nature.

The structure of our education system itself is one of these problems. With each technological panacea, it is assumed that by merely putting some high tech gadget in schools we will spur changes in classroom practices. This, however, is not the case. As we have seen, teachers tend to incorporate new technologies into their existing patterns of teaching, rather than changing those patterns to achieve optimal use of the technology. Without sufficient research into the use of a particular technology within the context of the classroom, and the more fundamental understanding of the processes of human learning, teachers have little guidance to do anything but incorporate the new technology into their existing practices. Had such information been available to teachers, they might have had more success in integrating instructional television into the curriculum.

Most of the discussion presented here has focused on teachers and their failure to use and accept instructional television. Their use of technology, however, is not entirely in their control. The rigid nature of our educational system with its patterns of grades, 50-minute periods, and shuffling secondary students from one class to another for each subject created problems for teachers' use of instructional television. Teachers only have control over the instructional time of the day. The length of periods, recesses, and the entire class day is out of their hands. Trying to schedule instructional television lessons within these confines was difficult and not always possible. The pattern of greater use of instructional television in elementary schools supports this claim. Elementary school teachers have greater control over the curriculum and the entire day's schedule than do secondary teachers. The structure of education, in this case, limited teachers' use of instructional television. Teachers' own aversion to technology was not the only barrier.

Instructional television did not live up to the initial claims that it would revolutionize our educational system. It is clear that this failure cannot be blamed solely on teachers. Teachers were in the unfortunate position of having to use a technology that was inadequately researched, insufficiently funded, poorly implemented, and imposed on them. This chapter does not intend to say that instructional television as a medium was a failure, or to disregard the fact that there were individual success stories. The intention is to show that instructional television did not live up to the claims that were made about it, and that there were several factors, unrelated to television itself, that contributed to this failure. Although the computer may be a far more powerful and flexible tool than television, we will see that it is hardly immune to the ills that befell instructional television. We will come back to these lessons throughout the book.

economic
benefits
of education
technology

On a recent bus trip to upstate New York, the driver and a passenger were chatting. The passenger, who owned the Amoco gas station in Tarrytown, said he had seven repair bays. The driver asked how he liked his job. The passenger replied it was good, but he had had to learn more in the last five years than in the previous 30. It was all due to the new high-tech ways to service and repair cars today. The bus driver said he used to own the Amoco station in Rye, but sold it in the early '70s. He asked how he might get back into the business. The station owner from Tarrytown replied, "Educate the hell out of yourself."

There is no question that in the future, better-educated workers will get the better jobs and will earn more money. The escalating skill requirements for individuals is demonstrated by the average incomes of 30-year-old men with a high school diploma and no college education. In 1972 they earned $34,000 (in 1995 dollars) compared with about $22,000 in 1995.[91] Children may be learning as well as they have in the past, but it is not good enough anymore. James Pinkerton summed it up in a piece for the *Los Angeles Times* when he said, "In the new information economy, what you earn is based on what you learn."[92] To the extent that students learn more of the traditional disciplines while using technology, they will have more of the basic skills that are required in "good" jobs. According to Richard Gagliardi, director of career and vocational education for the Manchester, Connecticut, public schools, "Employers are looking for portable skills that allow an individual to be readily adaptable to a variety of situations and circumstances."[93]

Former Secretary of Labor Robert Reich recently noted that, "If you have the right skills, technology and globalization really are on your side. You have a greater capacity to add value to the global economy. On the other hand, if you don't have the right skills, if you don't have the right education, technology may be your enemy."[94] As the New York bus driver discovered, *technology itself* is almost certain to be an aspect of any future job market that students of today will enter. According to the Children's Partnership, 47 percent of jobs in 1993 required computer and/or networking capability—up from 25 percent in 1984. By the year 2000, this study forecasts 60 percent of jobs will require these skills.[95] And we are not talking only about jobs in computer hardware and software companies. Everyone from auto repair people to cashiers to secretaries now must be able to use technology. According to Chris Clifton, executive vice president of the Memphis Area Chamber of Commerce, "There is no doubt that automation and technology have created a different type of demand for and sophistication of skill levels. While these skill levels are much higher, the pay levels are higher as well."[96]

Many high-technology companies cannot find enough skilled employees to meet the needs of their growing industry. The problem is so serious that the Northern Virginia Technology Council has requested the state legislature to enact a law that would require all teachers, principals, and guidance counselors to be certified in technology by the year 2001 in order to renew their licenses. To receive the certificate, they would have to be proficient in Internet research, electronic mail and word processing, as well as database and spreadsheet programs.[97] Because high-tech companies are unable to find the skilled labor that they need, they are working toward developing their own local technologically literate labor pool.

The Northern Virginia Technology Council has requested the state legislature to enact a law that would require all teachers, principals, and guidance counselors to be certified in technology by the year 2001 in order to renew their licenses.

Businesses are already having difficulty in finding people with enough basic skills even to be trained. *Financial World* magazine's cover story of August 12, 1996, was titled "Fixing Education." According to Richard Notebaert, chairman of Ameritech Corp., business needs "...people who have a high-school reading capability who can handle basic algebra. We'll do the training. We spend over 100 million a year on it. We are more than willing to teach you how to splice fiber optics, how to work on a computer, handle software. But for us to do that, you have to be able to read." Forty-three percent of organizations provide remedial or basic education, and this percentage rises with firm size. Seventy-two percent of firms trained employees in personal computer applications in 1995. Cecil Ursprung, president of Reflexite Corp. in Avon, Connecticut, has found that "there is a big gap between the preparation that is needed to be a winner in the global marketplace and the preparation we are finding in the general population."[98] This is not only the case for large employers; in 1995, 25 percent of small and mid-sized business owners said that finding qualified people was a significant challenge, up from 20 percent in 1994 and 13 percent in 1993.[99] The private sector is spending billions of dollars every year in lost productivity and teaching individuals what they should have learned in K-12. According to the National Forum for Information Association, "poor work performance and low productivity now cost American businesses an estimated $25 billion to $30 billion a year."[100] If investments in the individual were made earlier, when the individual is younger and learns more easily, businesses could save a significant amount of money on training and lost productivity. It takes much more time and effort (and money) to teach an adult how to read, understand basic math calculations, or to operate a computer, than to teach a child.

Having more education not only benefits the individual, it also benefits the employer in the form of increased productivity. Data from the National Center on the Educational Quality of the Workforce compared the changes in productivity associated with: a 10 percent increase in the book value of a company's capital stock, a 10 percent increase in the number of hours worked, and a 10 percent increase in employees' average education (which is equal to just over one year of additional schooling). The increase in capital stock resulted in a 3.4 percent increase in productivity while increased hours resulted in a 5.6 percent increase in productivity. An 8.6 percent increase in productivity was associated with the increased schooling of employees. In the nonmanufacturing sector this effect was even greater. The one additional year of schooling is associated with a whopping 11 percent increase in productivity.[101]

Benefits of a More Educated Population

Education technology, when implemented correctly, is more than a vocational tool; it is a learning tool. Increased learning in general results in a more educated population, which in turn has economic benefits to society as a whole. In addition to savings on remedial education, there are other economic benefits of having a more educated population that are well documented in economic literature. Reduced crime, better health, and consumer choice efficiency are all benefits of a more educated population, and we could argue that these benefits have a significant positive impact on the economy. When less money has to be spent on remedial education, crime, and illness, more resources become available for other, more satisfying uses.

Without question there is a strong negative correlation between education and criminal activity. Eighty percent of prison inmates are high school dropouts, with many of them illiterate or able to read only at an elementary school level.[102] Individuals with more education or specific skills have the opportunity to earn a legitimate income, and thus have less of an incentive to participate in crime. At the same time, lack of training and schooling are not barriers to enter illegal activities. Therefore, someone who is not educated will have more of an incentive to get involved in crime, because neither education nor specialized training are prerequisites to participate. On average, we spend $20,000 a year per prison inmate (compare this with the $6,993 that we spend annually per school student).[103] With over 1.4 million inmates, this amounts to over $28 billion *annually*.[104] How many people could have been kept out of crime if they had had a decent education and had been given the tools to earn an honest living? In so doing, the savings to the public would be enormous.

Health is also highly correlated with an individual's educational level. This is probably due to the fact that increased schooling contributes to information acquisition, occupational and locational choices, and medical care usage. Better health benefits more than the individual and the individual's family. It also translates into greater productivity in terms of hours worked and the quality of that work. This generally benefits the individual in the form of higher wages, but there are positive effects for the community as well. Employees with better health are more productive and cost their employers less in terms of health care. When individuals are unable to provide themselves with health care, that burden falls on taxpayers. Reducing contagious disease is another positive outcome. Though difficult to quantify, each of these has a cost to the private sector or to the community at large.[105]

Eighty percent of prison inmates are high school dropouts, with many of them illiterate or able to read only at an elementary school level.

Finally, a better educated population is more well informed and is in a better position to process information and make more intelligent consumption decisions. Many would also say that education leads to better investment decisions, which make capital markets work more effectively.[106]

Benefit/Cost Model

One of the main themes of a recent book on school improvement, Erik Hanushek's *Making Schools Work: Improving Performance and Controlling Costs,* is that educational innovations must be evaluated continuously to assure that money spent is yielding a rate of return sufficiently high that the benefits of a program exceed its cost.[107] As reasonable as such a recommendation is, there may be situations in which very expensive proposed innovations cannot be justified unless some *speculative* benefit/cost analysis is conducted prior to implementation. In the case of technology, our recommendation is that funding be provided to fully implement plans for educational technology in all 50 states. As we have seen, some experiments have been conducted and evaluated regarding computer usage in schools, but the full breadth of most states' plans have never been implemented in a state and rarely even in a single school. The success of technology in schools will depend upon much more, and different, teacher training, software, hardware, and network infrastructure than currently exists. After-the-fact evaluation is impossible at the present time.

Now we ask instead whether there is a reasonable set of assumptions that enables us to conduct a *hypothetical* benefit/cost analysis of one likely benefit of the proposed technological revolution in our nation's public schools, namely increased labor productivity and earnings. It is our view that such an analysis is possible. In this chapter, we estimate the benefits of individuals attending new, technology-based public schools in terms of their increased productivity in the labor force after leaving school. By summing the increases in productivity for each worker, we obtain a measure of the total national growth of output that is the result of the better, more technology-based education of the prospective labor force.

This calculation derives from a series of assumptions, each of which could be altered. For the most part, in order to determine total labor market productivity benefits from school technology, we made assumptions that usually would err on the side of lowering our estimate. The question is whether, with different assumptions, the results would change our recommendation to provide the funding currently needed to implement the states' technology plans for their schools. Our answer is that it would not change our conclusions.

We begin with the assumption that all students who obtain at least a high school diploma in new technology-rich schools will see their productivity in the labor force increase. Economist Alan Krueger[108] estimates that workers who use computers on their jobs earn 10 to 15 percent higher wages.[109] This premium is due to the relative scarcity today of workers with computer skills. If all workers (or most) had such skills, it is reasonable to assume the premium would fall. In the extreme case where *all* workers were more productive due to their technology training, there would be no earnings advantage for them (i.e., there would be no one to have an advantage over), but their productivity would have risen, goods would become cheaper, and their real purchasing power and standard of living would increase.

We assume that demand for technological skills rather than remaining constant will continue to grow at almost the same rate as the growth in their supply.[110] Additionally, we assume labor productivity will increase due to technology in the schools. Such an assumption does not seem unreasonable given the prevailing "buzz" about the new "knowledge/information society" and the rapidly expanding use of technology in manufacturing and in the provision of services.[111] Moreover, students will be entering the labor market with much more than a new ability to use computers (which is what Krueger measured); not only will they be able to use a variety of technologies and information retrieval systems but they also will have acquired greater competency in traditional subjects (writing, science, math, etc.) due to improved teaching and learning of such disciplines through the use of technology. Therefore there should be significant gains in noncomputer-related productivity that are considered only implicitly in our analysis. Despite a huge upward shift in the supply of technology-advanced workers, we assume that all workers will be more productive and will earn more (in terms of purchasing power) than the nontechnically trained workers of today. Further, this productivity will be reflected in higher purchasing power of those with at least a high school diploma, which we assume will be 5 percent higher than otherwise. Our assumption of a 5 percent productivity increase due to technology is one-half to one-third of the differential Krueger found, although assuming these new workers would have skills in addition to being able to use computers, one might expect at least the same rate of return. Thus, our assumption is conservative.

To find aggregate U.S. benefit of an across-the-board 5 percent increase in labor market productivity due to workers' being educated in technology rich schools, we focus on youngsters who were between 0 and 14 years of age in 1996.[112] Details of our model are provided in the Appendix, so we shall just touch on the highlights here. We assume that today's 0-14-year-olds will progress through and terminate school to enter the work force in the same patterns as we now observe for those between 16 and 30 years of age. That is, the same share will be high school dropouts, college graduates, and so on. We then assume that in real terms (i.e., ignoring inflation) our current 0-14-year-olds will earn the same amounts that their predecessors with the same schooling now earn over their lifetimes. Since such earnings presumably represent current productivity, we increase earnings every year by 5 percent to reflect the labor market benefits (increased productivity) due to technology. Since these increments will occur over many years in the future, we convert each year's 5 percent benefit for each person to its present value and then add them up for all people in all years.

These admittedly crude assumptions and rough calculations reveal that total productivity over the lifetime of 0-14-year-olds now living would increase by $202 billion in present value terms, 1996 dollars (see Appendix, Table A-5). This gain is to be compared to a cost of $50 billion, perhaps to be spent over four years. However, even if the benefit/cost ratio of about 4:1 is reduced significantly, the full funding of technology for our public schools appears to be a good investment.

Earlier we referred to a statement that poor work performance and low productivity now cost U.S. businesses an estimated $25 billion to $30 billion a year. How do these figures relate to our estimate of a $202 billion gain in productivity from school technology? Let us consider the savings in lost productivity if our cohort of those aged 0-14 in 1996 were educated in technology-rich schools.

We estimate the gains from better work performance and higher productivity to be $147 billion dollars in present value terms over 50 years, which is about 23 percent of the projected loss (see Appendix for details). Remember our 0-14-year-olds are only a fraction of the labor force. This figure is less than the $202 billion of productivity increase estimated above using a quite different approach. Combining our two results, we are very confident that our estimates of productivity increases due to a better-educated labor force, trained in technology-rich schools, are reasonable and probably greater than $150 billion but not much higher than $200 billion.

A report analyzing the benefit/cost ratio of government investment in post-secondary education under the World War II GI Bill estimated that ratio to fall between 12.5:1 and 5:1. The assumptions yielding the lower figure seem more realistic.[113] Given that the GI Bill is considered one of the most successful public expenditure programs in our history, the conservatively estimated 4:1 ratio for funding school technology implies that our investment in education technology would yield benefits of similar magnitude to those of the GI bill.

Moreover, the benefit considered is in terms of increased labor productivity and earnings only—we ignore a whole array of possible nonmonetary benefits, both private and social. Similarly, we do not allow for any increase in nonlabor market productivity and we do not include benefits to anyone yet to be born or who does not attain at least a high school diploma. Finally, we have not considered new immigrants who will be enrolled in U.S. public schools and subsequently benefit from school technology when they enter the labor force. These omissions add to the downward bias in our benefits calculation.

There are several assumptions in our model that may tend to bias the benefits estimate upward. For example, population estimates are used to represent the total number of students enrolled in public education. Although private education constitutes a small proportion of total school enrollment, we have overestimated benefits from public school technology by the proportion of each age-education cohort that enrolls in private schools. Also, we have not allowed for deaths or incapacity in the current 0-14-year-old population. Third, we assume full employment for all individuals with a high school degree or better after the age of 30. To the extent that some of those people now aged 0-14 never enter the labor force or work part-time or seasonally, our estimates are too high.

Furthermore, our estimates of the costs of implementing state technology plans ignore the marginal deadweight loss caused by the tax system. Twenty percent might be added to the cost for this reason. Nevertheless, in considering all the possible biases we have identified, we conclude that even the 3.6:1 benefit/cost ratio resulting from adding a 20 percent deadweight loss is conservative.

This and the preceding chapter are meant to suggest that in the right environment arguments can be made that should lead to federal and state funding of all states' school technology plans in one fell swoop. As this rapid infusion of public funds is unlikely, later we will investigate other ways the states might obtain some of the necessary funds. Before that, we ask what the schools must do to enable their students to obtain the benefits that school technology can provide.

GI JOE AND THE POST-WORLD WAR II ECONOMY

"If the 16 million veterans of World War II had descended on the labor force at one time, the result would have been economic chaos."

—DAVID R. SEGAL,
UNIVERSITY OF MARYLAND SOCIOLOGIST

Historical Perspective

The United States has compensated its veterans for their services since the earliest days of our country's history. As far back as the Pilgrims and the Continental Congress, pensions have been given to both disabled veterans and dependents of soldiers who lost their lives in battle. However, educational benefits that give a monthly education assistance allowance to veterans who are disabled have only dated back to the end of World War I.

During World War II, there were postwar predictions of economic depression and the prospect of the loss of millions of jobs at the end of the war, resulting from employee layoffs at military manufacturing factories that would no longer be needed and from the influx of millions of veterans that would eventually return to the labor force after the war ended. America was faced with the task of developing a solution to offset the potentially dangerous situation. Task forces were commissioned to investigate and study the anticipated postwar problems. The answer

came with the recommendation of programs for education and training.

The first GI Bill was signed into law by FDR. This legislation became known as the "GI Bill of Rights," and has since been accredited as one of the most important acts of any Congress. Since its inception over fifty years ago, the government has invested billions of dollars in education and training for millions of veterans.

Officially called the Servicemen's Readjustment Act of 1944, the bill was signed two weeks after D-day, as American soldiers were dying by the thousands in France. Even though we now know that the invasion of Normandy was the beginning of the end of World War II, the passing of this bill had a special meaning, marking the beginning of the creation of a "new social order" in the many years of peace that were to follow. On the 50-year anniversary of the GI Bill, President Clinton remarked to an audience at the Department of Veterans Affairs, "Just as D-day was the greatest military action in our history, so the GI Bill arguably was the greatest investment in our people in American history."[114]

The First GI Bill

The first GI Bill provided six benefits:
- education and training
- loan guarantee for a home, farm,

or business
- unemployment pay of $20 a week for up to 52 weeks
- job-finding assistance
- top priority for building material for VA hospitals
- military review of dishonorable discharges[115]

To be eligible for education benefits, a veteran had to have served 90 days or more, and to have other than a dishonorable discharge. The Veterans Administration paid educational institutions up to $500 a year for tuition, books, fees, and other costs. A single veteran also received an allowance of up to $50 a month, later increased to $75 a month. Since the GI Bill's inception in 1944, it has been amended with provisions associated with World War II, the Korean Conflict, and the Vietnam War.

Resistance
The GI Bill did not pass without any opposition. Many members of Congress did not believe that servicemen went to war for money. However, strong public support in letters and telegrams to Congress demanding veterans be compensated with some type of benefit helped erode any resistance that the legislation was facing. Opponents saw it as handouts for bums, socialism, or another "New Deal" boondoggle. Even several of the most influential veterans groups opposed the

bill as unwise legislation. But the public was for the bill, prompting the House and Senate to pass versions quickly to be signed into law by President Roosevelt. Even during the first year after the inception of the GI bill, many policy makers and educators felt it was too expensive and would encourage veterans to become lazy. Others feared that it would lower standards in education. This rhetoric quickly diminished when the United States began to see the benefits.

Benefits to Society
The original program ended July 16, 1956. In the peak year of 1947, veterans accounted for 49 percent of college enrollment with over half of the 15,440,000 veteran population enrolled in some type of education or training program:
- 2,230,000 in college
- 3,480,000 in other schools
- 1,400,000 in on-the-job training
- 690,000 in farm training[116]

The total cost of the GI Bill education program for World War II was $14.5 billion.[117] The deferment of so many veterans entering the labor market after World War II helped reduce extensive joblessness during this difficult period of our nation's history. When the veterans did enter the labor market, most of them were better educated and "were better prepared to contribute to the support of their families and society."[118] The GI Bill opened the gates to upward mobility for the veterans who took advantage of it. The federal government's investment became one of human capital.

The GI Bill was very costly. By 1947, the national debt was larger than the U.S. GNP. During the years that followed, however, the debt began to shrink as a percentage of the nation's output, largely due to the growth of the economy in response to the multibillions of dollars made available to returnees through the GI Bill. The GI Bill was believed to provide the necessary stimulus to expand the economy and absorb the veterans into the labor market.[119] A government study found that the ratio of the benefits, defined as the increase in the nation's total output, to the costs of the government's investment in education under the GI Bill, an estimated $7 billion just for the 2.2 million GIs who used the funds to attend college or graduate school, was at least 5 to 1 and at most 12.5 to 1.[120] Assuming that only 40 percent of the veterans went to college because of the bill, and would not have gone otherwise, then the 1952 present value of the net benefit came to $35.6 billion.[121]

Education

Besides having a direct influence on the labor market, the GI Bill had profound effects that could not be measured by our society. The GI Bill eliminated the concept of an educated elite. The GI Bill caused colleges and universities to expand enormously. In absorbing more than 2.25 million veterans, new groups of the population were reached that were never previously served. The bill created a newfound "appreciation for the practical and dollar values of a college diploma" which helped drive higher education to a new level.[122]

Higher education was democratized; college enrollments doubled and tripled within two years. These college-educated veterans enriched our society in ways that would not have been possible without the GI Bill. These GI graduates were men and women who would have been factory workers or secretaries, at best, in pre-World War II America.[123] Statistics from the Veterans Administration show the GI Bill produced 456,000 engineers, 180,000 doctors and dentists, 360,000 school teachers, 156,000 scientists, and 107,000 lawyers. These college-trained veterans helped create one of the longest economic expansions in the United States, which continued for more than a generation.[124] Our society and our country have become the beneficiaries of the GI Bill, as well as the individuals who benefited directly from it.

the cost of education technology

"A billion here, a billion there, pretty soon it adds up to real money." — SENATOR EVERETT DIRKSEN (1896-1969)

Many states are realizing that they must have a technology plan in order to take advantage of funding available through the federal government and of potential discounts through the new Telecommunications Act. Most are also aware that if they do not implement technology in their schools, they will fall behind other states in the quality of education they provide for students and the quality of workers they provide for their businesses. Unfortunately, many states are just at the beginning phases of their technology planning and have very little sense of how much it would cost to install technology completely and effectively in their schools. Most are shocked by the bottom line and find that they had grossly underestimated the cost of implementing education technology.

In the past three years both RAND and McKinsey & Co. have researched the costs of K-12 technology plans.[125] RAND took the more detailed approach, looking at eight schools that use technology extensively to facilitate instruction, and at the components of their technology plans. The cost elements were then standardized to make comparisons among the schools. RAND's study does not provide a model or cost estimate for more aggregated levels than the individual school but does give insight into the necessary components and the share of the costs that is attributable to each. It also demonstrates the cost variance that exists to achieve similar goals.

McKinsey & Co. approached the problem by modeling various levels of technology infused into a school. After creating a model for the average school's technology, and pricing out that model, they then extended the cost to every school in the country. Their estimate for the full classroom model was $47 billion in initial costs and $14 billion in annual operation and maintenance costs for the United States as a whole.

We began our own analyses by developing a cost model for the California Education Technology Task Force. The Benchmarks Subcommittee was asked to determine what a model technology school should have, without worrying about budget constraints. Integrating technology into the curriculum and into every classroom was a key premise. The benchmarks were in three main categories: hardware (computers and associated equipment, audio and video equipment, and connectivity); software (courseware, materials, and services); and training, staff development, and support (see the Appendix for details on elements of the cost estimate). With these benchmarks as a guide, we then generalized a slightly modified version of this model to every state.

Using a four-year deployment model, we first estimated the cost of each benchmark item, creating an inventory and price list for the average school setup. These prices are based on the most recent prices from retailers and school-based estimates from studies by RAND, the American Association of School Administrators, and McKinsey & Co. For some items, particularly computer hardware, we assumed that the cost of the item would decrease over time.[126] Then, taking into account the differences in average school size from state to state, and the number of schools in the state,[127] and adjusting for projected growth in enrollment,[128] we scaled the cost up to a state level. Additionally, the ongoing costs, which include maintenance and repair of hardware, software upgrades, technical support personnel, and monthly connectivity charges, were added into the calculation for initial costs through year 4. We also assumed that computer hardware would last four years, so in year 5, the computers from year 1 will be replaced. The total cost is $84.6 billion to implement technology in every school in the country over four years, and $23.2 billion annually for ongoing operations and maintenance costs (including replacement costs) in years 5 and following. State totals range from $230 million to $10 billion. This total represents how much it would cost today to implement a model technology plan in each state, assuming nothing had been done yet (see Table 4-1).

Table 4-1 Full Model: Total Four-Year Plan Cost

STATE	TOTAL COST OF 4-YEAR PLAN	ANNUAL COSTS YEAR 5+	COST PER STUDENT AS % OF EXPENDITURE PER STUDENT
Alabama	$1,261,157,008	$352,572,600	10.6%
Alaska	379,405,536	109,028,507	8.5%
Arizona	1,436,594,078	384,585,802	8.5%
Arkansas	728,778,935	209,240,441	9.4%
California	10,046,197,269	2,746,417,021	9.4%
Colorado	1,228,932,401	344,995,095	9.2%
Connecticut	979,003,618	269,439,692	5.6%
Delaware	230,007,491	63,590,012	8.0%
District of Columbia	137,179,930	37,290,185	4.2%
Florida	3,756,403,415	997,364,571	7.8%
Georgia	2,424,308,814	648,202,305	9.4%
Hawaii	390,098,327	102,567,008	9.5%
Idaho	439,121,220	125,304,345	11.1%
Illinois	3,944,733,600	1,088,892,639	8.7%
Indiana	1,982,282,053	540,731,128	9.0%
Iowa	953,401,120	273,848,772	9.0%
Kansas	904,438,839	262,697,567	8.6%
Kentucky	1,189,487,013	329,003,276	9.1%
Louisiana	1,387,219,327	377,107,892	9.8%
Maine	510,906,826	142,267,031	9.6%
Maryland	1,710,971,261	460,124,960	8.4%
Massachusetts	1,848,569,200	500,221,841	7.3%
Michigan	3,114,910,816	860,994,522	7.1%
Minnesota	1,468,722,176	412,778,788	7.8%
Mississippi	891,417,781	245,100,630	10.5%
Missouri	1,665,539,483	465,629,948	9.4%
Montana	367,814,311	115,533,380	9.7%
Nebraska	786,708,678	231,323,398	13.1%
Nevada	470,593,011	128,629,694	8.8%
New Hampshire	364,570,424	100,696,538	8.4%

Table 4-1   Full Model: Total Four-Year Plan Cost—continued

STATE	TOTAL COST OF 4-YEAR PLAN	ANNUAL COSTS YEAR 5+	COST PER STUDENT AS % OF EXPENDITURE PER STUDENT
New Jersey	2,716,948,331	739,050,738	5.9%
New Mexico	650,653,571	181,022,606	11.6%
New York	4,886,100,433	1,310,340,190	4.7%
North Carolina	2,273,070,068	620,364,382	10.0%
North Dakota	273,155,146	82,327,507	14.3%
Ohio	3,489,230,321	958,007,794	7.9%
Oklahoma	1,005,191,592	294,779,501	8.7%
Oregon	1,145,271,923	319,549,343	9.8%
Pennsylvania	3,412,753,912	917,006,782	6.8%
Rhode Island	329,445,547	88,433,701	7.7%
South Carolina	1,177,078,031	321,186,267	9.7%
South Dakota	336,583,727	104,809,840	12.7%
Tennessee	1,738,883,332	471,235,566	10.5%
Texas	6,157,486,442	1,705,214,285	8.6%
Utah	839,422,204	227,643,157	12.9%
Vermont	319,869,092	88,495,665	11.4%
Virginia	2,341,687,157	632,395,525	10.6%
Washington	1,890,446,103	532,248,854	8.6%
West Virginia	721,756,223	199,449,376	10.3%
Wisconsin	1,613,463,128	446,348,349	6.9%
Wyoming	235,002,402	68,875,621	10.4%
TOTAL	**$84,552,972,645.77**	**$23,234,964,635.84**	**AVERAGE 9.1%**

It is clear that few, if any, states will be able to find the full funding for this ideal setup for every one of its schools. When we look at these figures annualized (1/4 of state total) as a percentage of yearly state expenditures per student, the average is 9.1 percent, a significant percentage. Many of the items that are on the benchmark list, particularly in the audiovisual section, may seem unnecessary and therefore candidates to be cut to reduce cost, but they serve a very real educational purpose. For example, some people see the list and ridicule the idea that headphones would be included in a technology plan. Imagine a classroom with six computers and a student at each, all trying to practice spelling with a program that says the word out loud and prompts the student to type the correct spelling. Are we going to seclude the computers so that the sound does not disturb other students? We could similarly rationalize the use of every item on the benchmark list, but our main point is that there is much more to creating a technology plan than computers and peripherals. What each school needs will depend on how it plans to use the technology. The purpose of this chapter is not to advocate specific hardware or quibble about the current cost of each item, but to increase awareness of the ballpark cost of school technology plans in each state depending upon the elements included in its plan.

To bring costs down to a more manageable level, we created a scaled-down version of this model by raising the ratio of students per computer from five to six; removing all hardware except computers, printers, the school network, and connectivity; and removing the district-level technical support. The national total for this version is $62 billion for initial costs and $17 billion for ongoing costs (see Table 4-2).

Table 4-2 Reduced-Cost Model

STATE	TOTAL COST OF 4-YEAR PLAN	ANNUAL COSTS YEAR 5+	ANNUAL COST PER STUDENT AS % OF EXPENDITURE PER STUDENT
Alabama	$926,824,241	$259,366,131	7.8%
Alaska	284,372,694	82,111,555	6.4%
Arizona	1,043,489,597	277,721,039	6.2%
Arkansas	546,612,855	158,111,324	7.0%
California	7,293,824,963	1,986,011,792	6.8%
Colorado	911,971,205	256,793,185	6.8%
Connecticut	719,514,547	198,210,327	4.1%
Delaware	167,373,025	46,118,075	5.8%
District of Columbia	101,186,834	27,552,471	3.1%
Florida	2,714,970,922	715,752,982	5.7%
Georgia	1,752,108,275	465,178,678	6.8%
Hawaii	280,287,642	72,947,976	6.8%
Idaho	329,134,142	94,369,215	8.3%
Illinois	2,899,129,711	801,031,819	6.4%
Indiana	1,447,396,705	394,734,279	6.6%
Iowa	719,623,374	208,446,839	6.8%
Kansas	685,069,441	200,757,009	6.5%
Kentucky	877,336,091	243,089,522	6.7%
Louisiana	1,018,009,217	276,305,353	7.2%
Maine	381,910,728	106,805,349	7.2%
Maryland	1,238,861,255	330,988,525	6.1%
Massachusetts	1,354,499,573	365,821,909	5.3%
Michigan	2,293,258,191	634,737,798	5.2%
Minnesota	1,100,873,904	310,871,984	5.9%
Mississippi	656,295,462	180,691,782	7.7%
Missouri	1,241,814,198	348,518,435	7.0%
Montana	289,521,199	92,229,542	7.6%
Nebraska	600,598,338	178,334,734	10.0%
Nevada	344,286,055	93,899,809	6.4%
New Hampshire	270,553,039	74,952,326	6.2%
New Jersey	1,977,269,944	535,989,792	4.3%
New Mexico	479,895,505	133,751,552	8.5%
New York	3,547,882,194	947,544,036	3.4%
North Carolina	1,656,264,750	450,607,901	7.3%
North Dakota	212,792,111	64,847,496	11.1%
Ohio	2,564,421,984	704,747,831	5.8%
Oklahoma	767,393,380	227,255,109	6.6%
Oregon	843,141,172	235,576,465	7.2%
Pennsylvania	2,490,134,993	667,144,951	4.9%
Rhode Island	240,382,823	64,337,689	5.6%
South Carolina	859,954,013	234,060,381	7.1%
South Dakota	264,929,590	83,669,010	10.0%
Tennessee	1,267,087,233	342,286,687	7.6%
Texas	4,525,303,179	1,254,422,017	6.3%
Utah	610,182,524	164,851,070	9.4%
Vermont	236,868,319	65,701,129	8.5%
Virginia	1,700,827,007	456,671,934	7.7%
Washington	1,396,967,338	394,183,644	6.4%
West Virginia	533,385,680	147,712,261	7.6%
Wisconsin	1,197,373,683	332,234,330	5.1%
Wyoming	178,678,017	52,859,191	7.9%
TOTAL	$62,041,842,860	$17,042,916,242	AVERAGE 6.8%

Both estimates are significantly higher than McKinsey & Co.'s estimate of $47 billion. This variance is easily accounted for by differences in hardware included in the estimates and McKinsey's significantly lower levels of technical support (1 1/2 full-time employees [FTE] shared across a district versus our 1 FTE per school and 1/10 FTE per school at the district level). Additionally, the McKinsey estimate is at a national level and does not take into account differences among the states. Calculating costs by state and taking into account different school sizes result in different totals. In general, lower units of calculation will lead to greater costs.[129]

Some districts—Clark County in Nevada, for example—have come up with creative cost-cutting solutions such as sending high school students for computer and networking training and having them wire the school and maintain its computers.

Our initial estimate for each state represents the cost for the state to implement a model technology plan, assuming that nothing has been done yet. However, several states have made progress. In order to account for the existing base of technology in each state, we created a discount percentage based on the number of multimedia computers the state's schools already have, and the number of schools that are on-line.[130] This discount ranges from 8.2 percent to 50 percent. Based on this level of completion, we calculated the total cost of implementation for each state, after taking into account its installed base (see Table 4-3). The nationwide total for these adjusted figures is $66.4 billion for the full model and $48.7 billion for the low-cost model. The $48.7 billion figure is close to the McKinsey estimate despite a very different approach. This implies an annual expenditure on technology equal to 5.2 percent of educational expenditures. To put some perspective on this figure, we compared annual expenditures on equipment and training as a share of total revenue in the private sector with the proposed public schools' investment in technology and related training. The share of revenues in the private sector is 9.5 percent compared to education's 5.6 percent.[131] Clearly the amount of funding needed here is substantial but not unreasonable.

Table 4-3 Adjusted Full-Model and Adjusted Reduced-Cost Model

STATE	ADJUSTED FULL-MODEL COST	COST PER STUDENT AS % OF EXPENDITURE PER STUDENT	ADJUSTED REDUCED-COST MODEL	COSTS PER STUDENT AS % OF EXPENDITURE PER STUDENT
Alabama	$1,046,528,294	8.8%	$769,093,607	6.5%
Alaska	258,104,166	5.8%	193,454,681	4.3%
Arizona	1,131,475,786	6.7%	821,862,787	4.9%
Arkansas	606,036,139	7.8%	454,550,932	5.8%
California	8,421,218,055	7.9%	6,114,043,833	5.7%
Colorado	743,768,035	5.6%	551,938,438	4.1%
Connecticut	828,208,267	4.7%	608,688,144	3.5%
Delaware	173,718,253	6.0%	126,412,185	4.4%
District of Columbia	117,702,487	3.6%	86,819,857	2.7%
Florida	2,255,278,321	4.7%	1,630,020,630	3.4%
Georgia	1,841,110,021	7.1%	1,330,616,003	5.2%
Hawaii	313,971,392	7.6%	225,590,050	5.5%
Idaho	364,295,305	9.2%	273,049,940	6.9%
Illinois	3,219,031,953	7.1%	2,365,784,897	5.2%
Indiana	1,566,261,380	7.1%	1,145,908,756	5.2%
Iowa	694,043,906	6.5%	523,861,580	4.9%
Kansas	624,688,949	5.9%	473,172,193	4.5%
Kentucky	1,022,065,619	7.8%	753,850,227	5.8%
Louisiana	1,249,368,001	8.8%	916,847,189	6.5%
Maine	396,303,155	7.4%	296,242,717	5.5%
Maryland	1,387,416,784	6.8%	1,004,585,487	4.9%
Massachusetts	1,596,715,296	6.3%	1,169,959,008	4.6%
Michigan	2,661,165,398	6.1%	1,959,201,951	4.5%
Minnesota	1,007,238,839	5.4%	754,971,207	4.0%
Mississippi	818,218,196	9.6%	602,403,161	7.1%
Missouri	1,414,826,805	8.0%	1,054,884,637	5.9%
Montana	259,292,371	6.8%	204,099,285	5.4%
Nebraska	402,487,001	6.7%	307,271,332	5.1%
Nevada	344,764,450	6.4%	252,229,824	4.7%
New Hampshire	294,162,081	6.7%	218,301,978	5.0%
New Jersey	2,340,198,163	5.0%	1,703,088,512	3.7%
New Mexico	479,500,698	8.5%	353,660,135	6.3%
New York	4,175,132,505	4.0%	3,031,636,062	2.9%
North Carolina	1,186,985,905	5.2%	864,893,230	3.8%
North Dakota	136,599,963	7.1%	106,413,497	5.6%
Ohio	3,020,047,122	6.9%	2,219,594,157	5.1%
Oklahoma	857,335,355	7.4%	654,515,498	5.7%
Oregon	890,846,663	7.7%	655,835,076	5.6%
Pennsylvania	2,970,347,572	5.9%	2,167,330,731	4.3%
Rhode Island	265,144,600	6.2%	193,465,075	4.5%
South Carolina	947,707,481	7.8%	692,379,630	5.7%
South Dakota	251,517,953	9.5%	197,973,172	7.5%
Tennessee	1,334,340,539	8.0%	972,305,519	5.9%
Texas	4,468,852,799	6.2%	3,284,280,683	4.6%
Utah	607,415,233	9.3%	441,534,854	6.8%
Vermont	266,128,446	9.5%	197,072,487	7.0%
Virginia	1,724,821,058	7.8%	1,252,781,453	5.7%
Washington	1,299,796,967	5.9%	960,500,226	4.4%
West Virginia	657,487,408	9.4%	485,890,328	6.9%
Wisconsin	1,285,737,354	5.5%	954,163,776	4.1%
Wyoming	166,250,960	7.4%	126,404,631	5.6%
TOTAL	$66,391,659,445	AVERAGE 7.0%	$48,705,435,250	AVERAGE 5.2%

Despite our standardized model, we do not advocate a cookie-cutter approach to implementing education technology. The same approach is used in each state in order to provide an estimate for necessary funding at the state or national level. Each state, district, and even school will vary in its technology requirements based on its pedagogical goals and its estimate of how much money is likely to materialize. Further, costs for some items, particularly connectivity, vary significantly by location. A study by the American Association of School Administrators found that some schools spend as little as $250 per month for their T1 lines while others spend as much as $2,000 per month.[132] With this large variance, some schools might find it more cost effective to use ISDN or another alternative.

To get a more accurate estimate for each state, one would have to clearly define the benchmarks for that state; conduct a survey to determine what the existing base of technology, trained personnel, and technical support is; and, finally, determine local prices and available discounts for goods and services. Last year we assisted the state of Nevada in this process. The costs listed in this work for Nevada are higher than those we arrived at after customizing the cost estimate to the state's own benchmarks and taking into account its existing base, as identified by our survey. Similarly, after focusing on California specifically, the numbers that resulted from the ideal setup as defined by the California Education Technology Task Force are somewhat higher than those we have projected here, but both figures are within a reasonable range of the cost that can be expected.

Other items have been excluded from this model, but should be taken into account. The cost of asbestos removal and of upgrading heating, ventilation, and air-conditioning systems as well as electrical systems are expenses that need to be considered. However, without more detailed information at a state or district level, estimating the extent of these expenses is difficult.

How Much Has Been Spent?

Until recently, most states did not even include technology as a separate item in their education budgets, so it has been difficult to determine how much actually has been spent. In 1994 we conducted a survey of all 50 state chiefs, asking them how much they had spent on technology in the past five years (regardless of source).[133] At that time, on average, the states indicated that they had acquired 21 percent of the funds they needed. Since then, technology itself and the state school-technology plans have increased immensely in sophistication. More recently, we surveyed each *state* school-technology director to find out how much *state* money was being spent on technology. The total for 46 states for which data were available is $7.8 billion, which includes spending prior to 1994, bond revenue and general fund allocations from 1994 through the current year, future authorized funding, and proposed authorizations (see Table 4-4). These are very generous figures. The amounts prior to 1994 include other funding sources in addition to state funding. In addition, there is some overlap between spending prior to 1994 and figures provided by the states for ongoing projects. Despite this generous interpretation, the total comprises only 14.9 percent of the funding that is required using our lowest estimate ($48.7 billion). Even states that are considered to be at the forefront of technology utilization have not spent anywhere near the amounts in Tables 4-1 and 4-2, even though our figures are usually much higher than what has actually been spent because they include future authorized and proposed spending.[134]

Table 4-4 Past, Current, and Proposed Expenditures on K-12 Education Technology

STATE	TOTAL SPENT, AUTHORIZED, AND PROPOSED	ADJUSTED REDUCED-COST TOTAL	ADJUSTED REDUCED-COST MODEL	TOTAL SPENT & AUTHORIZED AS % OF ADJUSTED REDUCED-COST
Alabama	$1,046,528,294	8.8%	$769,093,607	6.5%
Alaska	258,104,166	5.8%	193,454,681	4.3%
Arizona	1,131,475,786	6.7%	821,862,787	4.9%
Arkansas	606,036,139	7.8%	454,550,932	5.8%
California	8,421,218,055	7.9%	6,114,043,833	5.7%
Colorado	743,768,035	5.6%	551,938,438	4.1%
Connecticut	828,208,267	4.7%	608,688,144	3.5%
Delaware	173,718,253	6.0%	126,412,185	4.4%
District of Columbia	117,702,487	3.6%	86,819,857	2.7%
Florida	2,255,278,321	4.7%	1,630,020,630	3.4%
Georgia	1,841,110,021	7.1%	1,330,616,003	5.2%
Hawaii	313,971,392	7.6%	225,590,050	5.5%
Idaho	364,295,305	9.2%	273,049,940	6.9%
Illinois	3,219,031,953	7.1%	2,365,784,897	5.2%
Indiana	1,566,261,380	7.1%	1,145,908,756	5.2%
Iowa	694,043,906	6.5%	523,861,580	4.9%
Kansas	624,688,949	5.9%	473,172,193	4.5%
Kentucky	1,022,065,619	7.8%	753,850,227	5.8%
Louisiana	1,249,368,001	8.8%	916,847,189	6.5%
Maine	396,303,155	7.4%	296,242,717	5.5%
Maryland	1,387,416,784	6.8%	1,004,585,487	4.9%
Massachusetts	1,596,715,296	6.3%	1,169,959,008	4.6%
Michigan	2,661,165,398	6.1%	1,959,201,951	4.5%
Minnesota	1,007,238,839	5.4%	754,971,207	4.0%
Mississippi	818,218,196	9.6%	602,403,161	7.1%
Missouri	1,414,826,805	8.0%	1,054,884,637	5.9%
Montana	259,292,371	6.8%	204,099,285	5.4%
Nebraska	402,487,001	6.7%	307,271,332	5.1%
Nevada	344,764,450	6.4%	252,229,824	4.7%
New Hampshire*	294,162,081	6.7%	218,301,978	5.0%
New Jersey	2,340,198,163	5.0%	1,703,088,512	3.7%
New Mexico	479,500,698	8.5%	353,660,135	6.3%
New York	4,175,132,505	4.0%	3,031,636,062	2.9%
North Carolina**	1,186,985,905	5.2%	864,893,230	3.8%
North Dakota	136,599,963	7.1%	106,413,497	5.6%
Ohio	3,020,047,122	6.9%	2,219,594,157	5.1%
Oklahoma	857,335,355	7.4%	654,515,498	5.7%
Oregon	890,846,663	7.7%	655,835,076	5.6%
Pennsylvania	2,970,347,572	5.9%	2,167,330,731	4.3%
Rhode Island	265,144,600	6.2%	193,465,075	4.5%
South Carolina	947,707,481	7.8%	92,379,630	5.7%
South Dakota*	251,517,953	9.5%	197,973,172	7.5%
Tennessee	1,334,340,539	8.0%	972,305,519	5.9%
Texas	4,468,852,799	6.2%	3,284,280,683	4.6%
Utah	607,415,233	9.3%	441,534,854	6.8%
Vermont	266,128,446	9.5%	197,072,487	7.0%
Virginia	1,724,821,058	7.8%	1,252,781,453	5.7%
Washington	1,299,796,967	5.9%	960,500,226	4.4%
West Virginia	657,487,408	9.4%	485,890,328	6.9%
Wisconsin	1,285,737,354	5.5%	954,163,776	4.1%
Wyoming	166,250,960	7.4%	126,404,631	5.6%
TOTAL	$66,391,659,445	AVERAGE 7.0%	$48,705,435,250	AVERAGE 5.2%

*There has been no state funding for education technology.

**Includes 10 percent of a facilities bond for $1.9 billion.

If we use Quality Education Data's figures on the number of multimedia computers per student and the number of schools that are on-line as a measure of completion, we find that, on average, states are roughly 20 percent of the way toward meeting the technology goals that we advocate. This is probably a slight overestimate, given that the number of multimedia computers per student and schools that are on-line (often in only one location at the school) cannot account for classroom wiring, teacher training, and other items that may not have been invested in. In this light, the amount that has been (or is planned to be) spent does seem to correspond to the completion rate derived from QED figures.[135]

McKinsey & Co. estimated that the sources of funding for technology were 20 percent state, 40 percent local, 25 percent federal, 10 percent business, and 5 percent other. While there is need for increased funding at the state and local levels, the federal and business contributions are not a function of the amount contributed by the state and local governments. Federal funding is constrained by competition for other uses, pressure to lower taxes, and the desire for a balanced budget. Private giving is based on the financial constraints of the company or individual. As spending increases at the state and local levels, federal and private contributions are unlikely to continue to maintain their current shares of technology funding. Assuming that the 14 percent of funding that has come from the state level is matched 2:1 at the local level, that the business community continues to contribute 10 percent,[136] and that the federal contribution is 10 percent, the total comes to only 62 percent, far short of what is required.

Possible Cost Savings
Given the level of funding required, many states will be unable to support the comprehensive technology program that we are modeling here. What other savings can be taken into account to bring the cost down? In addition to the cuts that are shown made in Table 4-2, there are other potential sources of cost savings. We would not recommend reducing the student-to-computer ratio beyond 6:1, but the cost of some computers could probably be reduced. Donated computers are an option that can save a significant amount of money. Several states have well-established programs that provide high-quality donated computers to schools for $200 to $500 each, a fraction of the cost of a comparable new computer. Donated computers can reduce costs, but they should be used with caution. They may be more likely to break down than are new computers. They also are likely to be older models than those currently being used in the business world. Computers that are somewhat out of date may present software compatibility issues as well.

Significant discounts for large-quantity purchases of hardware and software can also be obtained to reduce costs. For smaller schools or districts, technical support might be shared among schools. Wiring to a wide-area network is another item that could be shared throughout a district or by a few schools, creating a significant cost saving in most instances. Sharing wiring with nearby universities or community colleges is also an option for some schools. Some districts—Clark County in Nevada, for example—have come up with creative cost-saving solutions such as sending high school students for computer and networking training and having them wire the school and maintain its computers. The cost of sending students for training is far lower than the cost of hiring a private contractor to install wiring or perform maintenance. Students are also given the opportunity to take some responsibility and learn marketable computer skills.

It is likely that the wiring done on NetDays will have some impact in reducing the cost of wiring within a school. Businesses and foundations are also stepping in to donate wiring, Internet service, and hardware, as well as money. We have already expressed doubt that businesses will be able to continue contributing as much as 10 percent of the total cost. To do so, they would have to provide greater amounts as more spending is made by state and local governments.

Allocation and Implementation Issues for Limited Funding

Given that no state has or is planning to spend anywhere near the amount of money that will be required for a comprehensive technology plan, how should available funds be allocated? Some of the options are to allocate by average daily attendance (ADA), competitive grants, socioeconomic status, grade level, or academic subject. Allocation by ADA appears to be the most common approach used by states, probably because it is perceived as the most equitable. Grants are also fairly common, but equity then can become an issue. Each method has its pros and cons and particular appeal to different states based on their specific needs.[137]

Another approach is to begin spending limited resources on creating the foundation for more effective spending later. This can be done by first investing in the infrastructure—wiring, electrical systems, and building upgrades—for schools before buying computers and software. This has somewhat less general appeal, because the results of this spending after one or two years may not be visible in the form of students sitting in front of computers. Preparatory spending ensures that schools will have a safe, dry place in which to put a computer, plug it in, and keep it from frying when there is a power surge, and that once purchased, computers will immediately become a source of information and outreach via the Internet. Teacher training could also start before funds are spent on major hardware purchases. Providing teachers with their own computers and training in basic computer skills as well as the integration of technology into the curriculum is another way to ensure that technology will be used immediately, and used effectively, once it becomes available in the classroom. More details on how to spend the money will come in Chapter 9.

To summarize, we estimate that a minimum of $48.7 billion will be required to bring education technology to every public school in the nation. Our best estimates indicate that less than half of the funding for this endeavor has become available. We believe that unless the states step up to the plate and make more funding available, our schools will continue to go without technology.

Chapter Appendix 4-1

HARDWARE

Computers and Associated Equipment	Quantity	Cost per unit ($)

NETWORKED MULTIMEDIA COMPUTERS
  minimum MPC2 or Apple Power PC
  2 GB harddrive with 32 MB RAM
  CD ROM, Ethernet card (most current buys
  are at the 32 MB RAM, 4 GB harddrive level)
  15" monitor
	5 per classroom[+]
	5 per library[+]
	5 per office[+]
		1,200.

ADAPTIVE TECHNOLOGIES for persons needing disability access features	per room	500.
*SCANNER	1 per classroom, 1 per library	300.
NETWORK LASER PRINTER	1 per classroom, 1 per library	1,000.
COLOR PRINTER (Inkjet)	1 per 5 rooms (excluding office)	350.

Audio and Video Equipment		
* TAPE RECORDER	1 per 5 rooms (excluding office)	50.
* HEADPHONES	1 per computer	30.
* VIDEO CAPTURE BOARD	1 per 5 rooms (excluding office)	300.
* CAMCORDER	1 per 5 rooms (excluding office)	400.
* 31" TV MONITOR	1 per classroom, 1 per library	650.
* VCR	1 per classroom, 1 per library	250.
* OVERHEAD PROJECTOR AND SCREEN	1 per classroom, 1 per library	400.

Miscellaneous		
* FAX MACHINE	2 per school	300.
* TELEPHONE	1 per classroom, 1 per library	40.
FURNITURE AND SECURITY EQUIPMENT	1	355. per computer[***] 350. per room[***]

Connectivity		
T1 LINE (materials and installation fee)	1	3,000.
SCHOOL NETWORK (with Network Server, coaxial, wireless, hybrid technology)**	1	Costs vary

  + This number was reduced to 4 in the reduced-cost model.
  * These items were omitted from the reduced-cost model.
 ** See School Network Model.
*** McKinsey

COURSEWARE, MATERIALS AND SERVICES

Cost Element	Quanity	Cost per unit ($)
+COURSEWARE	5 per classroom, 5 per library, 5 per office	500.
MATERIALS AND SERVICES	1 per classroom, 1 for library, 1 for office	1,000.

+This number was reduced to 4 in the reduced-cost model.

Cost Element	Quantity	Cost per unit ($)
INSERVICE TRAINING FOR TEACHERS, LIBRARIANS, MEDIA SPECIALISTS, AND ADMINISTRATORS		
Cost of trainers	1 session per 10 teachers	4,500. [1]
** Staff support, materials, manuals, mileage, etc.	1 per classroom, 1 for library, 5 for office staff	2,000.

Technical Support		
*DISTRICT TECHNICAL SUPPORT	0.1	50,000. [2]
SCHOOL TECHNICAL SUPPORT	1	50,000. [3]

* These items were omitted from the reduced-cost model.
** This item was reduced to $1,000 in the reduced-cost model.

Notes
[1] 6 hours/wk for 15 weeks @ $50/hr.
[2] .1 FTE per school at district level.
[3] 1 FTE at school site.

1) MAINTENANCE/REPAIRS/UPGRADES	15% of the outlay on hardware (excluding connectivity) * the % of implementation completed e.g., Year 2 = [.15 (Hardware Costs -Connectivity) x Number of Schools x .25]
2) REPLACEMENTS	Year 5, the computers from year 1 are replaced

Courseware, Materials, and Services	
3) UPGRADES	Year 3 courseware from year 1 is upgraded at 50% of the initial outlay e.g., Year 3 = [(Year 1 Total for Courseware, Materials and Services) x .5]
4) COMMUNICATIONS COSTS	(($1000 monthly T1 fee)+($125 Internet access fee x 12 months) x Number of schools x *Number of Schools*% of implementation completed e.g., Year 3 = [(($1000x12)+($125x12)) x Number of schools x .5]

Training, Staff Development, and Support	
5) TRAINING	After their first year of training, teachers will receive 2 weeks of training a year e.g., Year 2 = [(Cost of 2-week course x Number of Schools)x.25]
6) TECHNICAL SUPPORT	Technical support * % of implementation completed e.g., Year 2 = [Technical Support x Number of Schools x .25]

Each Classroom

WIRING	2 outlets to building closet
1 12-PORT HUB	
TWISTED PAIR WIRING	100 feet (connects each computer)

Each Building

1 PATCH PANEL

1 16-PORT HUB

Each School

1 ROUTER

NETWORK SERVER

*Varying number of rooms, 3 buildings

Description	Quantity*	Cost ($)
OUTLETS FOR CLASSROOMS /library/office (per room)	Number of rooms	100.
GATEWAY ROUTER	1	2,000.
12-PORT NETWORK HUB	Number of rooms	100.
16-PORT MANAGEABLE HUB (per building)	Number of buildings	200.
NETWORK SERVER	1	7,000.
UTP between buildings	Number of buildings	1,000.
CLOSET WIRING per building	Number of buildings	700.

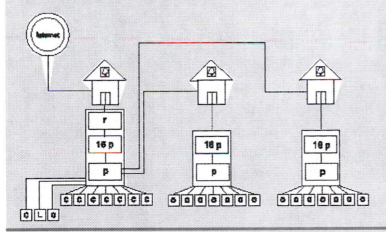

School Network Model

c=classroom (see classroom set-up)

o=office

L=library

p=patch panel

16p=16 port hub

r=router

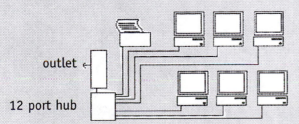

Classroom Set-up

outlet

12 port hub

the imperative
of
teacher
training

"We are restless because of incessant change, but we would be frightened if change were stopped."

— LYMAN LLOYD BRYSON, PROFESSOR AT COLUMBIA UNIVERSITY

Teacher education is probably the most important element of successfully integrating technology into our schools. We have learned from the failure of past attempts of schools to introduce technology that unless teachers are supportive, involved, and prepared, the innovation will fail.[138] In order for teachers to embrace new technology, they will have to be involved in design and planning from the start. They will have to understand the technology—its operation and its possibilities—and most important, they will have to know how to integrate it into their curricula. Education of teachers must occur both pre-service and in-service.

Pre-service Training

Clearly, training incoming teachers to use technology in the classroom is one of the most efficient ways of getting technology into the schools. Teachers who are accustomed to using technology will be a driving force to have it available to them in their classrooms. Additionally, they will require less intensive training after they begin teaching.

We conducted an informal review of fourteen graduate and teacher certification programs in education.[139] A few colleges of education have been successful in incorporating technology into their teacher education curricula; the majority have not. Of the schools that we reviewed, only one, the University of Texas at Austin, requires that education students pass a "Computing Tools for Educators Competency Test" in order to complete the program. This test requires that students demonstrate competency in the use of word processors, spreadsheets, databases, the ability to retrieve information from databases such as ERIC and University of Texas Catalog (UTCAT), send e-mail messages, and evaluate instructional software. One of the fourteen schools (Clark Atlanta) made no mention of technology in their education programs.

Many college education courses teach *about* technology rather than teaching students how to use technology as a tool in the classroom. There appear to be minimal "hands-on," experiential opportunities for the teacher education student; yet, this is exactly what is needed to produce a technologically proficient workforce. Research indicates that students benefit most from technology when the teacher is most knowledgeable about the computer system being used.[140] In order to be effective, teachers must be taught to use information technologies for instructional purposes.[141] A 1996 survey by *Electronic Learning* found that despite the fact that 76 percent of education professors surveyed responded that "information technology was now a very important aspect of education," 50 percent of recent teacher-education graduates surveyed "reported that they were either not prepared—or poorly prepared—to use information technology in the classroom." Among those who felt prepared to use technology at all, many felt comfortable with education games and drill and practice, but far fewer "felt able to collaborate over networks, use e-mail, or take advantage of distance-education services."[142] Given these bleak statistics, how can we expect schools of education to provide adequate technology training for future teachers?

Unless a student is specializing, minoring, or specifically seeking a degree in media or computers in education, technology is not a part of the standard teacher education curriculum. Even Harvard University has found itself providing a less than adequate knowledge base in education technology for its general teacher-education students. Harvard's teacher-education program, like that of many other schools, offers courses in computers and technology, but does not integrate technology into its general education courses. Professor John B. Willet commented that Harvard's education technology classes are electives, and "may not have been designed with their [pre-service teachers] needs in mind. What we're proposing is that teacher-education and educational-technology people get together and customize offerings, so that all teachers will be exposed to technology."[143] Though not surprising, these findings are unsettling and point vividly to the need for the inclusion of technology in teacher education curricula.

Several reasons might explain why teacher education programs are failing to teach instructional uses of technology. To begin with, much of the higher education faculty is not prepared to teach such courses—to education students or to any other college students. Professors who do not feel comfortable using technology might resist its use. There may also be a feeling that their inability to use technology devalues their own less-technical skills. We must remember that most education professors (and most current teachers) did not grow up using modern technology in their own schooling environment. It takes a significant amount of time and adjustment before they will be comfortable using it. Faculty use computers primarily to type, for research (particularly for statistical analysis) and, to a much lesser degree, for teaching. This is easily explained. As a word processor, the computer reduces the need for support staff and speeds up word processing. For statistical analysis, the computer enables more sophisticated analysis quickly and cheaply. For teaching, however, the computer requires *extra work*. It is clear that the first two uses make the professor's job easier while the third option makes it more difficult, at least in the short term. This might explain some of the reluctance to use technology in teaching.

There is also a prevalent feeling among faculty that technology is a subject to be taught by itself, rather than a tool that can be used to teach other subjects. In a sense, this becomes the root of the problem and the beginning of a vicious circle of ignorance. A 1995 study conducted by the

Technology, Teaching and Scholarship Project at the University of Southern California[144] found that, in general, only one in six college courses was taught in a computerized classroom or laboratory. This should not surprise us, because there are few incentives for college faculty to take the time to learn about technology or to revise their curricula, given that they are rewarded primarily for publishing. Moreover, tight budgets preclude most higher education institutions from purchasing all the equipment required for faculty to use it in their teaching. Even fewer classes were using technologies such as electronic mail and CD-ROM. If college faculty served as role models by using technology themselves, we would be more optimistic about its use in K-12 education. We believe that this is an area where the state and federal governments should step in to provide funding and incentives for faculty to develop technology-integrated curricula for teacher education. Even if private grants and donations can provide equipment, rarely do corporations provide significant funding for training.

There is also a prevalent feeling among faculty that technology is a subject to be taught by itself, rather than a tool that can be used to teach other subjects.

It is also important to acknowledge the placement of teacher education within the academic hierarchy. Colleges of education, in general, do not have high status in the higher education system. Education is considered a professional field rather than an academic discipline, and as a result it draws faculty from a number of different areas. Often that faculty is composed of former practitioners and is not predominantly tenure track; consequently it has little influence in the higher education power structure (i.e., Academic Senate). Further, schools of education typically do not bring in a large amount of research money. Given their professional emphasis and past job experiences in the field, research is usually not the primary goal (or the comparative advantage) of those within colleges of education. Thus they do not need to learn how technology could help them with research. Unfortunately, teacher-education programs experience a magnification of the two characteristics described—few tenure track faculty and little research interest or money for it—and so, are at the bottom of the pecking order of programs in colleges of education. Less research money also means that teacher-education programs are less likely to have funds to purchase equipment. Faculty in teacher education also have the lowest status within education schools. Top education research faculty generally prefer not to teach in teacher-education programs because they are too time-intensive and are of lower status. As a result, teacher education programs have minimal influence on the larger scope of higher education decision making.

The ramifications of this lack of status are many. To begin with, teacher education seems to get overlooked in the discussions of K-12 school reform. There has been little incentive to link reforms in colleges of education with K-12 reforms.[145] As a result, although technology can serve as a mechanism for helping to reform the schools, teacher education may lag behind in incorporating technology, thereby slowing reform efforts at the K-12 level. Colleges of education have more limited power than other departments to acquire funding and support for incorporating technology into their curriculum. Further, nontenure track faculty are more transient than tenure track faculty; as a result, they may have less institutional commitment and not be as willing to fight for funds to provide technology in their colleges or departments. Additionally, teacher training faculty who come from practice and do not do much research have had little need to use computers, and so, very little incentive to learn about technology.

There are several reasons that might explain why these schools are failing to teach technology. To begin with, teachers are unique in that the jobs that they are applying for generally require a piece of paper rather than a specific skill set. When a prospective teacher applies for a job, the only real requirement is that they have, or will be obtaining, a teaching credential, whereas an engineering student must learn and be able to demonstrate certain skills before being offered a job. Additionally, prospective teachers do not have to graduate from an accredited teacher-education program as a criterion for participation in the profession. As a matter of fact, under 50 percent of the schools of education are professionally accredited.[146] Those that are accredited are sanctioned by two types of organizations. Some are accredited by state standards boards—these exist in eleven states—and others by the National Council for Accreditation of Teacher Education (NCATE).[147]

The District of Columbia and fifteen states require coursework in computers as part of their broad academic requirements for the initial teaching certificate. Study of technology in teaching (content, not necessarily a separate course) is required in 30 states for the elementary teaching certificate and in 29 states for the secondary teaching certificate.

Within the state standards boards there is a great deal of variation. Membership varies from political appointees to professional educators. Standards set by NCATE and state boards are often duplicative and are all voluntary. As a result, they have minimal impact. Several states currently have coursework and content requirements for teaching certificates that include computers and technology. The District of Columbia and fifteen states require coursework in computers as part of their broad academic requirements for the initial teaching certificate.[148] Study of technology in teaching (content, not necessarily a separate course) is required in 30 states for the elementary teaching certificate and in 29 states for the secondary teaching certificate.[149] The content and quality of these offerings vary significantly from school to school. Many courses merely discuss the possibilities of using technology and offer students no opportunity to work with it or to apply it to their lessons.

A state requirement that a course be offered in "computers" or that "technology in teaching" be covered in a course does not ensure that these teacher trainees actually learn to use technology in their own teaching. After taking a course in instructional media, Tina Wallace, a recent graduate from Grambling State University's teacher-education program, said she'd like to learn more about integrating technology into her teaching, but "we didn't even work on the computers," she said.[150] This is fairly typical of required technology courses. If there is a state-mandated requirement, schools of education respond by offering a course, but not necessarily a course that allows teacher trainees to practice using technology in a classroom setting or integrated with other subjects.

There have even been stories about schools of education renaming classes that have had very low enrollment so that they meet a state-mandated requirement. The professor continues to teach the original content, but students enroll to meet their requirements. The school also satisfies the need to offer the required course without having to develop a new one. This is an extreme example. The point is the title of a course or the number assigned to it does not guarantee specific content. Additionally, there is no way to assure that the same level of rigor is being applied from school to school.

Michigan has mandated that teachers have "a working knowledge of modern technology and use of computers."[151] Schools of education must demonstrate their students' knowledge of technology to the satisfaction of the local school or district before students can begin their student teaching.[152] Rather than requiring that teacher-education students take a course in education technology, this state requires students to demonstrate their proficiency.

Nevertheless, certification agencies are trying to include technology recommendations in their guidelines. The NCATE has included educational computing as one of eight areas that the teacher-education curriculum should encompass.[153] This suggestion includes using related technologies and computers for assessment, instruction, and professional growth. NCATE has also endorsed the curriculum guidelines recommended by the International Society for the Accreditation of Technology in Education (ISTE), a professional organization of educators interested in instructional technology.[154] Figure 5-1 outlines these guidelines. We must reemphasize that all of these standards, guidelines, and accreditations are voluntary—no school of education is required to put any of these agencies' suggestions into their curriculum. Clearly, this points to one of the barriers in incorporating technology training into teacher education.

Figure 5-1

Curriculum Guidelines for Accreditation of Educational Computing and Technology Programs

The Accreditation Committee of the International Society for Technology in Education (ISTE) in 1992 developed a set of "Curriculum Guidelines for the Accreditation of Educational Computing and Technology Programs," which was approved by the National Council for the Accreditation of Teacher Education. The basic guidelines suggest that all teachers should be able to demonstrate the ability to operate a computer system in order to successfully use software.

- Evaluate and use computers and related technologies to support the instructional process.
- Apply instructional principles, research, and appropriate assessment practices to the use of computers and related technologies.
- Explore, evaluate, and use computer/technology-based materials, including applications, educational software, and documentation.
- Demonstrate knowledge of uses of computers for problem solving, data collection, information management, communications, presentations, and decision making.
- Design and develop student learning activities that integrate computing and technology for a variety of student grouping strategies and for diverse student populations.
- Evaluate, select, and integrate computer/technology-based instruction in the curriculum of one's subject area(s) and/or grade level.
- Demonstrate knowledge of uses of multimedia, hypermedia, and telecommunications to support instruction.
- Demonstrate skill in using productivity tools for professional and personal use, including word processing, database, spreadsheet, and print/graphics utilities.
- Demonstrate knowledge of equity, ethical, legal, and human issues of computing and technology as they relate to society and model appropriate behaviors.
- Identify resources for staying current in applications of computing and related technologies in education.
- Use computer-based technologies to access information to enhance personal and professional productivity.
- Apply computers and related technologies to facilitate emerging roles of the learner and the educator.

Source: Excerpt from goals established by the International Society for the Accreditation of Technology in Education, Accreditation Committee, Eugene, Oregon, 1992.

There is also a mismatch between what occurs at the teacher education level and what occurs at the K-12 school site. Some argue that many K-12 schools have more advanced technology resources and more experienced technology-using staff than do education schools within colleges and universities.[155] "It's hard to be a leader when you don't have the equipment," says James White, a professor of instructional technology at the University of South Florida.[156] Corporations tend to donate more technology to K-12 schools than colleges and universities because in the public eye there is more of a "feel good" sentiment toward K-12 than toward higher education.

As an exception to this rule, in 1989 IBM donated a total of $30 million (in hardware, software, cash, and training) to 144 teacher-education institutions nationwide. Each school established a networked IBM lab. In the IBM evaluation study, one of the major problems was discovered. IBM had provided a generous amount of equipment, but the training that was available was of a very technical nature. The education schools found that the available technical support served to get the lab up and running, but there was very minimal support available in learning to use the computers for instructional uses. One site pointed out "IBM could have 'forced the colleges of education to provide...release time, or other perks as compensation for...learning the technology.' IBM had the clout to require this, they just didn't know it."[157] IBM's generous contribution has taught us some valuable lessons for higher education which are equally relevant at the K-12 level. Equipment without technical support is of fairly limited value to new computer users. When we are asking that computers be learned not just as word processors, but as tools for teaching, a more specialized type of support is needed. Additionally, teachers need the time to figure out how to learn the technology and develop new curriculum. This is a problem for both pre-service and in-service training.

Whether K-12 schools are better equipped than colleges of education or vice versa is somewhat irrelevant. What is extremely relevant is that this mismatch prevents K-12 students from accessing the benefits provided by technology. The mismatch plays itself in two ways. In scenario number one, teacher-education students who have not been trained to use technology for teaching enter a school where there is extensive use of technology. These new teachers enter the classroom feeling underprepared and unable to utilize technology as an educational tool. In the second scenario, the new teacher who has had significant training in integrating technology into the curriculum is frustrated by the lack of opportunity to use the skills she had attained during her schooling because the school where she works has no modern technology. Further, this scenario does not allow teachers in training to gain that critical "hands-on" experience during their education process. Neither scenario should be acceptable.

It is clear that many changes need to be made in teacher-education programs and in teacher certification. To begin with, states should stop mandating content and coursework. Instead, teachers should be assessed on their ability in various content areas. Schools of education will be forced to respond by ensuring that students who pass through their program are competent enough to pass a certification exam, not just floating through the courses to meet requirements. Doctors are not allowed to practice based on the courses they have taken; they must pass the board certification exams before they are officially allowed to practice medicine unsupervised. Teachers will be shaping the thinking of our nation's children. Surely we want teachers who can *demonstrate* that they are competent. Certification of technology skills may be the first step toward teacher standards. Sooner or later schools of education will have to bow to outside pressure. At one end, aspiring teachers will begin to demand graduate education that can keep pace with rapidly evolving undergraduate programs. According to *Electronic Learning*, "As more colleges require undergraduates to use computers, education schools will be dealing with an increasingly sophisticated clientele."[158] At the other end, schools will begin to demand teachers with serious computer skills. Tom Layton, a technology teacher in Eugene, Oregon, says, "Schools are going to start saying, 'We have two kinds of teachers: Those who want to bring all of the educational opportunities out there in the world to their students—and those who can't.'"[159] Schools may have room for old teachers in the latter camp, but they won't be interested in hiring many new ones.

In-service Training

There are roughly 2.7 million teachers in our public schools today.[160] Although some of these teachers employ technology in their classrooms, most do not. This is the case despite the fact that more than 80 percent of U.S. schoolteachers now have computers at home.[161] In order for teachers to "buy into" the technology-rich school, they must be able to understand, firsthand, the potential benefits of these tools in their classrooms. But as Hattie Brown, principal of Detroit's John F. Bennett Elementary School, says, "Most of our career has been without" computers.[162]

Teacher training has been, perhaps, the most overlooked aspect of implementing technology in education. The focus has generally been on hardware and software. A 1995 survey by *Electronic Learning* found that on average schools and districts spend only 8.3 percent of their technology budgets on staff development. Case studies and interviews conducted by McKinsey & Co. indicate that even "model" technology schools "spend no more than 15 percent on training and support."[163] Hardware and software are tangible items that have specific costs, and when they are purchased the immediate task is accomplished. Training, on the other hand, is not as straightforward. Teachers are beginning with different knowledge bases and they learn at different paces. It is difficult to predict how much training will be required to bring different teachers up to speed, or to begin integrating technology into their curriculum. The goals for using technology at various grade levels and schools can also be dramatically different depending on their needs. Thus there are the questions of what to teach and how to teach it.

Teacher training has been, perhaps, the most overlooked aspect of implementing technology in education.

The majority of today's public school teachers are over 40 years old and have been teaching for more than ten years.[164] These people received their initial training when technology meant only instructional television and the overhead projector. Tom Stevens, director of Denver Public Schools' Career Education Center, commented, "When you ask someone to change their teaching style, it's like asking them to borrow a toothbrush."[165] People are accustomed to working in a particular way, with familiar tools. We grew up writing our essays with paper and pencil. Although we have been using word processors for years, both of us find that it is hard to break the habit of writing things out on paper first. To change these patterns takes effort and a lot of time.

In 1994 the average number of teachers that had at least nine hours of training in education technology was 15 percent, state averages ranging from 28 to 8 percent.

Teachers need to be given the time to get familiar with technology before they can begin teaching with it. In 1994 the average number of teachers who had at least nine hours of training in education technology was 15 percent, state averages ranging from 28 to 8 percent. Nine hours! Anyone who has worked with computers knows that it takes nine hours just to get familiar with the very basics of a particular computer. We would not expect our children to learn how to read after attending school nine hours or for one to two weeks. Why would we expect our teachers to be technologically literate after having such minimal training? Policy makers need to keep this in mind when they provide funding and expect immediate, visible results.

At the 1997 Milken National Education Conference, we recently had the opportunity to observe teachers at various skill levels in a computer training course. Some teachers who had previously used a computer and Netscape (a software package that allows users to browse the World Wide Web) were able to follow along, but many were lost from the moment class began. One teacher was staring at the screen on the verge of tears. When asked if he was having trouble, he responded, "The instructor clicked on something and I have no idea where he is now." Like a child that is behind the rest of the class, this teacher was experiencing extreme frustration and was too embarrassed to raise his hand and say that he had no idea what the instructor was doing. Several other teachers experienced the standard technical difficulties that can rarely be predicted. For these novices, it was difficult to determine if they had made a mistake or the computer was not working properly.

Another problem became apparent for beginners. Some educators were having difficulty manipulating the mouse. We focus on the use of computers and software, and integration into the curriculum, but often forget that there are basic coordination issues that need to be overcome. When Lew Solmon was dean at UCLA's School of Education and Apple Computer gave him a Macintosh, the technical support person told him that he was fortunate to have "good hand-eye coordination." When we see children who have grown up playing video games and using computers, we forget that the same agility with the keyboard and mouse does not always come naturally to adults. Another teacher at the Milken Conference couldn't understand why menus kept popping up on her screen instead of the pointer opening up the program. She was a Mac user and was using a PC for this course. The mouse for a Macintosh generally has only one button, while the PC mouse generally has two. She had been clicking on the right button instead of the left. Imagine the frustration if there were no technical support around to straighten out this confusion. Though a minor problem, this educator spent half the class fighting with her mouse! Even when it was pointed out that she should use the left button, it was physically difficult for her to do so. These are all challenges that will have to be dealt with slowly and patiently.

We believe that courses and training in technology are important for educators. However, this is only a start. Teachers will have to play with the computer on their own time to become truly comfortable with it. In the early stages one-on-one or small group peer training might be a more effective way to familiarize educators with the basics of computer use. Only after this point will training in specific software packages or computer-based lesson plans be of significant value. Concord, N.C., has a model staff development program that is based on the idea of interested teachers learning how to work with and going on to train other interested teachers. Jean White, the district's technology coordinator, directs a staff development program which began with her traveling around the district offering technology staff development to interested teachers. These trainers then became licensed technology specialists themselves and went on to train other interested teachers. Nearly every school in the district now has one of these trainers working in the classrooms. They work with teachers in their classrooms modeling the use of technology. This is a highly effective way of spreading the use of technology in our schools.[166]

The experiences of Phantom Lake Elementary School in Bellevue, Washington, provide another example of how technology can spread through a school by having educators excite and teach each other.

P H A N T O M   L A K E   E L E M E N T A R Y   S C H O O L

In Bellevue, Washington, a suburb of Seattle, in a school district feeling the effects of large-scale multiethnic immigration, a small group of teachers, with the input and support of the district's media specialist and assistant superintendent, brought technology into their classrooms in the hopes it would help them teach their ever-broadening, ever-more-challenging mix of students. Recognizing that educating students is problematic in an environment where 20 languages are primary, where children come from homes in poverty, and where the old school model prevails, members of the Phantom Lake Elementary School staff and community joined forces to completely remake their school.

The technology seed was planted in 1988 when Chris Held, a fourth-grade teacher at Phantom Lake, and John Newsom, the Bellevue district's technology specialist, attended a computer demonstration at an education conference. The two friends returned to the district full of ideas and excitement that started them thinking about ways they could use technology in the classroom. After sharing these ideas and his enthusiasm with the district leaders, Chris returned to Phantom Lake with six Apple IIes, and began his exploration of ways that computers could be used to enhance the curriculum and illustrate concepts in new ways.

Soon after, John, the district technology specialist, put out an invitation to other teachers: "Come see what Chris is doing, and if you're interested let us know." It was not long before three other teachers, each at different schools, showed an interest in bringing technology into their classrooms. With the technological support of Chris and the financial support of the district, these new pioneers were able to integrate technology into their curriculum. The following year, with growing interest sparked by the cadre of four technology leaders, the district successfully mounted a campaign for a $1.2 million property tax levy to purchase equipment, an Internet server, and begin networking schools.

With these funds, Phantom Lake was able to purchase the necessary computers and equipment to set up a local-area network. Operating under the aegis of site-based management, teachers and Principal Sylvia Hayden at Phantom Lake Elementary began a year-long philosophical discussion over their local-area network. They "talked," "met," and "argued" at length over electronic mail (e-mail) about how best to meet their own professional needs and, critically, the educational needs of their students. These teacher discussions were no small feat. In an elementary school, teachers are confined with their charges in classrooms from 8:00 A.M. to 2:00 P.M. At Phantom Lake, e-mail acted as a tool to help these educators establish the terms and conditions of the school they would restructure. Technology in the form of the local e-mail allowed these teachers to engage in something rare in the teaching profession: self-reflective thought among colleagues—no small task given traditional school boundaries of time and space. Ideas were bounced from one person to another; from teacher aides to principal to all members of the school staff. Everyone had equal access; all ideas had the same weight.

Phantom Lake's staff began its discussions with a vision of what they wanted their school to be. This gave the foundation for discussions on structural changes. Staff members brought with them ideas and knowledge from their years of experience and staff development courses. No specific plan, research theory, or expert guided their discussions. The initial result of this year-long conversation was the decision to trim class size from 26-31 students to 18-20. But *many* additional discussions and decisions critical to the successful restructuring followed as a consequence: Students would be grouped in a multiage and developmentally appropriate fashion, cooperative learning projects with teachers as leaders would form the nucleus of class time, and long-term group projects would focus on real-life questions. One of the ways of paying for these changes was to eliminate curricular specialists such as music, art, and physical education teachers, with regular classroom teachers assuming their responsi-

bilities. These decisions were controversial and did not have unanimous support. They did, however, represent the result of the joint decision-making process led, not directed, by Phantom Lake's highly effective principal, Sylvia Hayden. Teachers that were not happy with the outcome of this decision-making process chose to retire or transfer to other schools in the district, causing some turnover.

Phantom Lake took down the permanent walls that separated classrooms, replacing them with room dividers that allowed teachers to open rooms to different multi-age configurations; e.g., grades 3-5 were grouped as well as grades 2 and 3 with as many as 80 students and 4 teachers arranging themselves in different configurations for specific projects. Children were placed according to their individual abilities. Computer network access and multimedia stations were available in all classrooms.

These were all ideas Phantom Lake teachers believed in *before* technology entered their school. Technology did not make these ideas happen, but it did successfully support the process. Technology did not transform Phantom Lake Elementary; technology was used as a tool to facilitate the process.

As the dialog among educators was allowed to proceed at Phantom Lake, more teachers began to use technology as a learning resource. CD-ROMs, computers, videodisks, and the like were all extremely effective tools to promote the kind of group projects the restructuring called for. Technology allowed the Phantom Lake curriculum to become enriched and more broad. New sources, information, opinions, points of view, and individuals the students might otherwise never have been exposed to were brought into the classrooms.

Though it is too early to tell what the long-term effects on student achievement will be, the initial outcomes have been encouraging. The California Test of Basic Skills scores from 1994 for each grade have gone up. Averages have remained lower than the staff of Phantom Lake would like, but fewer students scored in the lowest quartile and more students scored in the highest quartile. Measurable gains have been made in one year alone. In addition to the improved achievement scores, there has been a definite improvement in the general school climate at Phantom Lake. At any time a visitor may walk through a classroom to find each child on task, able to explain what he is doing, and why he is doing it. Even during recess and lunch, students demonstrate respect for their peers and a sense of pride in their school. Playground fights and bigger kids picking on smaller kids are events that rarely occur.

Phantom Lake's success can be traced to the Bellevue District's decision to pass a technology tax levy. In Bellevue, the funds for technology came first—before the outcomes of technology in their classrooms could be assessed. The schools used technology to help them proceed with the restructuring process, to help educators engage in conversations about how they wanted to run their classrooms and schools. Technology's first use then was not to educate students, but to reform the education process.

The district took levy funds and applied them to a few teachers, who received training specific to their schools from both Chris Held and John Newsom. These teachers went back to their schools to integrate technology into their classrooms. Bellevue envisioned a few teachers learning to use the equipment, becoming comfortable with it—playing with it, becoming expert with it—and then spreading the word to other teachers. These teachers—or "leaders" as they came to be called—led classes to help train colleagues.

The Bellevue district has had technology tax levies for five years, amounting to $11.2 million. As mentioned above, the first levy was earmarked for equipment, networking 5-6 schools, and an Internet server. The second levy for $3.2 million was used specifically to upgrade buildings and electrical systems. The final levy for $6.8 million was for equipment and to network the remaining schools. Staff development and technology specialists have been provided through general district funds. Levy funds have been allocated on a per-pupil basis, assuring that even those schools that had some technology would continue to receive funds to further their efforts. Each school was required to submit a school-based plan for their use of technology, staff development plans, the name of technology leaders at their school, and a list of needed equipment. The plans were a way of getting schools to think about how they would use technology, and assure the district that they would not be asking the community to provide funds for idle computers.

Phantom Lake has received additional funds from the district because of the high level of involvement from its teachers, the role that those teachers play in developing new ideas in the use of technology in the classroom, and their role in spreading their knowledge to other educators in the district. The school used those additional funds to further their restructuring and exploratory efforts, not to financially reward teachers who were involved with technology. Since the passage of the levies, the selected teacher leaders have spread the word of technology throughout the system very successfully. The entire district administrative and school site system communicate on e-mail, and a large variety of hardware and software is utilized both in classrooms and in computer labs. At Phantom

Lake all staff members including teacher aides have access to e-mail. Because the levy funds are over five years, a fifth of the schools are networked each year. Thus there are still some schools that do not use e-mail to communicate.

Though the efforts to get technology into the Bellevue schools began at the district level, the process was not top-down. The district merely provided the opportunity for support, training and, quite significantly, funding. The real drive for technology at Phantom Lake was from teachers like Chris Held, who were using technology and sharing their excitement and knowledge with other teachers. At no time was there a technology mandate in Bellevue. In the beginning, only those teachers who showed an interest in using technology in their classroom did so. Teachers that were excited about technology used their own time to develop technology skills by attending voluntary staff development courses, provided free of charge by the district. To support these workshops and encourage greater participation the district also provides incentives to those who lead the workshops as well as those who attend. Some teachers are provided with small discretionary budgets from the district for their own development and to acquire new hardware and software to experiment with. In turn, these teachers lead workshops to pass on their knowledge to other educators. Teachers who choose to attend the workshops can apply the credit to their continuing education requirements.[167]

By having a policy where the use of technology was voluntary, and the specifics of each program left to individuals at the school site, teachers had ownership over their technology efforts and were empowered. More resistant teachers have not been forced to integrate technology into their classes. The Bellevue district's "trading" policy also gives these teachers another option. This policy allows teachers at different schools who teach the same grade level to trade schools without the approval of the district or the school administration. The result at Phantom Lake was that teachers who were not happy with their restructuring decisions or the technology-based format traded with teachers from other schools who had an interest in technology. This allowed teachers to trade to schools where the format suited their particular teaching style, and often where technology was not being utilized. However, as the district's expectations for the use of technology in the classroom have increased, these teachers have begun to feel more pressure. Some of the older teachers have simply chosen to retire.

The expectation for technological competency has also carried into the hiring of new teachers. Candidates must demonstrate some experience with technology to be seriously considered. As part of the hiring process, potential teachers must also submit a portfolio containing a hypothetical letter to the parents explaining how they will use technology in the classroom. The use of technology by teacher candidates implies a motivation and an interest in growing and learning new ways to teach. Though technological proficiency does not necessarily distinguish good teachers from bad teachers, it is one criterion that the district has used to raise the quality of its new teachers.

Phantom Lake has not limited its efforts to its students. Part of its restructuring effort has been to involve the parents and other members of the school's community. The school's staff firmly believes that having greater parent involvement and understanding will aid in students' success. Through a program titled Everybody's Schoolhouse, Phantom Lake uses the school facility after regular school hours to provide "lifelong learning classes and activities for all-age adults and youth; after-school classes and activities for children to enrich and support their learning; and a place for people to gain access to human services." Among other classes, Phantom Lake offers ESL and GED classes for their students' parents. Children realize the value of education when they see their parents having to attend classes and struggle with homework, just as they themselves do.

Another innovative part of this program is

the GranPal program that brings senior citizens into the school. Many seniors who were interested in learning to use computers found that the standard computer courses were too fast-paced for them. Phantom Lake offered the use of classroom computers after school hours so that seniors could lead their own classes at their own pace. In return, the seniors arrived half an hour early for each class to serve as mentors for the young students, assisting them in their various classroom tasks. This program brings the community, the school, and its children together. The community supports the Bellevue school district by backing the technology tax levies, and the school supports the community by opening its doors to its members and providing the courses that they request.

Everybody's Schoolhouse began without any funds, just the volunteer efforts of the school staff and community organizations. Once it began, the city and the district each contributed $10,000 to pay for a coordinator. Goals 2000 funds from the state were also available for six months. The remaining support has been through volunteers. Everybody's Schoolhouse has received little or no support from the business community. To maintain itself in the future, the program will have to seek out other sources of funds. Technology did not create nor is it a central aspect of the program; however, technology

did aid in the restructuring efforts at Phantom Lake, the communication between staff members, and the sharing of ideas like the one that created Everybody's Schoolhouse.

Yet technology is no cure-all. Technology's use has not been without its problems at Phantom Lake. During the first year, teachers not comfortable with the changes brought about by the restructuring efforts and the technology-based dialog left the school. Without diminishing the potential of technology, we must acknowledge key problems inherent in its use as an education tool.

How Will Teachers Be Trained?

To date, most training has taken place through traditional in-service training courses that are offered by the school or district. In most states, teachers are also required to take continuing education courses to maintain their certification.[168] These already established mechanisms are among the ways in which teachers might be trained to incorporate technology into their classrooms, but this is generally only a few hours per year. One class every few months does not come close to accomplishing what will be necessary to enable a teacher to feel comfortable with technology. The many facets of a technology-rich classroom require intensive training that includes a significant amount of hands-on instruction. If technology training is offered by the district trainers, do the trainers themselves have the appropriate knowledge to teach? Will the professional development staff have resources to hire the appropriate trainers, and will they do so, especially if this threatens the jobs of those already employed? This creates another set of challenges. Teachers often find that they are trained on one type of computer and have to go back to their schools and work on another kind. For beginners this can be more than frustrating. Another problem is access to technology. After returning from training, teachers need easy access to a computer so that they can continue to learn how to use it. The end result is often teachers eager to try out their new skills and no equipment to work on.

Other resources for providing professional development are local community colleges as well as four-year colleges and universities. Instruction on educational technology should be offered through traditional schools of education, through other higher education departments (such as computer science or mathematics), as well as through private education centers such as the various test-taking enhancement centers that are popular across the country. Of course, we must be cautious in providing funds to already existing supplemental programs. The funding must be accompanied by a mode of accountability to ensure that moneys are being spent solely on technology training. There would need to be a guarantee that funds would not be used to underwrite an existing course that was renamed to give the appearance of assisting teachers.

Firms that develop hardware and software might also serve as sources for training teachers to participate in the technology revolution. Several hardware and software companies are offering package deals that provide the technology training and technical support for specified lengths of time. One drawback to using hardware and software firms to provide teacher training is that they may only be willing to teach about their own products. On the other hand, who better to train a teacher to use a computer program, for example, than the company that developed it?

In addition, who will fund the development of the courses themselves? Is this something the districts should undertake? Should we expect institutions of higher education to develop the required courses? Given the reward structures in higher education, is this realistic? In community colleges, faculty get paid for the number of courses they teach rather than for creative course development. In four-year colleges and universities, faculty usually are rewarded for publishing. Thus, unless college faculty are compensated, it is not realistic to expect them to develop new curricula. Courses might be developed in the for-profit sector, where firms would offer them for a fee. Again, as we discussed in Chapter 4, the question is whether the teacher or the school would pay the fee, particularly at high private-sector rates.

We also propose that administrators (i.e., principals, assistant principals, superintendents) be exposed to technology training. A 1996 Quality Education Data Report indicates that superintendents, district technology coordinators, and principals are the most frequent decision makers in selecting technology (hardware) and software that is necessary at a school.[169] Clearly, if these groups are making decisions for entire districts and schools, they should be knowledgeable about the classroom uses of these items. Educators seem to be in agreement with this idea. A 1997 Milken Family Foundation poll found that 88 percent of teachers in schools using computers "believe that all teachers and administrators should be required to have some training in computers."[170] If such a requirement were to be made, as in the case of pre-service credential requirements, care should be taken to make sure that these requirements are not met by taking classes that have less than adequate content.

Another major difficulty is the lack of sufficient technical support. Few offices with dozens of computer users would rely on part-time technical support, or have a regular employee act as part-time technical support. However, this is frequently the case at schools. For many schools the only available technical support is a teacher or a librarian who spends part of the day helping others with their computer problems. For the initial years of technology usage, schools not only need a full-time person available to answer computer questions but they also need to have someone who is familiar with teaching and how technology can be applied to teaching. This support needs to be available on demand, not at scheduled times when the district's one technical support employee makes rounds to that particular school.

A final point on in-service training. Training teachers to use technology is not like a one-shot inoculation; it is an ongoing, unending process. Technology changes constantly, and with every change there will be new, exciting educational uses. This is not to say that teachers should always be up on the cutting edge of technology, but skills will become outdated if there is not the opportunity to update them. Jean White, technology coordinator of Concord, North Carolina, says, "Look at anything, look at basketball. Anybody who is good does it year after year, developing his or her skills. Why would anyone think that it would be any other way with technology? Otherwise you just end up pulling on the edges of it."[171]

can the private sector solve the problem?

"Who the hell wants to hear actors talk"

— H. M. WARNER, WARNER BROTHERS, 1927

Corporate Responsibility Through Collective Partnerships

Former Labor Secretary Robert Reich recently has advocated a movement toward "corporate social responsibility," whereby corporations would address issues concerned with the well-being of their employees, customers, and communities rather than focusing only on their bottom lines or profits. This notion conflicts with a long-held view of economist Milton Friedman, who said that the social responsibility of corporations is to increase profits. Adam Smith made the same point about the businessman centuries ago when he said, "By pursuing his own interest he frequently promotes that of society more effectually than when he really intends to promote it."[172]

Ultimately a profitable firm benefits shareholders, employees, managers, and customers alike. Moreover, a business's expertise relates to the good or service it produces, not necessarily to improving education or advancing other social causes. If a company is good at making widgets, who is to say that it also has competency in improving schools? Presumably, more profitable companies pay more taxes and thereby provide the means for government "experts" to take care of issues for the good of society. If a CEO's job and remuneration, as well as the jobs and salaries of her workers, depend upon this year's profits, she is not going to want to divert her workforce toward social goals as opposed to corporate profits, to say nothing of spending much of those profits on schools.

In the discussion of corporate responsibility the function of private, profit-seeking corporations in our society is important to rationalize. The role of these corporations is fundamentally different from that of charities or government. Milton Friedman defines the role of a corporate executive in a free-enterprise, private-property system as an employee of the owners of the business (i.e., of the shareholders): "He has a direct responsibility to his employers. That responsibility is to conduct the business in accordance with their desires, which generally will be to make as much money as possible while conforming to the basic rules of the society, both those embodied in law and those embodied in ethical custom."[173]

Indeed we must acknowledge that the corporation is operated by people who assume many other responsibilities voluntarily—whether they be to family, the community, or the education of their children. Here the individual acts as a principal, not as an agent. These are the "social responsibilities"of the individual that must not be confused with a "corporate responsibility." It is our contention that it is very important for private companies to continue their support for education and help with the infusion of technology into schools. However, we should not expect the business community to complete this task alone, nor should we expect it to bear all the cost.

Having said this, many corporations today do have a "social conscience." They feel they have the responsibility that all citizens have, to make this country better. They often even hire people who do have expertise in various social issues not directly related to their primary business activities. To the extent that firms do have a social conscience, this is one incentive for them to contribute to school improvement efforts including technology. Such efforts are good public relations or marketing ploys as well, and so can affect the bottom line.

The most talked-about benefit to business from their investments in education is the higher quality labor force that will result from better-educated graduates. The U.S. has a relatively high-tech labor force. In 1970, we were the leader in the share of our labor force in high-tech manufacturing. By 1991, we had fallen behind Japan, and other countries are catching up (Table 6-1). We are also behind several countries in high-tech employment as a percentage of total business sector employment. We will continue to lose our competitive advantage unless our schools move into the technological era. Indeed, using slightly different OECD data, we found that in 1980, the United States was second only to the Netherlands in share of manufacturing employment that was in high-technology firms. The U.S. share was 11.38 percent, and in third place was Great Britain at 9.86 percent. By 1992, Japan with a 12.52 percent share placed second to the Netherlands, with the U.S. having an 11.85 percent share that placed it behind Korea and Great Britain as well as Japan and the Netherlands. Between 1992 and 1994, the U.S. share of manufacturing employment that was in high-tech firms fell by more than the shares of Japan and Great Britain did, and Korea's share rose.

Table 6-1 Employment in High-Technology Manufacturing Industries

COUNTRY	NUMBERS (000s)	PERCENTAGE OF MANUFACTURING EMPLOYMENT		PERCENTAGE OF TOTAL BUSINESS SECTOR EMPLOYMENT		AVERAGE ANNUAL GROWTH RATE IN PERCENT OF EMPLOYMENT IN HIGH-TECH INDUSTRIES		
	1991	1970	1991	1970	1991	1970-80	1980-91	1970-91
United States	3,874.6	17.6	21.0	4.9	4.0	2.0	-0.4	0.7
Japan	3,441.3	16.0	21.8	4.9	4.2	0.6	3.1	1.9
Germany	1,823.7	16.5	20.1	7.1	6.5	-0.5	1.2	0.4
France	804.5	14.0	18.4	4.5	4.8	0.6	-0.2	0.1
United Kingdom	1,031.6	16.3	19.4	6.8	6.1	-1.1	-1.7	-1.4
Italy	553.5	10.2	10.9	3.1	3.3	1.6	-1.4	0.0
Canada	190.7	10.4	10.0	2.6	1.8	0.5	0.6	0.6
Denmark	62.2	9.6	12.3	2.8	2.9	-0.8	1.9	0.6
Netherlands	148.2	13.4	15.7	4.0	3.5	-0.7	-0.3	-0.5
Finland	44.7	5.7	10.5	1.5	2.7	4.4	0.1	2.1
Norway	26.9	6.6	9.9	1.9	2.2	1.7	-0.6	0.5
Sweden	125.1	12.0	13.8	3.6	4.5	2.0	-0.8	0.5
Australia	119.1	11.9	10.7	3.3	2.1	-1.6	-1.3	-1.4
Total	12,246.1	15.5	19.1	5.0	4.3	0.7	0.5	0.6

Sources: OECD STAN database; OECD Economic Outlook database; Secretariat estimates

Table 6-2

Share of Employment in High Technology Firms Firms Relative to Total Manufacturing

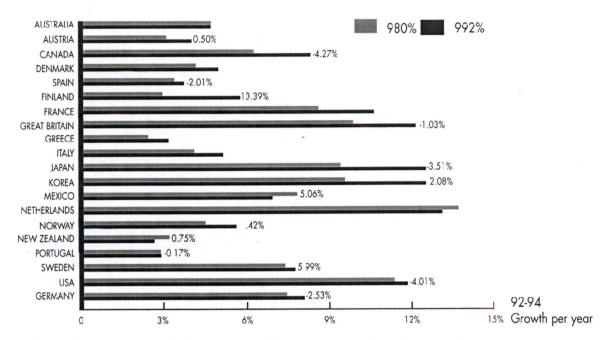

*Share of Employment in High Technology Firms Relative to Total Manufacturing
**Share of Employment in the Highest Technology Firms Relative to Total Manufacturing

The labor-force issue has impacts on many levels. Not only will business be unable to compete in the international economy, but also a poorly educated pool of workers forces companies to provide remedial training to workers so they can obtain skills they should have received in school. Ten percent of business's training costs today is for remedial training in basic skills.[174] Technology in the schools would save business money by improving the basic skills of graduates.

There is also a national security element to a well-trained workforce. This is similar to the argument made in support of the Interstate Highway System, which was supported in part as a mechanism to transport equipment and materials in the event of war. Similarly, after Sputnik, the support for training of scientists and engineers came in the form of the National Defense Education Act. The scientists and engineers who were trained in the 1960s with federal support will retire soon, and unless they are replaced by graduates of the same quality, there is the possibility of a shift of power on the international front. An unstable world is simply not good for business.

Finally, a better educated, more productive labor force will not only improve our nation's competitiveness, but it will also enhance the standard of living of our citizens. Every citizen is a potential customer for U.S. business. If they are better educated, and so better off, they will be better customers.

All these benefits to business are important, but they will be evident only in the long term. If an improved labor force will result from integrating technology into the classrooms, can the corporate sector afford to pay for that technology *now* in anticipation of more highly skilled workers fifteen years from now? Hence, not helping the schools does not necessarily mean that a firm is "bad." It is difficult to argue to a company whose costs have risen and whose sales have declined that an investment in our schools, particularly in our elementary schools, will turn their company around soon. A first grader won't enter the labor force for at least twelve years. Even if corporate efforts were targeted at the high schools, the payoffs in terms of an improved labor force or greater purchasing power are at best several years away. Thus, despite the importance of the labor market arguments, it is difficult to believe that, by themselves, they can convince the business community to make significant contributions to getting technology into our schools.

There are other incentives that have shorter-term payoffs for businesses. The telecommunications industry could benefit from ongoing fee-for-service payments from schools if they were to wire the schools at low or no cost. Hardware and software companies might increase their sales in the home market if they provide their products to schools where students use them and then ask their parents to purchase similar ones for their homes.

When Apple Computer decides to donate computers to schools, one motivation is to familiarize students and their parents with their products so that they might buy an Apple computer for their homes. The discounts that Apple offered to college students often had the intent and effect of creating brand-name loyalty. When these are the motivations, what reason does a firm have to donate computers to low-income schools, where parents cannot afford to purchase computers? At minimum, businesses expect their donated computers to be so effective that the schools receiving the donations and other schools will buy more of their products. Again, that motivation would lead Apple to give to wealthier rather than poorer schools.

When Lew Solmon was the dean at UCLA's School of Education, he approached many companies in an effort to raise funds for the school. Many corporations said that they give contributions where they have plants, where employees live, or where they have customers. For example, Ameritech has invested $168 million for broadband infrastructure support and distance learning, for schools in *its* territory. Given these circumstances, it is unlikely that the goal of implementing technology in *all* of our public schools will be accomplished by relying on businesses. There are many areas of the country where no large companies exist. Some areas are advantaged by the existence of technology firms or head offices of major telecommunications companies in their midst. As we will see below, NetDays and various business partnership experiences have demonstrated that relying upon corporate support for school technology will yield vastly different results in different schools, depending upon the location and income level of the schools and the populations they serve.

If a tax levied in California will raise prices there, and so encourage consumers to buy from companies in lower-tax states that can charge less, why should a California company support a tax hike? If another tax increases cost of doing business in California, and so makes profits lower than they would be if the company relocated, why should corporations in California support the tax? Both technology companies and firms that are not directly involved in the technology industry are likely to be among the most outspoken critics of new taxes. They are affected both as sellers and as buyers of technology. Some of these companies propose the opposite of a tax—namely, tax incentives to provide greater encouragement for business to help schools with technology.

Tax incentives already exist, of course. Businesses get tax deductions when they donate used computers to schools. Indeed, assuming the value to the firm of obsolete computers is zero (or negative if there are costs of disposal), any deduction for their contribution to the schools is an incentive. Moreover, firms that manufacture technology products also get deductions from donating new equipment. To the extent that they can deduct more than the marginal production cost (for example, wholesale or retail price), this is a strong incentive also. Incidentally, when Lew approached computer makers for funds for UCLA, they were willing to donate computers. When it came to donating money to train the users, the companies were not helpful.

We often see equipment donations to schools—but there is a great need for money to accompany these donations to provide for teacher training, software development, and the like. Since corporations can "shelter" pre-tax profits in corporate foundations and then donate money from their foundations, or if firms can consider cash contributions to schools as sales or marketing expenses, this reduces taxes as well. Despite these tax incentives, we see too few corporate contributions other than equipment.

The Private Sector and School Reform

The headline in a June 14, 1995, article in *Education Week* proclaimed "Businesses' Enthusiasm for Reform Seen Flagging."[175] The main thesis was that the corporate community, accustomed to fast results, is growing restless with the slow pace of school reform. Problems include the size of the task, the political climate in some states shifting toward indifference or even hostility, a scaling back by some corporations and corporate foundations of their education-related activities, stagnation of efforts by groups like the Business Roundtable to change state policy, conservative opposition to the development of national education standards, and proposals to dismantle the U.S. Education Department and scale back the Goals 2000: Educate America Act.

Nevertheless, many corporate leaders remain committed to school reform for the long haul, according to the *Education Week* article, primarily because they feel our economy is at risk without it. According to a 1992 *Business Week* article, education reform is still a top priority for corporate leaders that were surveyed.[176] Apparently, this is less true for smaller businesses. Groups such as the Business Roundtable and the National Alliance of Business continue to sponsor meetings on school reform and to publish progress reports. By 1995, five states had even enacted reforms that encompass all nine points of the Roundtable's agenda. We tried to get an update on the number of states that had enacted the Roundtable's agenda by mid-1997, but the Business Roundtable no longer keeps track of that number. Since the passage of Goals 2000, most states have adopted some of the agenda's goals, so enacting the full Roundtable agenda may not be as newsworthy as in the past. We have to wonder whether the Roundtable members would have felt it important to let people know if a large number of states actually had adopted their plan. Some states, like Kentucky, have committed to massive reforms with the strong support of major corporations; but in others, like California, efforts have stalled. The results of business support for reform are mixed; and so, we must question those who argue for relying principally on the corporate sector to support, both rhetorically and financially, a national effort to put technology into all of our public schools.

Some corporate people have taken leadership roles in advocating reforms that would fundamentally change public schools, if not destroy them. Here we are thinking of public/private school choice.

There is no consensus in the business community about what the "right reform" is for our public schools. Some corporate people have taken leadership roles in advocating reforms that would fundamentally change public schools, if not destroy them. Here we are thinking of public/private school choice. In California, a 1993 choice initiative was led by, among others, Joseph Alibrandi, CEO of Whittaker Corporation; and a future initiative is being sponsored in part by John Walton, one of the heirs of Sam Walton, the founder of Wal-Mart. Despite these efforts, opinion polls indicate the majority of Californians still are not ready for choice, and as the saying goes, "As goes California, so goes the nation."

Other business leaders are unwilling to give up on the public schools and so seek changes in them that are less radical and more consistent with the status quo. They often resonate with the schools and their recent efforts to bring about reform. Such leaders support changes in the organization, governance, and management of schools, including the sharing of policy-making responsibility among administrators and teachers (and sometimes parents) and site-based management because such strategies have been tried in industry with some success. However, it is important to recognize the differences between public schools and for-profit firms: the different bottom lines (profits versus student achievement), competition in the private sector, no tenure in the corporate world, and the ability there to reward private-sector employees for productivity and achievement. In a word, the incentives in the private sector render it more conducive to reform and improvement.

Business has also advocated curricular reform, in part because it finds that the new graduates hired each year are unprepared for the labor force. Business leaders are often strong advocates of standards and assessment, which they relate to the corporate bottom line and the accountability of public corporations to their shareholders. Business has helped schools focus on outcomes (particularly student achievement) rather than on inputs. However, without sanctions for not meeting goals or rewards for meeting them, this is a meager achievement.

Many "policy recommendations" have been made, and business has had input in making them, but frequently with inadequate follow-up and few positive results. This is not to say that particular efforts of specific firms have been failures. But to implement technology or any real reform, more money is needed along with equipment and advice. Many people from industry sit on panels and commissions to discuss reform, but often those doing the talking don't have the power of the purse. And when we talk about reform, we are talking about all public schools in the country, not just one or two schools in the city where the corporate headquarters is located.

The Center for Economic Development argues "Business' access to and involvement in the policy councils of education seem assured. Business-education compacts and collaboratives are active in most urban communities. The process of state policy making in education has changed substantially with business participation and approval." On the other hand, in a Conference Board report, Ted Sizer, one of our nation's leading school reformers, says: "...very little investment is made in reform. There is a lot of rhetoric but little serious, political action. In many cases, action means money. You cannot expect a faculty to rethink and change its school without serious time and money, any more than General Motors thought it could build the Saturn without an upfront investment of more than eight years and billions of dollars."[177]

The Appropriate Role of Business

There is a role for business in the education technology movement, but it is not going to be as the primary source of funding. Curtis G. Weeden, vice president for Corporate Contributions at Johnson & Johnson commented recently that "The reengineering of American business is taking its toll on corporate giving. While companies are continuing to make respectable profits, many are reducing the percentage of earnings set aside for philanthropy. One reason is that it simply does not seem right to pump up contributions at a time when employees and other resources are being squeezed."[178] Mr. Weeden also points out that "Businesses are inclined to couple in-kind services and volunteer time with their cash contributions, which adds important value to their philanthropy." Although the latter point is correct, we must remember that technology will not get into our schools unless substantial cash dollars are available, and in-kind services, while useful, are not a substitute for the required funding.

Federal legislation during the Bush Administration in 1990 established the New American Schools Development Corporation (NASDC) as an independent, nonprofit group. Its purpose was to promote and encourage school innovation by awarding grants to stimulate new education programs. It was to be supported, managed, and financed by private business. The goal was to raise $200 million. As of February 1993, the organization had raised $48 million.[179] By March 1995 the budget had grown to $105 million, but $50 million of that came from the Annenberg Foundation.[180] The 1997 total was $120 million. Thus in about six years, NASDC raised $70 million from the corporate sector, about one-third of its goal. This was a clearly defined effort that might have been a magnet for corporate funds, even for funds corporations would like to target to specific geographical areas. A 33 percent rate of success does not augur well for relying on the corporate sector to fund school technology to the tune of $50-$70 billion.

How Is Business Working with the Schools?

At Juarez-Lincoln School, in Chula Vista, California, twelve-year-old Ryan Garcia has enough ability to trek through the information superhighway to know that it is well worth the trip. "Sometimes we find things we don't even know," says the excited sixth grader. Three miles from the U.S.-Mexico border, downloading a vast amount of new information on the Internet via computers and high-speed data lines has become a part of the daily routine. The sixth graders are researching ancient Egypt by examining the architectural detail of the old pyramids from Web sites. The third graders are e-mailing bird experts all over the country to answer their questions about the American bald eagle. The first graders are able to research information about Alaska on the Internet. Juarez-Lincoln is on the cutting edge of information technology with the help of $250,000 worth of equipment and training from Pacific Bell, AT&T, and Apple Computer.[181] This pilot program is part of Pacific Bell's "Education First" initiative. Pacific Bell has committed to installing as many as five high-speed data lines to the 8,600 public and private schools and libraries in its territory. When President Clinton visited California in 1996, he embraced public-private partnerships such as Education First, asserting they were imperative to achieving the goal of providing all classrooms with Internet access by the end of this decade.

Given businesses' primary goals and ambiguous role in school reform, it is clear that they should not be relied upon to solve the entire problem of education technology. But without question, there are several ways that they can and have already begun to help. Many businesses are actively pursuing support relationships with schools. In 1984, 17 percent of schools had "helping hand" relationships with schools in which businesses provided tangible goods and services to schools. By 1991, 40 percent of schools had such relationships. More than 140,000 partnerships in 30,000 public elementary and secondary schools now exist, and over half of these relationships are between business organizations and the schools.[182]

Donating Employee Time

Companies who have skilled employees can donate employee time to train educators—or even students—to use computers, help schools maintain their systems, or advise schools on planning, implementation, or purchasing decisions. The Seminole County Board of Education in Florida has had a Business Advisory Board for the past several years. When the school board decided to replace its outdated computer system, it sought the advice of the Business Advisory Board. This resulted in a technology committee headed by George Kosmac, an AT&T executive. John Tracy, another committee member and executive with Cincinnati Bell Information Systems, volunteered his and his company staff's time for the project. Instead of hiring an outside consultant, Kosmac and Tracy decided that they could provide the necessary services free, using their own resources and those of others they could call upon. Tens of thousands of dollars were thus saved.[183] This type of assistance could save schools an immense amount of money and give companies a greater opportunity to contribute to their community.

Employees might also appreciate the chance to help out at their children's schools. It will not always be the case, however, that business partners and their employees can provide the necessary assistance. Having technical skills does not necessarily imply that employees can teach the skills needed in an educational setting, to teachers or students. These volunteer services can be invaluable but will not be a substitute for a well-trained teacher.

NetDay

Even if it is not feasible to contribute employee time on a regular basis, specific events, such as NetDay, offer opportunities for businesses to participate directly and to encourage their employees and other individuals to participate. NetDay is a grass-roots volunteer effort to wire schools so they can network their computers and connect them to the Internet. Labor and materials come from volunteers and support comes from companies, unions, parents, teachers, students, and school employees. Virtually every state has had at least one school participate in a NetDay. There have been a number of national (and international) NetDays in the past couple of years.

Scenic Park Elementary School in Anchorage, Alaska, became the second school statewide to be wired for Internet access. More than 100 volunteers wired 26 classrooms and six offices in their NetDay efforts. The local International Brotherhood of Electrical Workers, Anchorage Telephone Utility, military, and school parents provided the manpower. "This really was a concerted effort," said Catherine Heady, administrative coordinator. "People set aside their egos and really worked together to pull this off. It was sort of a communal kind of experience."[184] NetDay enabled a small school in Alaska to have a very big experience that will benefit the entire community.

The estimated cost of wiring a classroom is more than $1,000. If a significant portion of classrooms could be wired with donated equipment and services, the savings for schools would be enormous. The $200,000 that was spent by the California NetDay office for the first NetDay is believed to have translated into a $35 million return on that investment in the form of donations, volunteers, and equipment provided by companies. MCI estimates that the company and its employees "donated more than one million dollars in cash, in-kind support, equipment and volunteers to help schools link to the Information Superhighway."[185] It is estimated that 25,000 schools have been wired through NetDay efforts. If this estimate is correct, that comprises nearly 30 percent of public schools nationwide.

In California, there were wide disparities between the schools that participated in NetDay and those that did not. More affluent areas had a disproportionate number of schools with sponsors and volunteers to help with the wiring.

There are some criticisms, however. In California, there were wide disparities between the schools that participated in NetDay and those that did not. More affluent areas had a disproportionate number of schools with sponsors and volunteers to help with the wiring. Castle Heights Elementary in the Cheviot Hills section of Los Angeles, for example, enlisted eighteen volunteers, was sponsored by Friends of Castle Heights, and was able to use 80 computers donated by parents. "We have five computers in our house, and when we upgraded last year, we brought in our old ones," said Jane Wishon, president of the Castle Heights PTA. She stumbled onto the NetDay site when she was working on her home PC.

In stark comparison, Compton, a low-income area, did not have a single school sponsor, and many principals had not even heard of NetDay. This may have had much to do with the fact that NetDay was organized over the World Wide Web. How were schools and administrators that do not have access to the Web to have heard about it? "We'd like to participate," said Esperanza Elementary Principal Rowena Lagrosa. "But we don't have a sponsor and we don't have the manpower. It's really a sad state of affairs."[186] At Huntington Park High School, Robert Correa, a math and science teacher, heard about NetDay by chance. Unfortunately, he was unable to get a sponsor for his school. "Where are those sponsors who can donate the routers or cables that are necessary for us to network Huntington Park High School, network within our cluster, network so we can talk to the rest of the world? The people who know about this stuff are not the people in our community. We don't have companies here. Maybe the sponsors don't know Huntington Park exists."[187] For communities that lack company resources or where parents are not technologically literate, efforts such as NetDay may have inadvertently widened the disparity between the "haves" and the "have-nots." We must keep in mind that the idea of NetDay was to raise the awareness of the importance of technology and its value to the schools—to serve as a catalyst to encourage the partnership between schools and businesses, not to ensure that all schools would be wired overnight. To an extent, that goal has been accomplished, and due to the increased awareness as a result of the first NetDay, subsequent NetDays have been able to reach schools in lower-income areas.

TECH CORPS

Several companies have also worked together to create and support nonprofit efforts such as TECH CORPS, which is a national organization that provides schools with volunteers who "offer technical expertise in hardware/software/wiring, mentor students and teachers, work side by side with teachers in the classroom, deliver teacher training, and offer advice on technology and network planning."[188] Outside of TECH CORPS, Digital Equipment Corporation has contributed $10.6 million to support high school computer science and computer literacy programs. Ameritech, IBM, AT&T Network Systems, Centel Corp., Prodigy Services, and Eicon Technology Corp. have sponsored a two-year pilot project called TEAMS, for Telecommunications in English, Arts, Math, and Science. All of these programs are examples of ways in which businesses can serve as a catalyst for further contributions and volunteer efforts.

Telecommunication Discounts

The telecommunications and cable industries also have stepped forward by providing wiring, Internet access, and other services at reduced rates, if not free. For example, AT&T has pledged $150 million to provide free Internet access and voice mail services to 110,000 schools nationwide. Last year, the cable television industry boldly pledged to provide nearly every school in the country with access to the Internet. As we mentioned in the opening of this chapter, California's Pacific Bell has volunteered to wire schools and provide a year's worth of free service through its Education First Program.

Unfortunately, some of these proposals are not as promising as they would seem. For example, two years after the announcement of Education First, only 600 of 8,600 schools have taken advantage of the program.[189] This may reflect schools' lack of funding for computers and other equipment to use with the lines. Pacific Bell can only make the offer available, it cannot force schools to accept it. Or, as several Los Angeles Unified School District officials concluded, the offer might not have been as good a deal as it appeared. Assisted by the RAND Corp., the district analyzed the proposal and discovered that it contained costs such as "connecting equipment required for ISDN lines, construction costs for the installation of conduit, and the cost of an ISDN connection to the Internet, through a service, something the district already provides to its schools free through its own wide-area network."[190] One skeptical administrator, Les Higger, said, "My issue is if you put in the line here free for a year, and I have no idea what it is going to cost me in the future, I can't make a decision based on imaginary numbers."[191]

Donated Equipment

Donating equipment, computers, and peripherals is probably the most common type of contribution from businesses. Over 12 million computers are discarded every year in the United States. Organizations such as the National Cristina Foundation, the East West Foundation, and the Detwiler Foundation collect computers from businesses, refurbish them, and pass them on to schools. According to the Detwiler program in California, as of December 1996 over 27,000 computers had been placed in schools.[192] For many schools, programs like this are the primary source of computers.

There are some cautions, however. Donated computers are more likely to break down than new ones, and need frequent repairs because they are old. In Texas, the Northwest Independent School District was given 1,200 computers by American Airlines. However, the maintenance cost to keep the used computers operational was high. As a result, the district decided to buy new computers if funding became available.[193] Schools are already full of computers that sit in closets. Such computers may be obsolete and thus not able to run modern software. Without high-quality software, computers will sit in schools unused or will be used suboptimally. Finally, we should ask what kind of message we are sending to children when we tell them they need to know how to use technology for the modern workplace but give them machines that employers consider obsolete?

Some observers suggest that firms be given a tax credit for donating computers or be allowed to deduct as donations more than the depreciated value of a machine. These policies are being recommended to increase business donations of computers, perhaps by covering the delivery costs. Skeptics might wonder why "public-minded" corporations require subsidiaries to get them to be charitable.

Intel Corp. has announced a program to donate 100,000 motherboards to schools that submit plans to use them. To date, and to Intel's surprise, only 10,000 of the boards have been requested. This may be due to inadequate publicity about the program, or to the fact that without other substantial resources, not much can be done with just the motherboards.

Part-time and Summer Jobs

Providing part-time or summer jobs for students, and even for teachers, would give them an opportunity to see how technology is used in the workplace. Marian Ibrahim, a student at Batavia High School in Batavia, Illinois, is a participant in Saturday Scholars. This program brings students together with a professional who describes her job. "I attended a session in the fall where a system engineer from Microsoft came and spoke to us. He influenced me so much that I got in touch with him. Two weeks later he called me back and offered me an internship," Marian explained. More important than the internship offer, however, Marian was excited by the exposure to people in the field. "We're meeting people who are actually applying the subjects we learn in school in their daily lives instead of just getting information out of textbooks," said Marian.[194] Companies also benefit from the partnerships. Firms get cheap labor and can "preview" potential recruits.

Many companies take advantage of this early student exposure to the labor force by creating School-to-Work programs that educate high school students part time while they are still attending school. Ford Motor Company is increasing its investment in high school students because too many graduates lack the basic and technical skills that Ford will require from its future work force. Ford designed its Ford Academy of Manufacturing Sciences (FAMS) specifically to introduce students to career opportunities in technology environments. FAMS offers students the chance to learn science, math, and technology skills, all in real-life contexts. High school juniors and seniors are introduced to manufacturing systems and processes, quantitative literacy, computer technology, and special-ized math operations. The program places students in internships during the summer of their senior year. Corporations other than Ford provide 55 percent of the internships. Larry Bruno, the FAMS program manager, believes, "The essence of FAMS is to provide graduated high school students with skills that will serve them well, whether they are college-bound or headed directly to work."[195]

Model Schools

Funding model schools or pilot programs and research are other extremely valuable contributions that business can make. Gathering evidence on the value of technology is an absolutely necessary, but very costly, endeavor, without which we are unlikely to gain broad-based public support and funding. Projects like the Apple Classroom of Tomorrow and Bell Atlantic's financial support of the reforms in Union City, New Jersey, have provided invaluable evidence of the changes that occur when technology is integrated into a classroom and the remarkable results that can be achieved.

One particularly successful example is the partnership between schools and the business community in Louisville, Kentucky. The partnership was born out of a fund-raising effort to provide the schools with computer labs. At the root of the partnership was a mutual need. Business leaders in Louisville were concerned about the future lack of a skilled work force to replace the city's declining "smoke-stack" industrial base. The school district was struggling over court-ordered desegregation and "white flight" as a result of the declining demand in manufacturing jobs. In an effort to resolve some of these problems, and to bring technology to the schools, Louisville's major business leaders, among whom were Liberty National Bank's Malcolm Chancey and Humana, Inc.'s chairman and chief executive officer, David A. Jones, formed the Jefferson County Public Education Foundation.

The result of several meetings was the realization that providing technology for elementary schools was a very expensive proposition, between $17 million and $19 million. Additionally, board mem-bers questioned whether technology was worth that large an investment, especially when the funds were not readily available. "Not many people had thought of education as a sort of salvation [for economic problems]," said Donald W. Ingwersol, former superintendent of the Louisville, Kentucky, School District. Many members were in favor of bringing computers into the classrooms but were concerned about the money, and about effective use of the technology, not wanting either to go to waste. "I said to the superintendent, 'We can't commit to spending $9 million on computers and then have them sit around gathering dust,'" recalled Liberty's Chancey.[196]

Fortunately, Chancey had a solution. "If I were doing this in the banking business, I'd pilot it and see what the results were." The result was a pilot program at an inner-city school, Roosevelt Perry Elementary, funded by Humana's Jones, who had grown up in that neighborhood. The result was a network of computers in classrooms connected with a new computer lab. Students were using the computers to keep journals, practice basic skills, and supplement textbook lessons. The results were improved test scores, higher attendance, more parent involvement, and better teacher morale. The pilot program at Roosevelt Perry was able to demonstrate to the community and business leaders that technology could work in their community and led to further fund-raising for education technology.[197]

There is a caution, however. These projects provide evidence about what is possible given appropriate funding, expertise, and support. In reality, very few schools will be able to generate the funding necessary to experiment with and continue programs like these. One of the lessons from the Hagerstown instructional television experiment was that business can support a program—and that program can have great success—but when the private funding is removed, schools are unable to sustain the program on their own budgets. We must keep in mind that model schools are unlikely ever to become representative of the average school.

Providing Information and Lobbying

Businesses can also play a role by informing students, educators, voters, and policy makers about how important technology is and will be at work. Partnerships such as Illinois's Corridor Partnership for Excellence in Education (CPEE) realize that this is an area where they can have an impact. According to Cheryl Gray, executive director of CPEE, "We have to impact public policy. We have members who have [the governor's ear] on educational policies, who lobby and who help the government help business and education."[198] MCI helped to demonstrate the capabilities of technology in education to educators and to community leaders by sending CyberEd to schools in fifteen empowerment zones. CyberEd is a converted 18-wheel truck "equipped with personal computers, Internet connectivity, presentation facilities, printers, video conferencing and more."[199]

Lobbying for new public funding or supporting bond initiatives is another way businesses can advocate for technology. But can business ever accept more taxes? In 1996 we participated in the California Education Technology Task Force, a group convened by the Superintendent of Public Instruction, Delaine Eastin. Lew Solmon was head of the subcommittee on funding. After several meetings and much thought, the conclusion of the group was that the only sources of funding that were substantial enough and feasible were a sales tax increase, bonds, and a reduction of the governor's proposed income tax reduction.

Before publishing the final report, the Department of Education decided it needed to have the endorsement of the California Business Roundtable. After presenting the facts to this group, the Business Roundtable concluded that the issue needed more discussion. The task force report was then published without any final recommendation on financing. It merely listed a series of options and stated, "We are heartened that the California Business Roundtable...has agreed to convene a small group representing business, education, and public policy experts to explore the most expedient and pragmatic funding options."[200] The Roundtable's contribution was to hire a public relations firm to convene a new task force on finance, in which we again participated. This group again began by listing all the possible funding options (over 60 were listed!), only to end up with the original recommendations to be presented to the Roundtable for its endorsement. This process took several months—and the Business Roundtable never did endorse the Task Force's funding recommendations.

The Roundtable endorsed this plan within one day. Clearly, the Roundtable was willing to support a plan that was already likely to have a lot of political support because it did not require a new source of funds, but was unwilling to stand up and support a new tax that was not politically salable and that might impact them or their customers.

Interestingly, soon after the finance panel completed its report, Governor Wilson introduced a plan to fund technology for all California high schools. The difference between the governor's plan and that of the task force was that the former utilized funds that had become available due to increased and unanticipated revenue growth as the state's economy recovered from the severe recession of the mid-nineties. No new taxes were required. Indeed, because of California's Proposition 98, these growth funds were *required* to be spent on education. The governor just decided to use some of the funds for technology. The Roundtable endorsed this plan within one day. Clearly, the Roundtable was willing to support a plan that was already likely to have a lot of political support because it did not require a new source of funds, but was unwilling to stand up and support a new tax that was not politically salable and that might impact them or their customers.

Taking a New Perspective
Finally, one of the most important things business leaders can do is take a longer-run view of an

investment in school technology. This is a process that will have enormous payoffs for private industry and for each state as a whole, but it is not something that will happen overnight.

There is a large number of business-school partnerships around the country. Some are national efforts affecting schools in many states, and some are as small as the local drugstore providing discounts to "A" students. Some provide goods and services to schools, and others provide forums for conversations. Sometimes companies join with schools to lobby for new funds or for fundamental operational changes in school systems. Despite all this, many school districts in the country have no opportunity to collaborate with business. Where collaborations do exist, many do little to advance technology in the public schools. The *effectiveness* of business-school partnerships is as yet unknown. Even when businesses have been involved in schools where student achievement has risen, we have yet to determine to what extent the partnership can be given credit for the rise.

Donated goods and services, discounts, volunteered employee time, and advocacy are all helpful, but realistically they don't amount to very much. They are less direct, less expensive, and less likely to be effective than are monetary contributions. Without question, the best thing that businesses can contribute is money which can be used to enhance whatever aspects of their technology efforts schools choose. Financial contributions allow schools to target the funds toward those areas most in need of money, and schools really are the best judges of this. Historically, most innovations that have been imposed on schools from outside have failed. When outsiders give what they think is necessary, it often is not what is needed and is viewed as an imposition by educators. Educators resent being told what to do. Significant thought goes into a technology plan, and each district and each school is the best judge of how best to implement that plan. This is why financial contributions are most likely to have the greatest impact.

Problems with Business Partnerships

We must understand that business partnerships are important but are not enough to provide what is needed for our schools. One of the key impediments to business partnerships is the presumption on the part of businesspeople that their expertise exceeds that of teachers. Just like top-down imposition, this can engender considerable resentment among educators. It can even lead them to resist assistance. The different institutional cultures of schools and corporations may also make interaction difficult. Reward structures, which are fundamental to the success of any program, vary significantly between these two institutions. Both sides need to understand that they come from different vantage points and need to listen carefully to the other side's perspective.

The models of grassroots collective partnerships should be the beginning of a community's efforts to implement a successful technology program. A prime example of this creativity and innovation is the Build PEN (Pennsylvania Education Network) Partnership. Build PEN is a grassroots effort to encourage community volunteers and corporate sponsors to work collectively to buy local area networking components. Although similar to the NetDay program, in addition to wiring school buildings and installing computers, Build PEN's goals are also to develop schools' LANs, encourage professional development for educators by identifying resources and, most important, bring communities together for discussion. The PEN Link to Learn education initiative provides $121 million from 1997 through 1999, to supply schools with computer equipment, planning expertise, and other resources. Lt. Governor Mark Schweiker believes, "Our Build PEN partners are private-sector and community volunteers who understand technology's importance and understand that we must embrace it to give our children every possible opportunity to succeed."[201]

Business leaders often can become involved in short-term, high-profile programs that have little educational substance. Cooperative programs should be based on more than a general desire to be helpful or visible. Too often, partners fail to set goals and establish evaluation criteria, making evaluation of their efforts difficult, if not impossible.

The fact that it is easier to recommend programs than to pay for them is another pitfall. Many educators believe that businesses often prefer to give advice or to get involved in gimmicky projects rather than make substantial investments of time, money, or both. A corporate CEO taking a few hours off to teach in a ghetto classroom during "partnership week" may provide good press for his firm but probably does not help children at the school.

Our experience with business representatives on various state and national committees—from State Superintendent of Education Delaine Eastin's C³ group in California to the Governor's National Education Summit in March 1996—does not make us optimistic about business partnerships to help schools obtain modern technology. Every business participant wants to "have input" and "be supportive." But when it comes to providing their resources, or to supporting public initiatives to tax or to issue bonds, they have serious problems.

This can be illustrated by two examples. First, the National Governors' Summit was supposed to have addressed standards, assessment, and technology. The first two areas require changing attitudes among educators more than money, whereas technology is limited primarily by the ability to pay for it. A cynic might use this difference to explain why the summit focused almost entirely on standards and why virtually nothing was said about technology. Second, one of us chaired a subcommittee on funding for Delaine Eastin's Technology Task Force in California, the other members of which were predominantly representatives of business. When we were so naïve as to recommend a tax to pay for technology, there was unanimous opposition—save for one businessperson. He agreed with us but never showed up again: His boss replaced him and reversed his vote.

Key Characteristics of a Successful Collaboration

A successful collaboration has four characteristics. First, collaborations should be mutually benefi-cial. Each partner should receive desired outcomes, and the giving should flow in two directions. Second, they should make use of the expertise of the collaborators. If someone is an expert at finance, assigning him or her to the manual task of wiring is probably not the best idea. Being an expert in one area does not make someone an expert in others. Third, collaborations should involve those with solid influence. Influence—or "clout"—is not defined by the absolute extent of one's resources or authority but rather by the extent to which participants have the ability to get the job done. Last, they should focus on what is possible. When defining the problem, it is probably best to think small and try to solve a problem with the resources at hand. Keeping these criteria in mind, business-education partnerships seem to promise benefits to both groups. But we also have expressed pessimism that the private sector will lead the implementation of technology in our schools. To be explicit, we cannot expect business to solve the nation's $50-$70 billion school technology problem.

However, just because business cannot solve the entire problem does not mean we should not accept their contributions or encourage their participation. There are clearly valuable contributions that they can make—not just multi-million-dollar contributions. We also should be grateful for small partnerships between business and the schools. Small, identifiable changes are what should be expected from collaborative efforts, rather than a sea of change in educational efficacy. In a 1984 paper titled "Small Wins," psychologist Karl E. Weick suggested that on many fronts much can be accomplished through small steps instead of waiting for the ideal solution. According to Weick, "People often define social problem in ways that overwhelm their ability to do anything about them: When the magnitude of problems is scaled upward in the interest of mobilizing action, the quality of thought and action declines, because processes such as frustration, arousal, and helpless-ness are activated....To recast larger problems into smaller, less-arousing problems, people can identify a series of controllable opportunities of modest size that produce visible results."[202]

We would suggest that the wisest course is to take small steps in the interim and find gratification—and results—in small wins. From a survey of state departments of education, we estimate that as of this writing, businesses have contributed about 6 to 10 percent of the funds spent for school tech-nology. When one considers the billions of dollars necessary to implement education technology nationwide, this is a large sum—but it is not nearly enough to get the job done.

Can the Government Stimulate Business Involvement?

Some businesses argue that if there were *more* or greater tax incentives, they would be more inclined to help the schools with technology. Additional tax incentives might increase such involve-ment, but there are larger adverse effects of such tax complexity that we ought not ignore. And such tax incentives almost certainly cannot distinguish between business involvement that is useful and that which is not.

In the larger context, the idea of new business incentives in the tax code is likely to be a nonstarter. The whole emphasis in Washington these days is flat taxes, value added taxes, and the like; in short, simplification of the tax code is the order of the day. Congress does not offer tax goodies free: The "business incentives" will come with strings, requirements, and unrelated demands that will not improve the prospects for success of computerization of the schools.

If we assume, nonetheless, that more tax incentives will encourage business to help the schools get technology, we still must consider potential pitfalls. Every technology firm would pitch its own products regardless of their relative efficacy for the schools. Moreover, by providing incentives as opportunities for them arise, certain systems might be favored over others. For example, if new cable channels were awarded conditional upon those receiving the channels making them available in schools, this might result, for example, in a school's committing to cable rather than to wireless telephone lines even if the latter were more effective or cost efficient.

Even with various incentives, the question arises as to where the motivated companies would provide assistance. Would it be concentrated where the firms have a presence, or where they have markets? If so, it has been suggested that incentives be targeted toward helping in inner cities or rural areas. If such assistance is viewed as having lower payoffs for the firms involved, the incentives to get them to provide that assistance will have to be greater.

Are there things government can do to encourage corporate involvement in school technology other than the imposition of a new tax or providing incentives? Several have been suggested as possibly appropriate roles for government. It has been argued that if governments at different levels reduced certain regulations, corporations would increase their involvement. Implicit in this argument is that less regulation would mean lower costs of getting technology into the schools, and so, whatever resources the corporate sector provides would go farther. All of this is true. However, the particular regulations often mentioned in this context must be considered carefully. A recent GAO report estimates that it would cost $11 billion over the next three years to comply with federal mandates to make all schools accessible to all students and to remove or correct hazardous substances such as asbestos, lead in water or paint, materials in underground storage tanks, and radon, or meet other requirements. In the case at hand, when walls are knocked down to put wiring in schools, there is often an asbestos problem that must be dealt with. Certainly, there are more and less expensive ways to deal with asbestos to which children are exposed in order to facilitate wiring of schools. But if lead paint removal is a prerequisite of putting technology in the schools, or if other regulations are enforced to the limit, this might become excessive.

Some have complained that building regulations preclude, or make prohibitively expensive, adding rooms to schools in which technology could be placed. Again, some building regulations are unreasonable. However, we are not advocating adding computer labs to schools; rather, technology must be made available in *existing* classrooms. And even if computer labs are worthwhile, how do relaxed building codes attract money for teacher training and software?

It has also been suggested that an appropriate role for the federal government is to develop model technology programs for schools based upon successful experiments. We encourage experimentation and evaluation. However, it is important to let teachers decide at the local level what the best approach for technology is in their particular school or district. Any imposition of technology on teachers may be resisted by them.

Finally, the corporate sector gets back to declaring that the proper role for the federal government is to develop standards for the schools. Again, are federal technology guidelines relevant for every school? Obviously not. If standards refer to student achievement goals, we must ask how they can be expected to be met without new tools—like technology. And what are the incentives to meet standards if there are no sanctions for not doing so? Standards are easy to advocate because they encourage discussion—and they do not cost real money.

CONCLUSION

The former chief state school officer of the state of Iowa has summed up the actual and potential role of business in educational reform very well.[203] His comments apply to school technology and are worth quoting at length here:

America's corporate leaders are frustrated with their inability to effect change in the schoolhouse... . The National Business Roundtable, the National Alliance for Business, The United States Chamber of Commerce and their respective state affiliates have all declared education a top priority. In addition, many more businesses from the local bank to the mom and pop burger franchise have jumped into the fray. The array of business involvement in education, their various forms and scope, are extensive... . The result of this flurry of activity is the equivalent of firing peashooters at elephants. With few exceptions most business efforts in public education have been good ideas and well intentioned: but they have also been limited, short range, ineffective, and more hype than substance. Too many of these partnerships have been "feel good" programs which have no substantive impact on student performance. They are nice, but they don't make a difference. These ineffective efforts also include "magic bullet" initiatives which intrigue some corporate leaders, but are mostly simplistic good ideas which strive to fix public education with sweeping mandates or programs. Unfortunately, they don't work either, yet a number of businesses or business groups have latched onto such quick fixes as their pet projects... . Corporations that choose to enter the educational reform area, and many more should, need to approach their involvement as if they were tackling an infrastructure problem no less complex than transportation, telecommunications, or the banking system. No corporation would propose that the country tinker at the margins as a way to address an infrastructure problem, yet many seem to want the cheap quick fix for education, because it is perceived to be a simple system... . Most corporations would never consider going it alone to address an infrastructure need of national scope. Typically they join with other companies in a trade or civic organization and attack the problem in a systematic fashion. They cooperate with their competition in their own self-interest. After careful analysis of the situation and the involvement of all the appropriate players (for example, researchers, government, financial institutions, professional associations, suppliers, and customers) a comprehensive strategy is established. A strategic plan is hammered out based on a strong consensus. All too frequently, however, corporate managers, who routinely require a business plan for any new initiative in their company, take on school reform programs with a seat of the pants approach... . A big mistake of those who want change in schools is to assume that a rational plan of action can have an impact on the strength of its logic alone. Because there are so many groups involved in public education, a good plan must include strategies to address the politics of multi-group support. Building consensus and trust among the many players in the education field is no easy task, but necessary to reaching desired results. The failure to assess and understand the political environment in which change is possible is a fundamental barrier to any effort to improve education. Partisan politics are great for cocktail parties, but large-scale change to the system of public education will require the approval of many diverse political camps. Corporate leaders who are so ideology-bound that they cannot work with people of differing philosophies, would do their company and their ulcer a favor by limiting their involvement to writing a check to the nearest philosophically attuned think tank... . As one views what is happening in some cities and states, there are signs for hope. But the task before the nation is enormous, complicated, cumbersome, and long-term. Education is an infrastructure problem which has been neglected for too many years. And, as with other infrastructure problems, until the business sector is involved, substantive change will not take place. The business community must roll up its sleeves on this issue. Systemic change on the order of magnitude needed to achieve the student learning we desire will be difficult and painful. It will require no less than a national commitment to this end, built on a community by community, state by state approach. Educators cannot do it alone; parents cannot do it alone; and government cannot do it alone. Business also must play its critical part in the systemic change of education.

can the federal government take on this task?

"What is more difficult, to think of encampment on the moon, or of Harlem rebuilt? Both are now within the reach of our resources. Both now depend upon human decision and human will." —ADLAI E. STEVENSON

Brief History of Federal Involvement in K-12 Education

Education has historically been a local issue. Spending per pupil, curriculum, length of school year, and certification requirements for teachers are all determined at the state and local levels. As a nation that greatly values freedom and independence, the United States has generally operated its education system under the rule that local communities are best able to determine their educational needs. Thus, prior to the 1950s, the federal government's involvement—"judicial, legislative, and executive"[204] —was minimal. During the period between 1954 and 1967, however, the federal government's role in education dramatically increased. Post World War II social, economic, and defense pressures stimulated the federal government's interest in improving the quality of K-12 public education. Since that time, the federal government has asserted itself in four major areas: "(1) desegregation; (2) education related to defense and to vocations; (3) aid to research; and (4) education of the economically and culturally disadvantaged, and of the handicapped."[205]

Prior to this period, the federal judiciary had generally been reluctant to intervene in educational issues that were matters of local authority, except in cases of "infringement upon constitutional rights or abuse of power with respect to federal states and executive guidelines."[206] The Supreme Court's 1954 decision on Brown vs. Board of Education is a case in point. Though not immediately, this decision had a major impact on state education practices. It was federal legislative action, the Civil Rights Act of 1964, that ultimately forced compliance with the desegregation ruling. The Civil Rights Act gave the attorney general the authority to intervene in and initiate school desegregation suits. The power for the Department of Health, Education, and Welfare to withhold federal funding from school districts that discriminated against blacks was also provided for in this legislation. This marked the beginning of a significant federal presence in K-12 education.[207]

The beginning of the Cold War era brought about another federal role in education. Fears of communism focused attention on the need for mathematicians, scientists, foreign language specialists, and more research. In the 1940s, the passage of the G.I. Bill and the creation of the National Science Foundation (NSF) chiefly addressed this issue at the higher education level, with some spillover to K-12 education. The National Defense Education Act (NDEA) of 1958 was passed in response to the Russian launch of Sputnik in 1957. This event created worry that the United States was not preparing enough scientists and engineers to compete with the Russians. NDEA provided funds to secondary schools to improve the quality of math and science programs and encourage students to pursue engineering, science, and foreign language studies.

Added to concerns about national security, in the 1960s education quality was of great concern because of an increased focus on the relationship between education and the nation's economic health. There was serious contemplation of major federal funding for education to prepare students for the rapidly advancing technological society.[208]

Another issue during this period was the growing income and employment disparity between blacks and whites. Though the nation's productivity increased rapidly following World War II, these disparities created national concern over the quality of education available to children of different racial and socioeconomic backgrounds. Say S. Bailey and E. Mosher, "These disparities came to be viewed not only as a deterrent to regional prosperity and a violation of the individual's right to the dignity of gainful employment, but as a blot on America's international reputation as a humane democracy."[209] The feeling was that the quality of education provided in the United States was not just a state issue or a matter of personal enrichment but a matter of national interest.

Again, the federal government stepped in to ensure that schools were in tune with national goals. In 1965 the federal government passed legislation to address these national concerns. The Elementary and Secondary Education Act, which is the largest K-12 federal aid program ever, today provides over $10 billion primarily to address inequities in funding and educational opportunities for low-income children. This piece of legislation established the most significant federal presence in education to date.

The Brown vs. Board of Education decision and the passage of the Civil Rights Act set precedents for the special education movement to build on, in the 1970s. Here again, the federal government stepped in to ensure that everyone regardless of economic and cultural background or handicap would be provided with an appropriate education. (See the case study on special education in Chapter 10.) With desegregation, ESEA, and education for the handicapped, the federal government has established its role as an enforcer of fair and equitable education.

The Federal Role in Education Technology

President Clinton, Vice-President Gore, even Speaker of the House Newt Gingrich—they are all talking about the importance of education technology and wiring schools to the Internet. The president's 1996 State of the Union Address challenged the public and private sector to work together to ensure that every classroom is "connected to the information superhighway with computers and good software and well-trained teachers." This challenge was reiterated in 1997. Former Federal Communications Commission Chairman Reed Hundt made telecommunications discounts for schools and libraries a central focus of his tenure at the FCC. The executive branch has clearly established education technology as a priority, but what *is* the role of the federal government in reaching the nation's education technology goals, and more important, what *should* that role be? The Clinton administration has defined the role of the federal government as a "catalyst and coordinator of efforts at the state and local levels."[210]

Federal Programs Providing Education Technology Funding
Several federal agencies currently support education technology through a variety of programs. These programs tend to fall into the traditional federally defined roles in public K-12 education: promoting equity in education, education related to defense and to vocations, and research.

> **Title I Basic Grant Program**
> **Title I Concentration Grant Program**
> **Title I "Targeted Grants" Program**
> **Title II Professional Development Program**
> **Title VI School Improvement Block Grant Program**
> **Head Start**
> **Special Education**
> **Rehabilitation Services**
> **Technology Literacy Challenge Fund**
> **Technology Challenge Grant Program**
> **Goals 2000: Education Reform Program**
> **Youth Training (JTPA)**
> **Summer Youth Employment and Training (JTPA)**
> **School-to-Work Transition Program**
> **Star Schools Distance Learning Program**
> **School Construction**
> **America Reads**

Equity
Addressing the equity issue, the Department of Education has several programs that provide funding to encourage the use of technology for disadvantaged and handicapped children. The National Challenge Grants for Technology in Education awards provided over $57 million in FY97 to "consortia which must include at least one local educational agency with a high percentage of children living below the poverty line... ."[211] The Star Schools Program is also targeted at underserved students. In FY97 this was a $30 million project focusing on distance learning. To provide technology projects

and centers for disabled toddlers, children, and youth, the Technology, Educational Media, and Materials for Individuals with Disabilities program offers funding through the Department of Education.[212] Though not specifically for technology, Title I of the Elementary and Secondary Education Act (ESEA) is perhaps the largest single source of funding for education technology purchases. Title I provides compensatory funds for schools with a high density of low-income children. Because these funds come with relatively few restrictions, many schools choose to use the funds for technology, primarily for basic skills instruction.

Created during an era when there was a fear that the United States was not training enough people to go into math and science fields, NSF's technology programs are targeted toward education in those areas. NSF's Comprehensive Partnerships for Mathematics and Science and Achievement is targeted at minority populations. It seeks to improve access to quality math and science education through partnerships with universities, the private sector, and other organizations. Focusing on rural, economically disadvantaged areas, NSF's Rural Systemic Initiatives Program also aims to improve science, math, and technology education.

Even the Department of Agriculture has programs that address equal access to technology in education. Located in mostly rural areas, agricultural communities are often unable to receive many of the modern telecommunications services. Telecommunications companies do not perceive great demand in these areas for their services, or at least not enough to make a significant profit, and therefore tend not to invest in infrastructure to serve them. Generally, schools in these areas would have to pay prohibitively expensive fees for telecommunications services. Thus, the Department of Agriculture has stepped in to ensure that residents and businesses in these rural areas have access to technology. The Rural Utilities Service Loan Program provides financing to rural telecommunications providers to expand existing telecommunications networks, reach customers in unserved areas, and provide the necessary technology for distance learning and Internet access. A second program, the Rural Utilities Service Distance Learning Grant Program, grants millions of dollars to rural schools, as well as other rural agencies, to develop advanced telecommunications systems. The Department of Commerce Telecommunications and Information Infrastructure Application Program and Public Telecommunications Facilities Program also aim to provide greater telecommunications access to education entities. FY97 appropriations for these two programs was $34.9 million.

Education Related to Defense and to Vocations

In previous decades, impending crises such as soldiers returning from the war without jobs or the threat of communism have spurred federal investments in education to support national goals. Recently, this crisis has been related to global competitiveness. Among U.S. policy makers and business leaders there is growing concern that our students are not being prepared for the technological era. A Department of Education report states that "Our children's future, the future economic health of the nation, and the competence of America's future workforce depend on our meeting this challenge."[213] As a result, the president and the Congress have funded new programs to promote the use of technology in schools. The president has outlined four goals for education technology:

1. All teachers will be trained to help students learn through computers and the information superhighway
2. All students and teachers will have access to modern computers
3. All schools and classrooms will be linked to the information superhighway
4. High-quality software and on-line resources will be part of the curriculum in every school.[214]

Specifically addressing the president's goal to use the federal government as a catalyst and coordinator of state efforts, the Technology Literacy Challenge Fund leverages the participation of communities, states, and the private sector by requiring a one-to-one match. Funding is provided to the states based on the ESEA Title I formula after submitting a plan for how they will use the funds to address national educational technology goals. Alaska has used its grant to expand its distance learning network to more remote areas, while Washington will use its funds by giving grants to districts for implementation of their own technology plans. Connecticut has chosen to focus much of its grant on professional development. Another approach is being tried by New Mexico, which will use the funds to leverage additional support from the private sector and other entities, such as museums, libraries, and institutions of higher education. In addition, New Mexico will use its grant to connect schools to the Internet, and to assure compatibility of equipment throughout the state.[215]

Given the great cost of technology, so much time, money, and effort can be saved if schools and districts can learn from their counterparts that have begun to implement technology. But collecting this information and making it available to schools is not an easy task.

NSF has many programs that fall into the category of promoting education related to defense and vocations. In addition to the programs mentioned above—which are intended for students—NSF's Teacher Enhancement Program focuses on the quality of teachers. This program promotes in-service teacher development in the areas of mathematics, science and technology for pre-K-12 teachers.

The Department of Energy also supports science and technology programs through its labs, technology centers, and research facilities. Every year, the Department of Energy offers its services to hundreds of thousands of teachers and students through its science and technology education programs. It also provides curriculum materials for both pre-service and in-service teachers.

Research

Another task that the Department of Education has taken on is to support research into effective technology practices, as well as practical information such as costs and implementation. This support has been critical to the dissemination of knowledge in this area. Given the great cost of technology, so much time, money, and effort can be saved if schools and districts can learn from their counterparts that have begun to implement technology. But collecting this information and making it available to schools is not an easy task.

The Department of Energy has also contributed to the knowledge base of technology practices. They have conducted long-term studies to determine the "effectiveness of specific educational technologies for classroom instruction."[216] NSF similarly funds research on how technology and telecommunications can be used to enhance instruction, as well its uses for administrators and policy makers.

A medley of other federal programs exists through the agencies we have discussed as well as others such as NASA and the National Endowment for the Humanities, providing support for research, acquisition of technology, and teacher training. The federal government's most significant piece of legislation for education technology, however, is probably the Federal Telecommunications Act of 1996. Senators Olympia J. Snowe (R-ME), John D. Rockefeller IV (D-WV), James Exon (D-NE), and Robert J. Kerrey (D-NE) sponsored an amendment that identifies schools as important institutions in extending the benefits of telecommunications service. The Telecommunications Act now includes schools and libraries in the list of recipients for universal service. This will provide schools with discounted telecommunications services based on the income level of the school's population.

This was a major step for education technology. However, how much do these various federal programs amount to? This is difficult to calculate given the fact that most of these programs are not specifically for technology but for compensatory education, professional development, and so forth. To get an accurate estimate we would have to know what percentage of funds for each program actually went to technology. From surveys that we have conducted, we estimate that no more than 10 percent of the funding for education technology has come from the federal level. Given the president's goal of acting as a catalyst, perhaps this is a reasonable percentage. And what about the Telecommunications Act? Won't this make the cost of state technology plans significantly lower? The passage of the Telecommunications Act has led some people to believe that education technology will now become more affordable. Well, the discounts are great, if they are true discounts, and not just a readjustment from the higher prices that will be brought on by deregulation.

TELECOMMUNICATIONS ACT OF 1996
A BACKGROUND AND CHRONOLOGY OF EVENTS

February 1996

On February 8, 1996, President Clinton signed the Telecommunications Act of 1996 into law. The 1996 Act updates the Communications Act of 1934 and provides a new framework that will be developed on competition and market forces to advance the deployment of communications infrastructures throughout the country. The Telecommunications Act includes a special provision for public education.

The Universal Service provision was the first federal legislation passed to guarantee through explicit principles and mechanisms a set of telecommunications services to be available to all at affordable rates. The "universal service" system was originally designed to make basic telephone service available to all of us at reasonable rates. The Telecommunications Act of 1996 calls for a revision of the universal service system. The revision was to expand both the base of companies that will contribute to offset telecommunications service rates and the category of customers who will benefit from discounts. The "universal service" package would be established by the FCC and was to evolve over time to take into account any future advances in communication technologies and services.

In addition to these broad principles, the Snowe-Rockefeller-Exon-Kerrey provision in particular identifies schools as important institutions in extending the benefits of telecommunications service. Schools and classrooms were to be targeted for preferential rate and/or discounts on services and the provision mandates a plan for deploying this into the schools.

The act established a Federal-State Joint Board on Universal Services that would make recommendations on the definitions and mechanism to deliver this universal service. The following is a timeline on the proceedings and implementation of the FCC.

March 1996

On March 8 FCC Chairman Reed Hundt named the Federal-State Joint Board on Universal Service. The FCC initiated a proceeding to recommend changes to universal service regulation. Comments were due April 12, 1996. Reply comments were due May 7, 1996. Recommendations of the Joint Board were due to the FCC by November 8, 1996. Between November 8 and May 8, 1997, the FCC would initiate and complete a proceeding on universal service, allowing for public input.

April 1996

Universal Service comments were filed to the Joint Board and the FCC by over 200 organizations. The comment summaries are documented on the Benton Foundation's Universal Service Internet Web site.[217]

June 1996

On June 5 the Joint Board on Universal Service heard testimony about universal service in the emerging competitive marketplace. On June 19 the Joint Board on Universal Service heard testimony on wiring public schools.

November 8, 1996

The Federal-State Joint Board made its recommendations to the FCC on changes to universal service regulations. The Board outlined its recommendation on how the funding mechanism would work.

Every telecommunications carrier that provides interstate telecommunications service shall contribute, on an equitable and nondiscriminatory basis, to the universal service fund.

The FCC will provide the list of carriers that qualify. These companies' revenues will then be evaluated and provided with a ration that will determine how much the company will need to pay into the fund.

The fund will be set up to create a competitively neutral environment with a projected $2.25 billion cap.

All companies must contribute to the fund, but only eligible companies that can provide the outlined "core services" will be able to use the subsidy.

A company uses the subsidy by deducting any discounts to the amount that is required to be paid into the fund. If the amount is greater than what the company is mandated to pay, the company may be reimbursed from the general universal fund.

The Joint Board's recommendations provide for:

- A sliding scale of discounts that range from 20 to 90 percent and are based on a school's or library's ability to pay. The deepest discounts will be provided to the least-well-off institutions.

- Discounts on any available telecommunications service to meet the varied needs of schools and libraries.

- A universal service fund whose unexpended resources can be carried over from year to year.

- Discounts for classrooms and internal library connections (whether wired or wireless).

- Discounts on monthly rates for telecommunications and Internet services.

- The recommendation also provides schools with the maximum flexibility to purchase the package of services they believe will be most effective to meet their needs.[218]

May 7, 1997

The Joint Board made its final recommendations on the specifics to the universal service provision. The Joint Board recommended that schools be able to purchase at a discount any telecommunications services that are commercially available, internal connections, and access to the Internet. Public and private schools would be eligible to receive support. Department of Education data estimates that 113,000 schools would be eligible for benefits. The level of discount a particular institution receives would be a percentage of its communications costs based on its location and level of wealth. Discounts would be 20 percent for the wealthiest schools and libraries and as great as 90 percent for the poorest.

In order to receive support, a school would have to meet three requirements:

- Self-certification that it has a plan for securing access to all necessary resources.

- Submission of a request for support that can be posted to attract competitive bids.

- Signature of a statement that it is eligible and will observe the rules associated with the universal service funding mechanism.[219]

Total expenditures of universal service support for schools and libraries is capped at $2.25 billion per year, with a rollover into following years of funding authority, if necessary, for funds not disbursed in any given year.[220]

There already is a question of how firm the $2.25 billion figure is. On May 8, 1997, the FCC reduced its estimates of the future costs of wiring the schools. The FCC said that connectivity installation to the Internet will be a "gradual process" that will consume only $1 billion—rather than $2.25 billion in the first year. The purpose of this revised assumption was to hold the line against more aggressive price increases to other users that would have been required to come up with the full $2.25 billion. We have to wonder what other "adjustments" will be made in the future. Granted that the allocation for schools is not capped at $1 billion for the first year, rather, it is just anticipated that the states will not be able to gear up quickly enough to use more than that amount so early in the process. Apparently, the difference between $2.25 billion and what is used will be rolled over to the next year.

Nevertheless, when price increases elsewhere get blamed on the fact that schools have been included in universal service, or when the telecom companies start to feel they are giving too much to the schools, will the $2.25 billion plus rollovers be maintained year after year? Perhaps, but the schools must be somewhat cautious in making future commitments of this money.

What happens next?

Several steps remain before the discounts become available. First, the interim fund administrator process needs to be set up and the applications need to be distributed.

Second, every state is required to hold its own proceeding on universal service. This will enable schools, libraries, and the Public Utility Commission to create rules for the program.

Finally, any legal challenges potentially can prolong implementation of the discounts. All funds to support the discounts were available starting on January 1, 1998. An approved technology plan is necessary to apply for the discounts.[221]

Where Are We Now?

Even with the present recommendations of the Joint Board, it isn't very clear when any of these might actually be implemented or when any school might be able to benefit from these insignificant discounted telecommunication rates.

How Helpful Will the Telecommunications Act Be for the Schools?

Total expenditures for universal service support for schools and libraries is capped at $2.25 billion per year. The recent recommendations from the Joint Board are encouraging in many ways:

- Discounts for wiring are required not only to bring wiring to the school door, but also for wiring between classrooms.
- Intrastate and interstate services will be provided at a discount. Schools will have more options with service providers and, especially in distance learning areas, long-distance service will be provided at a discount.
- Schools can decide what services they need—bandwidth, internal networks and Internet connections.

Wiring for telecommunications is essential to using technology in the way that we envision it. However, it is just one component. Wiring is useless without a computer to plug into it, or a teacher trained to use it appropriately. In terms of cost, wiring is only a fraction of the total cost of implementing technology in our schools. The combined total cost of the internal and external connections eligible for universal service are 18 percent of total initial costs and 15 percent of ongoing costs.[222]

Discounts on telecommunications services is a critical step in getting technology into our schools, but this does not mean that all of the Joint Board's recommendations are helpful, nor does it mean that suddenly we will all have wiring in all our schools. There is no mandate that telecommunications companies actively seek out schools, or attempt to provide them with wiring unless it is asked for. Unless the companies perceive enough demand they are not going to pursue this market. As a result, the "have and have not" situation is unlikely to change. There is a problem with the lack of incentives for telecommunication providers to service schools, particularly in rural areas. For example, the new law affects distance learning programs. Long-distance providers can now receive reimbursement, so there is no incentive for local providers to put the wiring into local schools when part of the reimbursement money will go to the long-distance providers. Recently, we have seen ads on TV that say: When AT&T calls to ask you to change to your local service, ask them how much they have contributed to your local school district.

Along the same lines, schools are not required to have their schools wired. Unless the schools themselves ask to be wired, nothing will happen. Schools must adopt a plan for securing access to all of the necessary supporting technologies needed to use effectively the services purchased. This prevents waste. But what if a school does not have capability to write a plan or to secure supporting technologies? Although there are clearinghouses to help them, there still is a need for some expertise locally.

The FCC sets the floor for discounts, which depend on relative wealth and remoteness of location. Because the discounts will not be 100 percent, they may fail to enable participation by those schools that cannot allocate any of their own funds toward purchase of eligible discounted services. This may increase the disparity that exists among schools. The discounts are high, however the cost still depends upon pricing during a deregulated albeit competitive period.

Next, there is no timeline to wire schools. State Public Utility Commissions might step in here and require that a certain percentage of schools be wired each year. But then we have to ask the question, if we mandate that all schools should be wired within a particular time frame, what about schools that don't want the wiring (perhaps because wireless or cable are better solutions for them) and schools that don't have the money to pay the monthly fees, even with a 90 percent discount? What about the schools that cannot afford the computers or teacher training? And what about those that have no expertise or no interest in using technology?

Finally, we should ask why is it that wiring is mandated to be provided at a discount when hardware and software providers aren't required to give a discount? Two reasons: (1) There is no ongoing benefit for hardware and software providers, unless subsequent parent purchases at home—after they see their children using computers at school—are analogous to monthly fees which provide an ongoing revenue stream after the initial investment. Similarly, software providers can consistently sell upgrades. (2) Some say that because hardware and software companies are competitive while phone companies are regulated, the latter can be obligated to provide discounts whereas the prices of the former's products will be as low as possible due to competition. Well, now that there is competition in the telecommunications industry, why are we mandating discounts?

Just because schools now get a discount on telecommunications services does not mean they will all be wired. Now that there is deregulation driving prices up, this act may just be protecting schools from highway robbery by the telecommunications industry. Nothing is being *forced* to change.

Can the Federal Government Do More?
The federal government's education technology activities seem to be meeting the goals specified by the president, namely to act as a catalyst and to provide support for state and local technology activities. However, is there an argument to be made that there is a great enough need for technology in

our schools—a national need—to warrant a national funding plan? We believe there is.

The plan we suggest for using public funds for the installation and networking of computers and related technology in schools across the country accepts the premise that the best way to spend marginal dollars available for education is for technology. Economists will raise a question: If those attending public schools will benefit from learning more and from their resultant increased productivity, why don't we expect them to pay for technology themselves? That is, private benefits should be purchased privately. A general tax program to fund school technology means, in effect, that all beneficiaries *are* paying, although if the tax is progressive, those more able to pay will pay more. Even those who do not benefit directly from learning more, by attending technology-rich classrooms, will benefit from a society of more educated citizens who are less prone to crime, and more to better health. Increased productivity, however, results in greater economic growth and so benefits all citizens, not just those receiving the productivity-enhancing education.

Computer networking in general involves significant "externalities." The addition of a new person or school to the network generates benefits for those already on the network, but those benefits are not considered by the entity when deciding whether to join. (A similar rationale led to subsidization of local telephone service at an earlier time.)

If we mandate that all schools should be wired within a particular time frame, what about schools that don't want the wiring...What about the schools that cannot afford the computers or teacher training? And what about those that have no expertise or no interest in using technology?

Successful implementation of technology for the schools cannot be achieved by individuals or their families deciding whether or not to pay their shares individually. Some families will have different private discount rates and will make benefit/cost calculations that could lead to decisions not to pay for school technology. Many families will face cash-flow problems as benefits accrue in the distant future, but costs must be covered immediately. If families can opt in or out, it is likely that some who could reap substantial benefits would decide not to participate. Unless all families agree to pay their full shares, insufficient funds will be available. Since the implicit calculation by families will ignore social benefits, they will "purchase" too little technology by comparing costs only to the benefits they themselves receive. There could be a "free-rider" problem as well, because assuming some level of technology is available in a classroom, it would be very difficult to prevent particular students from using it because their parents did not share in the cost of purchasing the technology. Further, there are likely to be significant economies of scale in implementing technology plans. Costs will be significantly higher unless all schools and all students participate.

There are other factors as well that may make a tax transfer result in more people joining the network. If schools can purchase computers at a lower cost than individuals can—due to quantity discounts—the funds moved from individual purchasers to schools will purchase more computers in schools than the same funds could buy for individuals. Of course, there is the caveat that schools must be careful not to eat up this advantage by bureaucratic waste. Each computer purchased by a school puts more people (students/teachers) on the network than does a computer purchased by an individual (assuming there are more users per computer in a school than in a home). As we have noted, when schools get students on the network, assuming their education is enhanced, we believe there is a wide range of private and social benefits.

The goal here is to enable *every* school in the nation to have the configuration of technology that would ultimately help *all* students reach their maximum potential, academically, socially, and in the labor market. Could a particular school opt out of this program? Certainly. Do we expect that, given adequate funding, many would forgo technology? Not if they recognized its potential benefits.

The fact is that money is not now available for all schools that believe they would benefit from technology. Certainly some schools have found ways to use existing funds to buy technology; others have been able to obtain new public money through state or local taxes or bond issues. Still other schools have had the good fortune of obtaining sufficient funds from corporations or private foundations. The availability of resources, however, is correlated only weakly with the desire for technology by schools. That is, many schools that would like technology and that would benefit from it do not have the necessary funding.

The fact is that money is not now available for all schools that believe they would benefit from technology; ...many schools that would like technology and that would benefit from it do not have the necessary funding.

In addition, in order for schools to optimize their use of technology, they cannot be the only recipients of funding. For example, teacher-education programs, district training centers, software developers, and others require money to produce programs that will support what is being done in the schools. If we continue to rely upon the hit-or-miss approach to getting technology into the schools, the process will succeed in some schools and fail in others. Also, schools and the teachers working in them will not have the full complement of resources necessary to make optimal use of what they are able to buy.

To get technology into every school, or at least into every school that wants it, will require a more systematic and dependable source of funding. This cannot depend upon the willingness of particular communities to support a new tax or bond issue in a particular year. Nor can it rely on the generosity (or perceived self-interest) of local businesses, which can change with every quarterly profit report or new public need for their charitable or marketing budgets.

We are looking for a long-term source of funds that will continue to be available until we get technology into all the public schools that want it. We expect that by the time those at the head of the line demonstrate success, the line will include most of our public schools. We also need a funding source that has the potential for continuing after implementation to enable maintenance and updating.

One Possible Tax Plan

One possible method of getting the $50-$70 billion necessary to bring technology into the schools is to raise funds through a national excise tax and then require states to match these funds if they want to use them.

It might be preferable to fund a program to place technology in schools through general state or federal revenues rather than by an excise tax because the latter increases the cost of the targeted product and so distorts consumer and producer choices. There are several potential problems with reliance on the general tax base at either the state or federal level. People's fear of increasing the federal deficit, their resistance to tax increases in general, their reluctance to give up other programs that currently use tax dollars, and the general dissatisfaction with how money is spent by public schools makes increased use of new or diverted general tax revenues unrealistic.

Although it might be preferable on some grounds for an excise tax to be levied by states rather than by the federal government, a national tax prevents tax avoidance by purchasing computers in low- or no-tax states and transporting them to high-tax states. (There is an analogy to the cigarette tax here.) Thus, this proposal begins with a national tax.

We seek increased funding for education to be used exclusively for computers, related hardware and software costs, teacher training, technical support, and networking. How can we raise the money and be relatively certain that it will be used for the intended purposes? It would be easier politically to raise the money through a specific, targeted excise tax than through a general sales or income tax. Voters would feel it is "fairer" to tax those who make computers and related products than to tax everyone, because the computer and related industries would be the beneficiaries of the increased sales of their products. The general public would see the tax as a reduction in the profit rate of the sellers to be compensated by a growth in the amount of sales to be taxed.

It will be easier to earmark the revenue from an excise tax that falls on a source that seems to benefit from the program. Earmarking is a very important issue in this case due to the fungibility of most tax revenues. If we look to lottery funds, for example, it is known that these moneys are often supposed to be used for education. It is often the case, however, that when lottery funds are available, state legislatures simply divert some of the funds already used for education. Thus, although the lottery funds are indeed used for education, the net increase in educational budgets is less than the revenue from the lottery. Moreover, teacher unions might press for the incremental funds to be used for salary increments and class-size reductions. It is essential, then, when authorizing the new tax, that state legislatures or Congress stress "effort maintenance," that is, make certain that spending for technology rises by the full amount of the new, earmarked revenue.

In 1996, the computer hardware and software industry generated more than $80 billion dollars in taxable sales. At a 5 percent tax rate, the revenue from the tax would be $4 billion at the start. How might this money be allocated to all the states to help fund technology for the schools?

In 1996, the computer hardware and software industry generated more than $80 billion dollars in taxable sales.[223] It has been estimated that by 1998 or 1999, sales of personal computers alone will reach $100 billion. Here we shall assume, conservatively, that when the excise tax is implemented, total sales of hardware and software will be $80 billion. As sales grow, so will tax revenues. At a 5 percent tax rate, the revenue from the tax would be $4 billion at the start. How might this money be allocated to all the states to help fund technology for the schools?

Assume the $4 billion is allocated according to each state's share of all students in the country (see Table 7-1). This would provide as little as $8.7 million to Wyoming, and as much as $490 million to California, because there are 98,777 students in Wyoming and over 5.5 million in California. The allocation of federal tax revenues to the states would be contingent upon the states' matching the federal contribution. The state contributions would range from 1.02 percent to 2.6 percent of the state's expenditure on K-12 education (see Table 7-1).

Table 7-1

Allocating $4 Billion from a Federal Excise Tax to the States

	State Expenditures on K-12 Education 1992-93 ($Millions)	Estimated Fall 96 K-12 Enrollment	% of Nation's Students	Federal $ Allocated to State	% of State K-12 Education Expenditures to be Saved & Used for the Match
Alabama	2,530	741,933	1.64%	65,616,377	2.59%
Alaska	1,089	126,015	0.28%	11,144,736	1.02%
Arizona	3,463	749,759	1.66%	66,308,506	1.91%
Arkansas	1,714	457,076	1.01%	40,423,692	2.36%
California	26,530	5,535,312	12.24%	489,541,667	1.85%
Colorado	3,291	673,438	1.49%	59,558,695	1.81%
Connecticut	3,777	523,054	1.16%	46,258,770	1.22%
Delaware	681	110,549	0.24%	9,776,927	1.44%
District of Columbia	621	79,159	0.18%	7,000,803	1.13%
Florida	11,160	2,240,283	4.95%	198,130,092	1.78%
Georgia	5,942	1,321,239	2.92%	116,850,061	1.97%
Hawaii	834	188,485	0.42%	16,669,568	2.00%
Idaho	837	245,252	0.54%	21,690,028	2.59%
Illinois	10,243	1,961,299	4.34%	173,456,814	1.69%
Indiana	4,923	984,610	2.18%	87,078,672	1.77%
Iowa	2,552	504,511	1.12%	44,618,832	1.75%
Kansas	2,392	465,140	1.03%	41,136,870	1.72%
Kentucky	2,595	663,071	1.47%	58,641,840	2.26%
Louisiana	3,372	777,570	1.72%	68,768,104	2.04%
Maine	1,187	218,560	0.48%	19,329,394	1.63%
Maryland	4,497	818,947	1.81%	72,427,476	1.61%
Massachusetts	4,972	936,794	2.07%	82,849,837	1.67%
Michigan	10,254	1,662,100	3.67%	146,995,726	1.43%
Minnesota	5,065	836,700	1.85%	73,997,547	1.46%
Mississippi	1,802	504,168	1.11%	44,588,497	2.47%
Missouri	4,104	883,327	1.95%	78,121,228	1.90%
Montana	810	166,909	0.37%	14,761,392	1.82%
Nebraska	1,606	292,121	0.65%	25,835,111	1.61%
Nevada	1,191	282,131	0.62%	24,951,598	2.10%
New Hampshire	1,016	194,581	0.43%	17,208,697	1.69%
New Jersey	10,020	1,221,013	2.70%	107,986,097	1.08%
New Mexico	1,403	330,522	0.73%	29,231,286	2.08%
New York	23,471	2,825,000	6.25%	249,842,323	1.06%
North Carolina	5,382	1,199,962	2.65%	106,124,352	1.97%
North Dakota	548	118,427	0.26%	10,473,655	1.91%
Ohio	9,842	1,841,095	4.07%	162,826,001	1.65%
Oklahoma	2,721	620,379	1.37%	54,866,170	2.02%
Oregon	3,098	537,783	1.19%	47,561,400	1.54%
Pennsylvania	12,448	1,807,250	4.00%	159,832,757	1.28%
Rhode Island	929	151,181	0.33%	13,370,411	1.44%
South Carolina	2,900	648,980	1.43%	57,395,636	1.98%
South Dakota	613	142,910	0.32%	12,638,926	2.06%
Tennessee	3,172	891,101	1.97%	78,808,759	2.48%
Texas	17,153	3,809,186	8.42%	336,883,497	1.96%
Utah	1,626	478,085	1.06%	42,281,723	2.60%
Vermont	550	106,607	0.24%	9,428,298	1.71%
Virginia	5,713	1,096,093	2.42%	96,938,202	1.70%
Washington	5,951	971,903	2.15%	85,954,868	1.44%
West Virginia	1,699	303,441	0.67%	26,836,249	1.58%
Wisconsin	5,431	884,738	1.96%	78,246,017	1.44%
Wyoming	594	98,777	0.22%	8,735,814	1.47%
	240,310			4,000,000,000	1.66%

Source: *Digest of Educational Statistics,* 1997; Table 35, column 4; Table 40, column 23

This begs the question of where the states would find the matching money. But with their share of $4 billion from the federal government awaiting their matching funds, we believe states would be more likely than they are now to find ways to raise their part.

Clearly, using the $4 billion in tax revenues combined with the states' contribution meets a major portion of the need by providing $8 billion per year, assuming it will take four or five years to fully implement a technology plan in a state. Of course, there will still be a gap. A $50-$70 billion price tag, over a four-year period of implementation, requires at least $12.5 billion a year to be raised—leaving $4.5 billion a year still to be generated even after the $4 billion from the federal excise tax and a similar amount from the states. However, as noted, a growing base of hardware and software sales will yield more and more tax revenues over time. Additionally, the residual burden will get smaller as the costs of hardware and software fall.

It may be necessary for states to contribute more than the federal government, or the federal government may feel that it is appropriate to generate additional funds through shifts in the current budget or through other types of taxes. However, considering that many schools already have made some investment in technology, and allowing for contributions from local public utility companies, hardware and software producers, and other businesses, it appears that this tax and matching plan goes a long way toward putting technology into all of our public schools. Remember, too, that as hardware and software sales continue to grow every year, the revenues generated by the national excise tax will grow as well.

This plan does not preclude finding ways to supplement the federal and state allocations. Schools that increase their previous per-student expenditures beyond what they are allocated should *not* be penalized by having their tax allocation reduced. The plan should aim to assure that the spending individual schools did before the tax will be maintained, but it should not discourage new spending by schools to supplement what they receive from the excise tax allocation.

Technology funds need not be viewed simply as an add-on to all other expenditures in the school. If other activities can be curtailed, or other supplies used less, additional funds may be available for technology. At the state level, technology might facilitate distance learning, for example, and so free up funds previously required for certain teachers to travel to remote areas of the state. Many of the ideas presented in the next chapter could also be considered to obtain supplemental funding.

Some might argue that the proposed tax plan would raise the cost of computers and software, and thereby price less affluent potential buyers out of the market. However, the more likely scenario is that as sales grow, the price of computers and software will decline dramatically as has been the case to date. The estimate that total dollar sales will at least double implies that increases in unit sales will more than compensate for falling prices in regard to generating revenue.

This tax also might be criticized because sales taxes are generally regressive. However, unlike taxes on food and other necessary consumer goods and services, advanced technology products are purchased more frequently by corporations and relatively wealthy individuals, and these groups are most likely to be constantly updating their equipment and software. Hence, despite our desire for all families to own computers, this tax may be more reasonably considered a luxury tax than a typical sales tax. The broadening accessibility of technology to less affluent families will come from falling prices.

Assume that a pool of money becomes available at the federal level, perhaps through a tax plan like the one we have proposed. One question is who should decide what the money should be spent for? Perhaps there are lessons to be learned from the approach used in funding highways.

The money in the Highway Trust Fund (obtained from the gasoline tax) is allocated to the states according to a formula (see the case study of the Interstate Highway System at the end of this chapter). For the states to get their highway money, they must submit a list of projects in priority order. In the case of school technology, these projects or activities are specified in the state plans for school technology. Here the allocation would be based upon each state's share of K-12 students nationwide. Then, the Department of Transportation decides how far down each state's list to fund, depending upon available money. The state is then required to contribute some percentage of the federal allocation.

Once the revenue from the targeted excise tax on technology products is set aside for the states (to be put into a separate technology fund), a federally organized group would have to sign off on the overall state plans, and on the staging of the implementation. For example, if the hardware configuration sought is satisfactory, but there is no credible plan for teacher training, that would require explanation and possibly revision of the plan. The educational establishment or related political bodies are disinclined or unprepared to determine which proposed plans have potential for success. Hence, an independent outside agency should be given the responsibility for deciding who gets funding, and for what. This group would review state plans to access funds for use of technology, and monitor progress in preparation for the funding of subsequent stages of their plans. It must be recognized that this review and monitoring process itself would require some funding.

The most obvious candidates are panels formed by the National Science Foundation, the National Academy of Sciences, or the American Association for the Advancement of Science. Any of these organizations could establish review panels to include representatives of professional teacher groups such as the International Society for Technology in Education (ISTE), or the teachers' unions, but the panels should be dominated by K-12 educators and higher education faculty who are knowledgeable about what is required and what works when technology is applied in the schools. It is possible that representatives from the hardware and software companies could be included if they are able to separate their corporate self-interest from their ability to identify what is best for the schools. These panels would be guided by the basic notion that all children deserve access to technology in their classrooms.

Once the plan (for the year) is approved, the money would be sent to the state, conditional upon the state's providing matching funds. These matching funds might prove to be a significant burden on the state, but the task at hand is so important that the money must be found, some of it perhaps through efficiency savings. Then a state committee would oversee activities for the year. It would review proposals from districts and schools and make grants to them. The federal review board would revisit the states' activities when deciding upon funding for the next year. This process allows the states to direct the implementation of their respective plans. Particular schools or districts could decide not to participate, but if the federal panel were to feel that there was insufficient participation in a state, they might reduce the allocation to that state for the following year. Thus, we have broad oversight without federal micromanagement.

Possible Problems with the Excise Tax
No tax plan can be proposed today without hearing cries of "waste," "misuse," "bureaucracy," "distortions," "misallocations," "strings attached," "loopholes," "will never end," and when the tax is federal, "too far from the use." All of these charges must be addressed. To begin, however, it must be acknowledged that each of these charges is true in regard to some taxes, and not true in regard to others. To accept them as definite is never to find *any* tax acceptable *ever*. They could be the rationale for those opposing any government involvement (or new involvement) in our society. On the other hand, in certain circumstances, such as wartime or natural disasters like earthquakes or floods, no one makes the charges noted above, and taxes are imposed readily, despite potential problems in order to make money available for emergencies. On June 12, 1997, the president approved a spending law that contains $8.6 billion in emergency funds including $5.6 billion to help more than two dozen states recover from recent floods and other natural disasters, as well as $1.9 billion for military activity aimed at keeping the peace in Bosnia and the Middle East.[224] The fundamental question here is whether the dismal state of our nation's schools is tantamount to a natural disaster or a potential military conflict, or whether it should be seen as just another opportunity for intrusion into the lives of citizens by the federal government. If next year is disaster-free and peaceful, could and would the federal government provide $8.6 billion for school technology?

Perhaps an intermediate ground is to ask whether the charges are true, or if they could be dealt with. The first issue to be considered is waste. The question could be raised as to how much of the

$4 billion revenue raised by the federal excise tax will actually be spent on technology for local schools. Will federal and state governments establish new bureaucracies to collect and distribute the revenues? Will the private sector be forced to waste time and money to handle new paperwork? If so, these are pure deadweight losses to society. Depending upon the nature of a particular tax and the mechanism for its collection and distribution, this loss could range anywhere from minimal to 40 percent of the revenue raised. But we must assume that some share of the revenue collected does not find its way into classrooms via technology purchases. We are not claiming that there is no waste in government programs. The question is whether 85 percent of something (assuming 15 percent waste) is worth more than 100 percent of nothing.

There are two aspects of the likely bureaucracy in the case at hand. The first is the collection and disbursement of the revenues. The more precise the definition of the taxable products, the more effort that will be required to decide whether to include or exclude specific items in the tax base, and the more time that will be spent by sellers to keep products out of the taxable category; that is, to find loopholes. On the other hand, if the spirit of the tax, namely to tax all hardware and software, is maintained, the products to be taxed could be quite easily identified. It should include all supplementary materials that serve to facilitate use of the primary products (including manuals and related books and pamphlets, for example). Thus, a simple calculation of 5 percent of total sales is all that is required, and the tax payment remitted. Each year, each state's share, based upon its share of all K-12 students, could be disbursed to the respective state departments of education, to the same office that receives other federal disbursements for education. The funds for disbursement could be put in a special trust fund similar to the Highway Trust Fund with a statute to ensure they will be used only for the intended purpose. None of this has to be overly burdensome.

The second bureaucratic costs relate to various review procedures. A relatively small grant to an independent agency like the National Academy of Sciences would enable the establishment of one or more review panels to look at each state's plan for school technology, determine if it is in compliance with some general guidelines, and evaluate progress over the past year. Assuming these are satisfactory, the money would be sent to the states. The states would have to identify matching funds. Then each state's already established office of technology would review proposals from districts, and perhaps individual schools, and distribute their funds according to criteria established in their state plans. It does not appear that any new bureaucracy would be required at the state level.

In a recent discussion of recisions on selected education programs, the Department of Education[225] discussed administrative costs of Title I grants to local education agencies. According to the analysis, states retain not more than 1 percent of the funding for state administration; school districts use only 4-10 percent of local Title I funds for district administration. The report goes on to say that according to a recent GAO study, districts devote a greater percentage of Title I funds to classroom instruction (73 percent) than they do with other district funds (62 percent). Title I funds are allocated to states according to a federal formula; the states then suballocate funds to school districts. Within districts, funds go to schools with the highest proportions of children from low-income families. A similar procedure could be implemented for technology funds.

Title I programs are more diverse and complicated than would-be efforts to put technology into the schools. Yet only 1 percent of Title I funds goes to administration at the state level and roughly 9 percent at the district level. This means 90 percent of the money which the state receives gets into classrooms.[226] The remainder is likely to be utilized programmatically for services provided at the district level (e.g., nursing services, various special instructors who move from school to school), rather than a particular school. Seventeen percent, what's left after 73 percent goes to classrooms and 10 percent is eaten up as administrative costs, seem to be spent by the feds. It is unclear whether that is pure waste, or whether it represents useful spending to supplement activities in the states (e.g., research, development, or evaluation). However, this example demonstrates that administrative costs can be kept relatively low for certain federally funded educational programs. We would expect the efficiencies in a federal program to get technology into the schools to be even greater.

The next question concerns the responsibility of the *federal* government for getting technology into the schools, even conceding that there are social benefits in doing so. The federal government traditionally has not been the primary funder of public education despite its social benefits; nor does it fund all public goods. However, the desire to get all states to participate (i.e., to prevent states from opting out) and to prevent tax avoidance suggests a tax at the federal level. It would also avoid putting those states that did impose the tax at a competitive disadvantage. It's not just the companies that make technology products that would be hurt. A state specific tax that increases costs of doing business in a state increases the costs of goods and services of any company.

Although some would accept federal responsibility for a *national* technology network, they cannot see the need for federal involvement in providing the schools with hardware, software, and teacher training. But if we agree that schools must be on that national network, without the hardware and software and the people who know how to use it, the wiring alone will be of no value to the schools.

Even conceding these points, it could be argued that if the absence of federal funding results in inequitable opportunities for school technology across the states, then allocation of federal funds based on the student population in each state is unlikely to effect greater equality. Money will flow to states with both high and low current capacities in school technology. The allocation mechanism proposed takes account of political realities in that without a per-student criterion, states that already have strong technology systems will oppose the plan because they will object to a new tax without commensurate benefits. Moreover, this is an objective allocation mechanism in the sense that particularly powerful politicians would not be able to influence the system to disproportionately benefit their constituents. No state is presently at or near the saturation level regarding school technology. Every state would benefit from the federal funds it receives. Moreover, as states approach the completion point of their school technology plan, they may be less interested in applying for federal funds despite being taxed, given the matching requirement. Finally, perhaps the goal is less equality than sufficiency. Inevitably some states will always have better technology in their schools; the goal here is that every state reach a level enabling them to improve student learning to acceptable levels.

Some argue that "federalization" of the program will lead to a multitude of problems. With federal dollars come federal strings; Congress will not be willing for long to take the heat for taxing while others (e.g., the local school boards) get the credit for spending. Inevitably, they believe, Congress will add increasing and increasingly complex requirements designed to satisfy its own constituencies. The reason for this belief is not clear. Opponents of the plan will claim that the $1 to $1 matching requirement is only the beginning, and it is dangerous to advocate a program that over time will evolve into one-size-fits-all. Furthermore, a federal tax and block grant program essentially is a cartel arrangement in which the federal government imposes taxes higher than those that the states would be able to impose if they had to compete with each other for business.

Should we not argue, they ask, for a bottom-up process encouraging more rather than less experimentation with hardware, software, training programs, classroom procedures, and the like? If so, the program ought to be established at the state/local level, with states, districts, and schools participating as they deem it appropriate to do so, and being allowed to experiment with alternative approaches.

The other side of the federal "strings" problem is the alleged creation of poor incentives for states and localities. The lure of federal dollars—even with a matching requirement—will create strong pressures for school districts to join the program even if the implementation and operation of the computerization curricula have been thought through poorly in light of local conditions. To put it bluntly: Federalization of the program creates at both the federal and state/local levels perverse incentives that will increase the probability of poor outcomes.

Each of these criticisms is plausible, particularly if we are not aware of them. In fact, if the tax plan proves to be successful, Congress will get credit, not "heat," just as it got credit for the G.I. Bill. There is no need for Congress to add increasing and increasingly complex requirements, nor will it be necessary for a one-size-fits-all program. We have suggested that the federal review panel only consider the appropriateness of each state's plan and progress to date. The state reviews would consider the merits of plans prepared by local districts and individual schools. Experimentation is indeed possible at the state and district level.

We agree that the federal plan results in higher taxes than the states would be able to impose on their own. That is precisely the point. Without such a tax, there would not be sufficient funds to do school technology properly. A federal program provides incentives for the states to incur the short-term costs for long-term gain, and it ensures that states that do so will not be hurt in the interstate competition for business in the near term. For example, if all states raise taxes in order to obtain the funds required to match their federal allocations, no one state would lose its advantage in attracting new business due to higher tax rates. The purpose is *not* to allow states to opt in or out of technology as they see fit, although states that decide not to match their potential allocation could do so. The purpose is to get *all* states to put technology in *all* their public schools. Nevertheless, districts or schools can choose not to submit proposals for funding technology.

The type of tax suggested, namely, an excise tax, has also caused some concern. It is argued that since technology in the public schools ought to be defined as a capital investment for educational purposes, because it will be used for some substantial number of years, it is efficient to spread the costs over time. Accordingly, it would be appropriate to borrow in order to finance the program. Then, since education quality is reflected heavily by local land prices—that is, housing is a complement for the demand for education—it is most appropriate that local property taxes be used to retire the debt used to finance technology. Local and state sales taxes are a second-best alternative.

Although this alternative proposal has some theoretical appeal, it also has a number of problems. Once again, we must keep in mind that our goal is to get technology into *all* our nation's public schools. Both the proposed bond issues and local or state tax plans give citizens in each state the option to do school technology or not, but if such an option is made available, technology is likely to be forgone (i.e., new tax or bond programs defeated) because many voters will not recognize the social benefits of school technology, cash flow problems, the free-ride problem, competition from other claimants to public funds, and other reasons stated earlier. Interest groups will advocate alternative uses of state and local bond revenues and taxes, or no additional spending at all, and given the strength of lobbies on behalf of such interests, funds will become available for school technology only infrequently. Moreover, even if successful, advocacy for state or local technology bonds and new taxes will require inordinate amounts of money and effort, and will take a very long time. Rather than a single appeal for a national excise tax, the alternative plan will require 50 attempts to get approval for bonds and 50 attempts to get a new or higher tax. And not all of them will succeed.

In California between 1983 and November 1990, there were 272 school-related tax and bond elections. Of these, 43.8 percent were successful.[227] Between 1983 and mid-1997, the total number of tax and bond elections rose to 822, of which 49 percent were successful. Thus, even though the success rate has risen slightly in more recent years, the probability of an election's being successful is still less than 50-50. In 1992, nationwide, we have identified 28 ballot initiatives that could be viewed as positive for education and 17 could be viewed as negative. Comparable figures for 1994 were 16 positive and 8 negative. These success rates of 62 and 67 percent indicate that, despite the fact that a majority has passed in recent years, attempts to fund school technology through the initiative process will meet with frequent disappointment. School bonds for elementary and secondary schools, after rising to a total of $39.8 billion in 1992, have begun to drop since then. School bond issues totaled $28.9 billion in 1993, and for the first six months of 1994, they totaled $11.4 billion, less than half the $23.3 billion in bonds issued during the first half of 1993.[228] As has been demonstrated in California, in the debate over Proposition 13, the short-term benefit of a bit more money in the taxpayer's pocket often is much more appealing than the long-term gains from better schools.

Since education quality is reflected heavily by local land prices— that is, housing is a complement for the demand for education—it is most appropriate that local property taxes be used to retire the debt used to finance technology.

If our goal is to put technology in all our nation's schools, relying on voters of each state to support this effort financially is problematic at best. Although individuals might be making choices that are in their own best interest, such reliance will not achieve the goal that is desirable from a broad societal perspective.

Another argument against the excise tax is that once implemented, taxes never end; that is, it is very difficult to repeal a tax once imposed. The classic example given here is the federal gasoline tax which yields more revenue than is spent on highways. That is only one case, and others at various levels of government can be cited to both support and reject the hypothesis. But taxes have been repealed. The "luxury tax" enacted as part of the 1990 deficit-reduction law was repealed in 1993. In 1988, Congress passed a law to expand Medicare benefits by taxing wealthier recipients and then repealed it under tremendous pressure in 1989. Until 1993, Michigan charged a top rate of 17 percent on the inheritances left by its wealthiest citizens, but in 1993, the legislature repealed it. The Board of Supervisors in San Francisco repealed a small-business tax after one year in 1994. A tax on snack foods, passed in 1991, was repealed by California voters in a ballot initiative in 1992. After the 1989 Loma Prieta earthquake in Northern California, the legislature met in special session and passed a quarter-cent increase in the sales tax. That levy expired 13 months later. More examples could be found, but it is clear that to argue that taxes never end is pure hyperbole. However, if the proposed national excise tax works well, we do not propose to end it any time soon. Once technology is in every school, the tax revenues can be used for maintaining and updating it. However, if sales of the targeted products grow enough, and assuming needs for the proceeds of the tax for school technology are lower in the future, it is highly likely that the rate of the tax could be reduced.

All the points just raised are general arguments against new taxes, particularly against targeted taxes and federal ones. We believe that a national excise tax on computer hardware and software is the best way to obtain the funds to put technology in all our public schools.

All the points just raised are general arguments against new taxes, particularly against targeted taxes and federal ones. We believe that a national excise tax on computer hardware and software is the best way to obtain the funds to put technology in all our public schools.

Before giving up on a federal tax, we should look at some recent evidence on the public's views. In late May and early June of 1997, Peter D. Hart Research Associates conducted a series of comprehensive telephone surveys for the Milken Family Foundation's Milken Exchange on Education Technology, on attitudes toward the role of computers and modern technology in public education. The study consisted of three separate telephone surveys, including a representative nationwide sample of 801 registered voters, with an overall sample of 211 registered voters in California (for a combined total of 309 California voters). The national poll has a margin of error of ± 3.5 percent. The goals of the research were to uncover respondents' attitudes toward the importance of computers in the future of today's young people, to determine how respondents perceive the current state of computer accessibility in the public schools, to see whether they believe that computers and modern technology can affect the quality of public education, and to learn how much they are willing to invest to equip the nation's public schools with computers and modern technology.

After being told that the initial start-up costs of equipping every public school in the country with computers and modern technology would amount to $50 billion, respondents were asked about their reaction to the idea of spending that amount (see Table 7-2). Thirty-three percent answered "very favorable," and 27 percent "somewhat favorable." The fact that 60 percent were at least somewhat willing to pay for school technology should give us encouragement. And 61 percent said they would be willing to pay $100 more in federal taxes if the additional money were used only to equip public schools with computers and modern technology (Table 7-3). If all 115 million tax returns filed did "contribute" an extra $100, that might mean $11.5 billion dollars per year. If this input could be maintained for five years, we could reach our goal.

Table 7-2   Public's Reaction to Spending $50 Billion on Technology

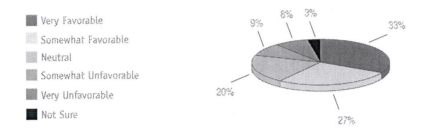

Table 7-3   Federal Taxes

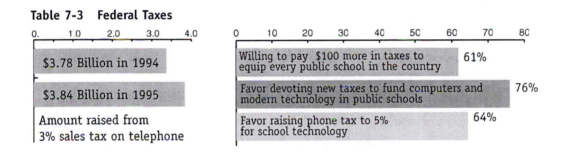

The survey then got more specific regarding a federal excise tax by focusing on one that already exists: the 3 percent national sales tax on telephone service, money that now goes into the federal general fund. One-third of those surveyed was aware of this tax and two-thirds were not. Thus, it is a tax that does not have much of an impact on people. Seventy-six percent of respondents would favor a proposal to use the money raised by this tax to specifically fund computers and modern technology in the public schools (15 percent opposed, and 9 percent not sure). Next, people were asked if they would favor raising this tax from 3 to 5 percent if the money raised would be adequate to equip every public school in the country. Fully 60 percent favored such action and 30 percent opposed it. This percentage is almost the same as the share willing to have the nation pay the $50 billion total and to pay $100 more in federal taxes themselves. This is encouraging evidence that the public might accept our funding proposal, or one similar to it, even though the option proposed in the poll would not fully pay for the technology and related costs required by the schools in a reasonable time period. A 5 percent telephone tax would require almost a decade to fully fund school technology. (The 3 percent tax yielded $3.78 billion in 1994 and $3.84 billion in 1995. Thus, if increased to 5 percent, the revenue would be $6.4 billion. That amount would enable full initial installation in 7.8 years, if all ongoing costs were ignored.)

If people were convinced that their tax money would be targeted for good purposes, they would pay willingly. It also indicates that the public believes that school technology is a good way to spend their tax dollars.

How can these seemingly optimistic results be explained in the light of almost universal reluctance to impose or pay more taxes? In one sense, they confirm our sense that if people were convinced that their tax money would be targeted for good purposes, they would pay willingly. It also indicates that the public believes that school technology is a good way to spend their tax dollars.

Finally, we believe the survey demonstrates that the public will accept taxes that do not seem too burdensome to them. One hundred dollars per year, or a 2 percent hike in a tax they did not even know they were paying, are acceptable. This was confirmed when respondents were asked about other possible taxes (Table 7-4). Fifty-seven percent would strongly favor raising the tax on cigarettes and other tobacco products, while 40 percent would strongly favor raising the corporate income tax. Since 57 percent of respondents probably do not use tobacco products and most probably believe (incorrectly) that taxes on corporations do not affect them, the most highly favored taxes seem to be those that voters believe impact them least. Alternatively, the proportions strongly favoring taxes that hit closer to home were much lower: state sales tax increase of one penny, 2 percent; tax on computers and technology-related equipment, 22 percent; and bond measures on property taxes, 10 percent.

Table 7-4 Strongly Favored Taxes

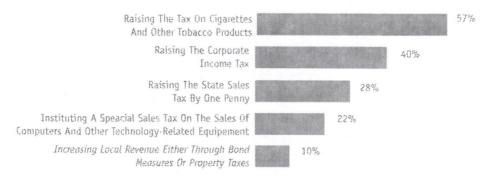

There are several implications to be drawn from these survey responses. First, we must continue to convince people of the value of school technology. Second, we must also convince them that any new taxes they pay will be used only for the stated purpose. And third, we should try to identify taxes that will be perceived by the public as not being too much of a burden on them. If we accomplish these three goals, we might well be able to sell our plan and buy modern technology for our schools.

This focus on federal funds does not stem from a desire to see a substantial new central involvement in the details of education, but rather from the desire to see the federal government do what it does well. Although the federal government has a history of controversial and disappointing attempts at micro-management, it has a far more illustrious tradition of rallying the nation around a bold vision for the future. When John F. Kennedy challenged America to put a man on the moon by the end of the 1960s, he relied not on evidence that it would be easy, but on a conviction that Americans achieve our greatest heights when the national spirit is energized by a common goal. The transcontinental railroad and later the national highway system were products, not of an airtight cost/benefit analysis, but of a vision of the United States worth striving for. Indeed, education technology offers enough stirring possibilities to rally the nation and has the added advantage of compelling evidence to back it up. We know a great deal more about the positive spinoffs of education technology than we knew about the benefits of the space program in the sixties. What we lack is not evidence or money; it is leadership and daring—a drive to do things, not because they are easy but because they are hard. However, given the current politics, we are not prepared to hold our breath waiting for bold and visionary guidance, so we must now turn to other possible funding sources.

THE INTERSTATE HIGHWAY SYSTEM

It is axiomatic that to get large infusions of public funds, a program requires strong advocates. Although this fact may seem obvious in today's political environment featuring political action committees (PACs) and periodic indictments of politicians alleged to have taken money illegally from those with special interests, the situation has been the same for generations. Lobbyists have been on the scene for a long time.

An expenditure for school technology of more than $50 billion by federal and state governments will require extensive lobbying to convince legislators of the merits of such action. Thus the question arises regarding the characteristics of successful lobbying efforts. To gain insight into such characteristics, we now review a highly effective crusade that extracted exceptional amounts of money from federal and state coffers: the highway lobby.

The Highway Lobby

In a recent book, Stephen B. Goddard[229] documents the century-long competition between railroad interests and the interests of road and highway builders, and the industries that supported each. By most assessments, the highway lobby was a tremendous success, as money from Congress grew from $10,000 in 1893 to fund an Office of Road Inquiry to $27 billion in 1956 for the interstate highway system. This amount is about $160 billion in 1996 dollars.

The initial impetus for good roads came not from automobile users but from bicyclists. In 1880, Colonel Albert A. Pope, a manufacturer of bicycles, realized that without good roads to ride on, the bicycle would soon become a white elephant. As a marketing strategy, Pope founded the League of American Wheelmen, which "led the first campaign for state funds for local road construction."[230] Unfortunately, the efforts of the Wheelmen were unsuccessful because of opposition from farmers who feared that roads for bicyclists would mean higher property taxes. In an effort to convince farmers that good roads would benefit them, the Wheelmen began a program to educate skeptics of the benefits of good roads.[231]

The premise to support road building was that good roads would enable farmers to get their produce to markets and bring needed materials back to their farms all year around, rather than be "stuck in the mud" when weather was bad. Advocates initially even co-opted the railroads by convincing them that good roads would enable more farmers to get their crops to the local rail depot for further shipping. Supporters also claimed that "good highways would raise land values, open new markets, provide access to manufactured goods, end rural poverty, increase political participation by farmers, and improve education."[232] Because the roads would be used by and would benefit many taxpayers, they argued that roads should be paid for by the general public through taxes. In addition, they reasoned that building new roads would cost less in the long run than existing maintenance programs.[233]

Another important characteristic of the road lobby is that it was led by (civil) engineers who believed in roads and wanted to build them. Those who would benefit the most—users and ultimately those who supplied materials for building roads and automobiles—were brought into the movement at a later time. The initial role of engineers in shaping highway policy dates back to 1893 when the Office of Road Inquiry (ORI) was formed. Because highways were strictly under the jurisdiction of local government, Congress created the ORI with the intention that it would gather technical data on roads, and serve as a source of expertise. However, under the leadership of Roy Stone, a guiding force in the good-roads movement, the ORI played a much greater role. Under Stone, the ORI sought to "build a reputation for technical knowledge, promote the gospel of good roads, and utilize cooperation to reach those goals."[234] Their reputation for apolitical technical expertise put the ORI engineers in an ideal position to advocate better roads. In contrast to the partisan reputation of self-interested manufacturers and politically motivated leaders in Congress, the engineers came across as individuals guided by the results of empirical research, which translated into a credible argument for good roads.

By 1903, drivers had bought 35,000 cars and the Automobile Association of America (AAA) began to thrive. But the drive for good roads still came from the engineers, who were by now employed by the federal government, particularly in the Office of Public Roads (OPR).[235] Many engineers moved from OPR to newly formed state highway departments to lead their road-building programs. They believed they were "doing good" rather than serving any special interest group or political program.[236]

The start of the second decade of the century saw the commercial value of the automobile grow, and so good roads were advocated not only by user groups such as AAA, but also by those with a financial interest in expansion. The highway lobby blossomed to include the engineers and user groups, as well as road contractors, road machinery manufacturers, road materials producers, auto manufacturers, makers of glass, rubber, steel, and concrete, fuel and service stations, insurance companies, and even the railroads.[237]

These interests soon coalesced into the American Association for Highway Improvement, which advocated federal aid to state highway departments. In addition, state highway commissioners and engineers formed the American Association of State Highway Officials (AASHO) to discuss legislation as well as economic and technical subjects. AASHO was really established to extract money from the federal government. In 1916, the Federal Aid Road Act set up state highway departments and provided $5 million for its first year. The bill had the support of both the state (AASHO) and federal (OPR) road advocates. This support occurred despite conflicts between the engineers who, according to Goddard, believed in their own intellectual and moral superiority over policy makers, and legislators who often resented them.[238]

of control but also make it easier to divert state gasoline tax revenues to other uses (like schools). Thus, in 1934, the Hayden-Cartwright Act ended federal road aid to states that used motor vehicle taxes for something other than building or maintaining highways.[240]

Another concern of the period was where to build new roads and highways. Villages, truckers, farmers, urban planners, highway engineers, and shippers, among others, all had their own agendas, but there was no mechanism for reaching agreement on where

By 1954, a 200,000-mile network of good roads gave the United States the best system in the world. Washington was taking in more money at the gasoline pumps than it gave back for roads...

The federal highway efforts were financed out of general revenues until 1932. Federal aid had only produced about 7 percent of total road mileage while linking all county seats in the nation. The next 20 or so years were characterized by debates about how to finance further expansion (federal and state gasoline taxes, property taxes, tolls, bonds, tire taxes, trucking taxes, and even "excess taking" by the federal government).[239] There was substantial concern that more money from Washington would not only change the locus

to build. Moreover, the composition of the road/highway lobby changed and the power of various constituents varied: Urban interests eclipsed rural; truckers came to dominate car owners; and new interests of the tourism industries (hotels and motels, restaurants, etc.), real estate, and Wall Street bankers all gained a voice.[241]

By 1954, a 200,000-mile network of good roads gave the United States the best system in the world. Washington was taking in more money at the gasoline pumps than it gave back for roads, which angered the governors who demanded an end to the federal gas tax. When this was rejected, the states decided to build their roads without reliance on Washington.[242]

To look into the development of a federal interstate highway plan, President Eisenhower created a highway committee, headed by General Lucius Clay, a military engineer who had supervised the Berlin Airlift. Though there was general agreement on the need for and benefits of a highway system, there were many differing opinions on how to achieve these goals. The committee found itself confronted with lobbyists forcefully representing the conflicting views of such groups as the AASHO, the AAA, the Farm Bureau Administration, and the Asphalt Institute.[243]

President Eisenhower proposed a $50 billion plan to build 40,000 miles of superhighways across the nation, this when the total federal budget was $71 billion. Although this move reduced the hostility of the governors, who dropped their opposition to the federal gas tax, state politicians still wanted to keep control over highway building in their states, whether by supporting the president's plan or by building their own toll roads. The battle for control was between the state's bureaucratic highwaymen and the president.[244]

Various ideas were floated, including a Federal Highway Corporation to finance and direct the interstate program, funding through higher gas taxes, tolls, tire taxes, or bonds, state allocations based upon various weightings of land area, mileage and population, and favoring cities over rural areas and truckers over automobile users. Finally, the Highway Trust Fund was established, which was intended to prevent diversion of federal taxes received and enabled revenues to be disbursed without need to go back to Congress for authorization. Though in recent years, some federal road user and gasoline taxes have been diverted for deficit reduction and other uses, funds that go into the Highway Trust Fund have been used only for transportation-related projects. Rural areas were to be favored for a time, then population would take precedence in the allocation formula. Small increases in the gas tax and modest levies on truckers enabled the extra burden on users to be minimal. Ironically, to strengthen support of a war-sensitive populus, Congress named the interstate program "the National System of Interstate and *Defense* Highways." Yet the system's value for defense proved to be slight. Moreover, the *interstate* system was more often than not a set of intracity highways to satisfy some urban interests.[245]

The above is a bare-bones description of a lobbying effort whose success can be measured both by miles of roads and highways built and by growth of federal expenditures from virtually nothing at the turn of the century to $68 million (1994 dollars) in 1916 to $147 billion (1994 dollars) in 1956. This is in addition to what the individual states spent. Can this success story provide lessons for those seeking to effect a massive infusion of technology into our schools today?

Although as a nation we are hugely dependent upon our system of interstate highways, and the path of urban and suburban development has been greatly influenced by them, it is possible to conceive of a nation far less dependent upon the interstates. Had the highway lobby failed to secure the funds they did, we might have seen a thriving interstate railroad system and strong urban and interurban commuter trains. The point is that the benefits of the current system of roads and highways were far from certain at the beginning, and no one could be sure that alternatives to it would not have provided at least, or almost, the same functions. Indeed, these alternatives might well have lessened the burdens our nation has endured in the form of pollution, traffic congestion, and the deterioration of our inner cities.

Could a case be made for school technology, given its undocumented potential for student learning, just as one was made for our system of roads and highways at a time when their benefits and superiority to alternatives were equally vague? The answer is "perhaps." But if such a case is to be made, and the requisite funding obtained, a strong lobby will be required to advocate it.

Is it ever possible to develop the necessary coalition to extract huge sums for educational initiatives from state and federal governments? As we will show later, such funding has been obtained for education in the past, primarily through a highly successful lobbying effort on behalf of handicapped and learning-disabled children. When we put what we can learn from that lobbying success alongside lessons from the highway lobby's accomplishments, our hopes for school technology may become more realistic.

Highway Trust Fund

If there are lessons to be learned from the successful lobbying efforts that resulted in funding for our national system of highways and roads, we must also ask if there are other lessons from the actual operation of the Highway Trust Fund. Critics of the plan proposed here for getting technology into our schools point to the problems and debates surrounding the Highway Trust Fund as arguments against a similar plan for school technology.

The concept that highways should be paid for by their users, through fuel taxes and automotive (or trucker) fees, dates back to the inception of automotive travel. The first gasoline tax was imposed in 1919 and, within ten years, every state taxed gasoline and used the proceeds for building and maintaining highways. Most states—either by constitutional provision or statute—earmarked motor fuel tax revenues to pay for highways. Even in the few states where highways are financed from the general funds, highway spending has corresponded closely to highway-user revenues.

The price controls of 1971 and the supply reduction of 1974 caused a fuel shortage in 1973-74 and a decline in tax revenues. Higher gasoline prices and a shift to cars with greater fuel economy, automotive fuel economy standards mandated at higher levels than would have prevailed otherwise, and a proposed "gas guzzler" tax all contributed to reduced gasoline consumption and revenues.[247] Moreover, highway construction costs rose dramatically in the mid-1970s.

The first gasoline tax was imposed in 1919 and, within ten years, every state taxed gasoline and used the proceeds for building and maintaining highways.

In 1956, the federal government joined the states in linking highway spending to highway revenue through the Federal Highway Trust Fund. The bulk of federal highway users' taxes were paid into the fund and federal highway aid was paid from the fund to the states. More than 80 percent of the funds disbursed by the states for highways annually came from state and federal road-user, energy-related taxes. The system worked well as new highways proliferated, at least up to the early 1970s and the OPEC oil embargo; road-user taxes have risen more slowly than have many other taxes.[246]

Thus, many states reduced their budgets and staffing in the highway maintenance area, and it was claimed that highways were deteriorating 50 percent faster than they were being replaced.[248] The response of the states was, unsurprisingly, to raise the motor fuel tax, and to seek other ways to raise tax revenues. Table 7-5 shows trends in federal and state gasoline taxes. Ultimately, demographic changes and other demand-enhancing factors alleviated the revenue shortage, and very different problems ensued. These will be discussed below.

(See Table 7-5)

The problems of revenue shortfalls have been raised in regard to the "school technology tax" as well. Specifically, what if sales of hardware or software decline, or prices fall so that revenue expectations from the tax are not met? Will that result in an increase in the tax rate or in the diversion of revenues from other uses? We expect that, depending upon elasticities of demand and supply, such a decline is unlikely given that the market is only in its embryonic stages. Nevertheless, lower revenue from the federal government will simply require that the states proceed more slowly than otherwise in implementing their school technology plans, using funds they raise themselves for this purpose. If, on the other hand, certain states wish to add revenues from other sources, that is their decision. Although our goal is national, there is no problem with states' proceeding at different paces as long as every state provides money to match whatever funds the federal government provides and achieves at least a minimal level of technology for its schools. Every effort should be made to keep the tax rate no higher than 5 percent; although this may be unrealistic given past history, the gasoline tax has risen quite slowly until recent years when politicians saw it as a way to pay for unrelated expenditures. Figure 7-1 shows the dramatic correspondence between the increasing gasoline tax rate and the increasing deficit in the 1980s.

(See Figure 7-1)

Another problem with the Federal Highway Trust Fund grants has been referred to as the "displacement effect."[249] A number of studies have shown that at current program levels, additional federal grants are mostly used to fund highway expenditures that would have been undertaken by the states alone, freeing state revenues for other purposes. In fact, one study shows that from 1976 to 1982 states were able to convert 63 percent of their matching grants into unrestricted resources. In the Meyers study, it was found that "there is statistical support for a hypothesis that unaided road systems benefit, as expenditures for these roads increase by about a dollar for every federal grant dollar targeted for primary, secondary, and urban systems."[250] There are strong local lobbies for the road system, which may explain why money displaced is still used for (different types of) roads. Or this may be due to the existence of strong bureaucracies at the state level making sure that federal highway assistance was totally spent, assisted by numerous earmarking systems that work against ready diversion of resources to other uses. An alternative rationale is that there is a strong complementarity between aided and unaided roads, and that enhancement of the former stimulates a demand for improvements in the latter.[251]

The lesson here for the schools is that the federal grants must be strongly earmarked for technology. Virtually every state has begun to work to get technology into its schools with its own state funds, at different levels of intensity. The federal money is intended to speed up the process and to enable states to do more than they can do with their own limited resources. If the federal money simply replaces money that otherwise would have been spent on school technology, the advocates of school technology in the states must make sure the displaced funds are used for complementary activities, perhaps software development and teacher training rather than buying computers and wiring the schools, for example. It is fairly certain that the federal money projected to be available from the excise tax will not cover all the costs of getting technology into the public schools, even when added to the states' own current budgets for this purpose. Hence, if the federal funds pay for the first things the states had planned to do, state funds can be used for the next steps.

Displacement aside, in recent years the Federal Highway Trust Fund has had significant "leakages." The Fund is generated not only from fuel taxes paid by motorists, but also from interest generated from surpluses that first appeared during the Vietnam War era. As these surpluses grew with compound interest, and as the federal deficit increased, beginning in 1980, fuel tax money began being diverted away from highway funding—

more than $42 billion has been diverted to date.[252] Some of this money has been used for nonhighway purposes such as Amtrak. Today, 4.3 cents of the 18.4 cents per gallon gasoline tax is diverted for "deficit reduction" (i.e., other spending) rather than for highways. The Trust Fund now has a balance of more than $9.5 billion, which some transport advocates claim is unspent solely to make the federal budget deficit look smaller.[253] These same advocates claim there is a $290 billion backlog of unfunded road and bridge needs.

The Highway Trust Fund is self-sustaining and among the very few federal programs that are user-financed and do not contribute to the deficit, according to Representative Bud Shuster of Pennsylvania, the new chairman of the House Transportation and Infrastructure Committee.[254] When the user-tax revenues are used for purposes other than those intended, however, the stated purpose may go wanting. Thus rate increases are proposed to enable more spending for highways while still using some of the revenues for other purposes. Without the leakages, there would be fewer unmet highway needs and less of a case for a tax increase.

Some people believe that a case might be made for more, not less, allocation of highway taxes to nonhighway expenditures.[255] Like all public services and public capital, highways represent tremendous amounts of wealth yet are subject to no taxation; as a facility, highways are tax-exempt, as opposed, say, to railroads, which are among the largest contributors to local property-tax revenues. The expansion of highways in the past removed an ever-increasing amount of land from the tax rolls. Highways generate revenues through fuel taxes. Hence, these taxes, or part of them, could be thought of as a compensating contribution of highways to the general tax base. But if this argument is to be made, it could also be made for all public capital. Nonusers of highways benefit from their existence as land adjacent to highways increases in value, as industrialization increases, and so forth. If nonusers already benefit, why should they be able to appropriate tax payments made by those who do use the highways? And how should we factor in the argument that because general revenues have been used to build highways in the past, it is only fair now to return revenues from the gas tax to the general fund.

Today, the debate centers upon whether or not to take the Highway Trust Fund "off budget" to make sure tax revenues are used for the stated purposes of building and maintaining highways. President Clinton and congressional budget leaders say no, the Highway Trust Fund—like all other trust funds except Social Security's—needs to stay in a "unified" budget "to make sure no one is spared in the delicate balanced-budget

dance."[256] Being "off budget" does not prevent Congress from taking revenue out of the Fund for other purposes. The only possible gain is that surpluses in an "off budget" Fund cannot be used to reduce the stated deficit, and so there is less incentive not to spend available funds.

The point here relevant to school technology is that a tax on computer hardware and software *cannot* be seen as just another revenue source to fight the deficit problem. We would suggest that the "School Technology Trust Fund" be established as an off budget item to help ensure that its funds are used only for clearly earmarked purposes. Although this would be a weak assurance at best, at least any diversions would be visible. If necessary, the tax could be revisited after perhaps ten years, with a requirement that it cease to exist unless it is reauthorized at that time. If the benefits are apparent, the tax could be retained. If more money is being accumulated than is used, the rate could be cut. Of course, skeptics will doubt whether Congress would ever cut the tax. Nevertheless, earlier we identified a number of taxes that have been reduced or ended. Apparently, Highway Trust Fund revenues grew faster than the nation's capacity to use them for a time, and that resulted in diversion. Great care should be taken to prevent that in the case at hand by making sure all available funds get spent for school technology. At least in the short term, it is unlikely that we will raise more money than is "needed" for getting technology into the schools. The highway example does not prove that our plan cannot work, but rather provides cautions about how to structure it.

Finally, there is the fundamental issue of waste or misuse of funds in government-run spending programs. Although the data we have seen do not allow us to distinguish between spending on asphalt and steel as compared to administrative costs, it does appear that over 90 percent of revenues to the Highway Trust Fund are allocated to programs that actually build and maintain highways. Some might consider use of these funds for air-quality improvement or highway safety to be far afield from their original purpose; however, air quality and safety do appear to benefit those who use the roads and pay the fuel taxes. Similarly, funds used for mass transit or Amtrak may be rationalized as reducing congestion on roads and highways, and thereby benefiting automobile users. How drivers gain from allocations to the Land and Water Conservation Fund and the Aquatic Reservoir Trust Fund is less clear.

Once again, our plan should try to put limits on administrative costs relative to direct expenditures on the technology and training. Care must be taken to ensure that spending be for stated purposes. Our plan is not intended, for example, to provide funds to reduce class size or to raise teacher salaries. Having said this, the Highway Trust Fund provides encouragement for our proposal, as well as caution flags about how to proceed. The statement that we do not want our proposal to turn into another Highway Trust Fund is only slightly true.

Table 7-5   Federal and State Motor-Fuel Tax Rates by Years, 1932-1994

YEAR	FEDERAL GAS TAX RATE (X 10)	STATE AVERAGE GAS TAX RATE	STATE HIGH RATE	STATE LOW RATE
1932	1.00	3.60	7.00	2.00
1933	1.50	3.65	7.00	2.00
1934	1.00	3.66	7.00	2.00
1935	1.00	3.80	7.00	2.00
1936	1.00	3.85	7.00	2.00
1937	1.00	3.91	7.00	2.00
1938	1.00	3.96	7.00	2.00
1939	1.00	3.96	7.00	2.00
1940	1.50	3.96	7.00	2.00
1941	1.50	3.99	7.00	2.00
1942	1.50	3.99	7.00	2.00
1943	1.50	4.05	7.00	2.00
1944	1.50	4.06	7.00	2.00
1945	1.50	4.10	7.00	2.00
1946	1.50	4.16	7.00	2.00
1947	1.50	4.25	7.00	2.00
1948	1.50	4.35	9.00	2.00
1949	1.50	4.52	9.00	2.00
1950	1.50	4.65	9.00	2.00
1951	2.00	4.74	9.00	2.00
1952	2.00	4.83	9.00	2.00
1953	2.00	5.10	7.00	3.00
1954	2.00	5.19	7.00	3.00
1955	2.00	5.35	7.00	3.00
1956	3.00	5.54	7.00	3.00
1957	3.00	5.58	7.50	3.00
1958	3.00	5.65	7.00	3.00
1959	4.00	5.86	7.00	3.00
1960	4.00	5.94	7.00	3.00
1961	4.00	6.09	8.00	3.00
1962	4.00	6.18	8.00	5.00
1963	4.00	6.22	8.00	5.00
1964	4.00	6.31	7.50	5.00
1965	4.00	6.41	8.00	5.00
1966	4.00	6.42	8.00	5.00
1967	4.00	6.45	8.00	5.00
1968	4.00	6.62	9.00	5.00
1969	4.00	6.84	9.00	5.00
1970	4.00	7.01	9.00	5.00
1971	4.00	7.09	9.00	5.00
1972	4.00	7.32	9.00	5.00
1973	4.00	7.53	9.00	5.00
1974	4.00	7.57	9.00	5.00
1975	4.00	7.65	10.00	5.00
1976	4.00	7.71	11.00	5.00
1977	4.00	7.79	11.00	5.00
1978	4.00	7.83	11.00	5.00
1979	4.00	8.01	11.00	5.00
1980	4.00	8.24	12.00	5.00
1981	4.00	9.15	13.90	5.00
1982	4.00	9.07	14.00	5.00
1983	9.00	9.75	16.00	5.00
1984	9.00	10.58	18.00	7.00
1985	9.00	11.08	18.00	7.00
1986	9.00	11.78	18.00	7.00
1987	9.10	12.75	20.00	7.50
1988	9.10	13.42	20.90	7.50
1989	9.10	14.19	22.00	7.50
1990	14.10	15.47	22.00	7.50
1991	14.10	17.55	25.00	7.50
1992	14.10	17.99	26.00	7.50
1993	18.40	18.34	29.00	7.50
1994	18.40	18.53	31.00	7.50

Source: *Highway Statistics, Summary to 1985,* Table MF-205; Office of Highway Management, State and Federal Motor-Fuel Tax Rates, 1981-1994, Table SS93-3

Figure 7-1 Federal Gas Rate Compared to Federal Deficit

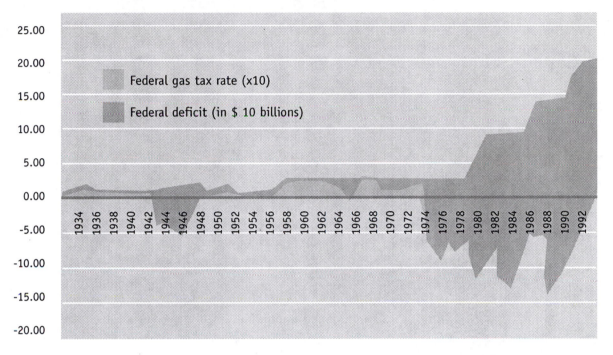

CONCLUSION

The experience gained from building America's highways and roads is very instructive as we contemplate how to extend the information highway into our nation's public schools. In a word, a strong, well-formulated lobby that reflected the strong public demand for roads and highways got the roads and highways financed and built. As the public funds to build and maintain the roads and highways were lined up, virtually every problem endemic to public financing was encountered. Nevertheless, the roads got built in a fairly efficient manner. Could the same things have been accomplished at lower cost? Probably. But would we have a *national* system of roads and highways wherein every state has roads and highways of similar expanse and quality as every other state? Probably not. Certainly particular states and congressional districts have benefited disproportionately from the "clout" of their senators and congressmen and others have suffered from a corresponding lack of influence. Not all funds were spent for the stated purposes. In the real world, however, this was probably the best way possible to achieve a national system of high quality roads and highways.

If we are able to be as successful in bringing technology into all our nation's public schools as we have been in building roads, our efforts will be justified. The program will not be without critics. However, we must not reject a "good" solution while we wait for the "perfect" one.

chapter 8

state
funding
for
technology

"He that will not apply new remedies must expect new evils."

— Francis Bacon

Given that funding from the private sector and the federal government is limited, a large gap still exists between the funds that states and communities need and the funds that are available. State and local communities will have to find ways to meet this significant funding gap by raising new revenue or scaling back some current programs in favor of education technology. How have states funded their technology programs to date? What are other options for raising revenue for education technology at the state and local levels? What are the state politics that affect the likeliness of obtaining state funding? We will discuss these issues in this chapter.

State Budget Appropriations

The majority of states have relied on money from the state's general fund, with income, sales, and property taxes being the most common sources. Allocations are made either to specific programs or into technology trust funds that also can accept contributions from outside sources and make allocations for various programs. In some states, such as California and Nevada, which have experienced considerable revenue growth in recent years, technology funds are being allocated from budget surpluses. In this situation, the main battle is against competing interests for the same funds.

Taxes

Though new and elevated property, sales, and income taxes are the most common methods of increasing revenue, strong taxpayer resistance makes each of these approaches difficult. In many states property taxes have been found to be an inequitable way to fund schools. The argument is that since wealthier districts have a stronger property tax base to support their schools, lower income districts must either operate their schools on less revenue or tax their community at exorbitant rates to gain revenue equality. This argument does not necessarily rule out the use of local property taxes to fund some school technology plans. The Bellevue, Washington, school district has raised over $11.2 million from its technology tax levies over the past seven years. However, evidence of a systematic trend toward wealthier communities having more technology in their schools would likely leave financing of technology by property taxes open to lawsuits.

Ever since California's Proposition 13 was passed in a "taxpayer revolt," opposition to increases in property taxes has been particularly staunch. In fact, when homeowners revolted against rapidly growing property levies they not only rolled taxes back, they substantially reduced the power of many states to raise them again. In California, for example, the legislature is effectively hamstrung with respect to property taxes because these can be raised only 2 percent per year.

Income taxes are number two on our list of taboo revenue sources. Again, it seems that lawmakers still are feeling a backlash that began in the 1970s. Whatever the cause, we see very few politicians today with the *chutzpah* to advocate openly a substantial increase in income taxes.

Politics clearly plays a role in getting technology funded. In 1798, Thomas Jefferson said to John Taylor, "In every free and deliberating society, there must, from the nature of man, be opposite parties, and violent dissensions and discords; and one of these, for the most part, must prevail over the other for a longer or shorter time." The situation has not changed significantly today.

Income taxes are number two on our list of taboo revenue sources. Again, it seems that lawmakers still are feeling a backlash that began in the 1970s. Whatever the cause, we see very few politicians today with the *chutzpah* to advocate openly a substantial increase in income taxes.

In education, this problem is sometimes exaggerated by the political differences of not only the governor and the legislature, but also by the state superintendent of education and the state board of education. All states have elected governors and elected legislators, but not all have elected superintendents. According to the Council of Chief State School Officers in Washington, D.C., 15 states have elected superintendents, 25 states have superintendents that are appointed by the state board, and others are appointed by the governor. Elected superintendents can be a significant problem if they are of a different party than the governor's. Appointed superintendents are more likely to be in agreement with the governor's education goals, and thus have political support to accomplish these goals. To make matters worse, the state board of education is generally appointed by the governor and may or may not be of the same party as the superintendent.

We have created a table outlining the various combinations of party affiliations for these groups across the country (see Table 8-1). We looked at the party affiliations of the state chief, the governor, and the two houses of the legislature. When we could not determine the affiliation of the superintendent directly, we made the assumption that if he or she was appointed by the governor, they were of the same party. In a few cases, the superintendent was listed as independent. The table shows some of the potential political problems. These various political party combinations can make for significant political squabbling and get in the way of choosing the most appropriate policy. This has been apparent in California's efforts to fund education technology (see the California Education Technology case study).

Table 8-1 Political Affiliations

Number of States	State Chief Party Affiliation	Governor	State House Control	State Senate Control
5	Democrat	Democrat	Democrat	Democrat
1	Democrat	Democrat	Democrat	Republican
2	Democrat	Democrat	Republican	Democrat
3	Democrat	Democrat	Republican	Republican
3	Democrat	Republican	Democrat	Democrat
1	Democrat	Republican	Republican	Democrat
2	Democrat	Republican	Republican	Republican
7	Republican	Republican	Republican	Republican
1	Republican	Republican	Republican	Democrat
3	Republican	Republican	Democrat	Republican
7	Republican	Republican	Democrat	Democrat
3	Republican	Democrat	Republican	Republican
1	Republican	Democrat	Democrat	Democrat
1	Independent	Democrat	(Unicameral)	(Unicameral)
1	Independent	Democrat	Republican	Republican
1	Independent	Independent	Democrat	Democrat
3	Independent	Republican	Republican	Republican
3	Independent	Republican	Democrat	Democrat
2	Independent	Republican	Democrat	Republican

CALIFORNIA EDUCATION TECHNOLOGY

California's Governor Wilson is a Republican in his final term. The Superintendent of Public Instruction, Delaine Eastin, is an up-and-coming Democrat, with aspirations to be a future California governor. This competition has led to paralysis in California's education technology goals.

Superintendent Eastin realizes that California's public schools rank near the bottom of every state comparison of student achievement, and she decided—correctly, we think—that technology would be very helpful in moving them from the bottom to the top 10 percent in such indicators. She appointed a statewide task force which concluded that $6.7 billion of new public money would be required to properly implement technology in California's schools. Over four years, that amounts to about 5 percent of the total now being spent for California's public schools.

There appeared to be three possibilities for raising the funds that would be devoted exclusively to school technology: a targeted excise tax on technology and related goods and services, including telecommunications and other public utility services; a one-half-cent increase in the general state sales tax; or a small reduction in the 15 percent cut in the state income tax that had been proposed by Republican Governor Pete Wilson. The governor's office was unwilling to break its pledge to cut the state income tax, felt donated

computers and other voluntary contributions could play a major role, and believed that a major reallocation of currently available funds along with natural funding increases from a growing economy could help make up the balance.

The education lobby opposed the governor's proposed tax cut but argued that the saved revenue should be spent on purchasing textbooks, repairing deteriorating schools, upgrading safety, and replacing those laid off by earlier budget cuts. Nothing was said about the revenues for school technology.

The governor presented his own plan for K-12 spending. With the state's growth-induced budget surplus, and later the Senate's killing Wilson's proposed income tax cut, $971 million was made available to reduce class size in grades 1-2, $387 million to provide every public school with a one-time $50,000 block grant to be spent according to site level priorities, $200 million to strengthen the teaching of reading, and $83 million for instructional and library resources. Only $100 million was allocated to technology, even though many of the other targeted problems could have been at least partially rectified if the money could have been spent on technology. Republicans in the state legislature wanted money to improve basic skills, which they saw linked to smaller classes but not to technology that was viewed as this year's gimmick. Democrats wanted unconstrained block grants to be spent as the local constituencies, including the teachers' unions, deemed best.

The competitive rivalry between the Republican governor in California and the Democratic superintendent of education has resulted in no major funding for technology until 1997.

In his 1997 "State of the State" address, Governor Pete Wilson called for a significant investment in technology—computers, Internet access and software—for every one of California's 1.6 million high school students. Either the governor had finally become convinced by Eastin and the Connect, Compute, and Compete Report or he independently recognized how important technology could be for California schools. For the state that is home to the Silicon Valley, that started NetDay, and that has been innovative in the technology industry, California had done a very poor job of putting computers in the hands of teachers and students.

As signed into law by Governor Wilson, the "Digital High School" legislation (AB 64) provides for the following:

A one-time grant of $300 per student, matched by local school districts, to install a comprehensive computer network on each of California's 840 public high schools and per-manent annual funding of $45 per student, matched by local school districts, for main-tenance and upgrade of these networks.

The governor and the legislature provided $100 million in funding for the first year of the program (1997/98), enough for ap-proximately 216 high schools to receive installation grants.

The governor's budget proposed for the fiscal year 1998/99 calls for $136 million in fund-ing; additional funding will be provided in the following two years. Every California pub-lic high school will receive a grant within four years—an unprecedented investment in the future of California's students.

With the local match, the typical high school will be able to invest approximately $1 mil-lion on its computer network—Internet access for every student and teacher, hard-ware, local networks and software.

There is now talk of a "Digital Junior High" program and even a "Digital Elementary School" program down the road.

For states in which either a property tax or an income tax increase is politically feasible, it is worth noting that both taxes share an important property—they are deductible from federal income tax. Thus, their net impact is tantamount to squeezing a subsidy out of the federal government. Says Joseph Stiglitz, "This means that if my community taxes me $1,000 to support public schools, the cost to me is far less than $1,000. If I am in the 50 percent marginal tax bracket (so that I pay 50 percent for each additional dollar of taxable income to the federal government), then by deducting $1,000, my federal taxes are reduced by $500. The net cost to me of $1,000 spent on public education is only $500."[257]

Put another way, it's as if these taxes come with partial matching funds. From the state perspective, this federal subsidy is an argument in favor of such taxes. Politically, however, property and income taxes will be difficult to sell.

Of the main state taxes, sales tax increases seem to face the least opposition. The principal argument against the sales tax is that it is regressive. However, by exempting products that dominate expenditures of the poor, like food, this point is weakened. The state of California has a history of getting approval to raise the sales tax for limited periods for disaster relief. This earmarking approach is especially effective in states with a ballot initiative system. If California's voters were to decide that there is a great enough need for technology in our schools, there is good reason to expect that a special sales tax could be implemented to pay for it. To appease an increasingly wary electorate, however, it is necessary not just to establish a compelling need but also to show that new funding will actually address the need.

Businesses generally oppose sales taxes because they increase the cost of doing business. Although such taxes do not apply to intermediate goods to be further processed and resold, they do impact firms that purchase goods for their own use. Thus, if a company purchases desks, paper, computers, or the like in a high sales tax state, its profit margins will be lower. When we were trying to find ways to fund school technology in California and suggested an excise tax on computer products, there was obviously opposition from that industry. There was just as strong opposition from a representative of Hughes Aircraft, however. As major consumers of computer technology, he said, the company could not afford to have increases in the cost of purchasing new computers. As a company that has to make competitive bids against companies in other states, they would be at a serious competitive disadvantage. State taxes on products that are not intrinsically local will give businesses an incentive to relocate, too, presenting a loss to the state's tax base.

In 1989, Kentucky's supreme court ruled that the state's education system was not fulfilling the state's educational mandates. In 1990, in response to this ruling, the legislature passed what is considered the nation's most sweeping state school-reform law—the Kentucky Education Reform

Act (KERA). This reform effort included equalizing funding for students across the state, as well as creating and funding the Kentucky Education Technology Trust Fund. The Fund has received annual allocations (appropriated in the state's biennial budget) from the state's general fund. To increase general fund revenue for the various components of KERA, including the Technology Trust Fund, the state legislature increased the state sales and use tax from $0.05 to $0.06 per dollar. Though this increase was mainly used to fund the significant increases in education spending, the increase was not passed as an earmarked source of revenue for education but as a source of general revenue. We can only speculate whether this sales tax increase would have passed if it were earmarked for education or if the state was not mandated to improve its education system. Regardless, it is clear that the state found this the most palatable method of raising revenue.

To make raising taxes easier at the local level, tax restrictions could be eased at the state level. Sometime this entails lowering the passing vote requirement or raising the cap on local tax authority. In Ohio, school districts have been given the authority to place local operating levies (taxes to pay for ongoing expenses) on the ballot. Nebraska's state government has authorized Educational Service Units to levy up to 5 cents on each $100 of their valuation to be used to purchase equipment for the infrastructure of their Internet system. This has allowed communities who are at their legal property tax limit to assess taxes beyond the ceiling.

Bonds

Second to taxes, bonds are a major source of capital. The key benefit of bonds is that they enable the issuer to raise a significant sum at one time. Bonds are ideal when large expenditures need to be made up front and the funding is not available all at once. This is a way to finance purchases that might otherwise be delayed by several years—the time it would take to raise the necessary revenues. Bonds are commonly used to fund technology infrastructure expenditures but generally should not be used to purchase hardware and software. Most hardware and software will be obsolete within 5 years while the life of most bonds is 10 to 20 years, so to replace obsolete computers, new bonds would have to be issued before the old ones are paid off. In contrast, infrastructure expenditures—which can include telecommunications wiring, upgrading heating, ventilation and air-conditioning systems, training teachers, furniture purchases and security systems—will go toward items with a much longer lifetime. Connecticut is one state that has used bonds for infrastructure. In 1995, Connecticut used $10.4 million in bond revenue to support activities related to upgrading electrical systems, wiring buildings and acquiring equipment.

There is nothing to prevent issuing five-year bonds. These are called "revenue bonds" and are guaranteed by general state revenues. They are generally used when funds are necessary up front, and there is a source of revenue attached to the bond, such as a bridge bond that is repaid by using toll fees. As there is no identifiable revenue source for education technology, revenue bonds are not an ideal funding source for this purpose.

Bonds cannot be completely ruled out for computer hardware purchases, however. In some cases it is necessary to spend significantly more up front to develop a critical mass of technology. For example, in 1995 voters in Maine authorized $15 million to establish a distance learning network. If the state were to try to put together such a network piecemeal, as funding from the general budget or education budget became available, it is possible that the distance learning network would never develop a wide enough net to be used to its full potential. Thus, any expenditures that were made toward the network would not be as effective as they could have been. Sometimes, it is necessary for projects to have greater funding levels in the beginning in order to get up and running. Bonds will allow for this. A distance network may have more of the qualities of infrastructure than of computers, since it is likely to last for ten or more years.

The main caution to keep in mind is that bonds should not be used for purchases or expenses that will be annual in nature or will need a constant stream of revenue to support, such as routine computer upgrades, teacher training, technical support salaries, and software upgrades. Ohio has an aggressive five-year $95 million set of bond issues that will be used to wire all classrooms in the state with voice, data, and interactive video communications.[258] Again, this is a one-time project and most effectively implemented by having funding available all at once.

At the local level, bonds have been used extensively to fund school and district technology programs. These bonds are generally school construction or school maintenance bonds that include technology expenditures. Unfortunately, as with any funding that is obtained at the local level, local bonds will result in unequal distribution of technology across the state's schools. Communities with more wealth who place greater value on technology and its role in education and the workplace are more likely to approve of bonds for technology. Similarly, in small communities where parents can mount a campaign to support the passage of a bond issue, success is more likely. Some communities rarely or never pass a bond for education in general. Education technology is not likely to fare much better.

State legislatures can work to make it easier for local communities to raise funds. When local bond issues require a two-thirds vote for approval, the legislature could lower the approval requirement to a simple majority. Caution should be used, however, in setting debt ceilings to ensure that communities do not pass excessive bond issues, since communities have sometimes viewed bond proceeds as "free" money. This has become a major problem in Arizona (see the Arizona case study).

DEBT FINANCING IN ARIZONA

The State of Arizona's experience with capital appreciation bonds (CAB) illustrates how extreme the abuse can be when bonds are issued irresponsibly.

In the case of CABs, interest is due and payable upon maturity along with principal. Thus, debt service can be extended without increasing annual debt service requirements in intervening years. However, excessive reliance on CABs can result in future difficulties because a large lump sum payment is required some years hence. To refund CABs at maturity, refunding bonds must be issued in larger amounts than the outstanding principal of the refunded bonds. Thus, more of the debt limit is used up over time. If the equipment or facilities originally financed need to be replaced before or at the date of maturity, new bonds will have to be issued to retire the earlier ones, and additional bonds will be required to build new facilities. Again, the debt limit will be pressed.

To avoid the debt limit, while obtaining more proceeds, CABs issued for refunding purposes are often issued at a premium so that the proceeds are greater than the principal amount of the bonds. A 20-year $1,000 bond with an $80 coupon every six months will sell for $2,000 (proceeds) to produce a yield of 8 percent per annum. In 20 years, a total of $4,200 is due, that is $1,000 in principal and $3,200 in coupons. One thousand dollars (i.e., "the

principal") is applied to the debt limit, so more proceeds can be obtained than what is put against the debt limit. In this case, there would be no impact on the current debt service requirements until the twentieth year.

With the CAB, the purchaser delivers payment at issuance and receives payment at maturity. Hence the prospective buyer may be relatively indifferent to the characterization of the portions of the two payments as principal or premium. The yield is constant; the nominal interest rate is higher the lower the stated principal and the higher the premium.

Allowing arbitrary allocation of principal and premium creates a problem, however. If the proceeds of the bond are treated completely as principal, voters will clearly know when debt limits are reached, and new borrowing will cease. However, if, say, only one-third of the face value of a bond is declared to be principal, with the remainder of the face value being defined as the premium and all accruing interest designated as interest, the spirit of the debt limit is soon violated.

Take as an example a ten-year $10,000 bond issued with coupons of $80 every six months (i.e., a 16 percent coupon rate) when the market interest rate is 8 percent. The obligation at maturity will be $42,000 (i.e., interest of $32,000 and principal of $10,000). Despite this obligation ten years hence, if one-third of the face value is defined as principal and two-thirds as premium, the debt limit is impacted by only $3,333. Three factors combine to yield this small figure: the coupon rate being higher than the market rate of interest, the fact that only one-third of the face value of the bond was counted as premium, and the fact that all interest is due at maturity.

If a school district can receive $20,000 while encumbering its debt limit by only $3,333, it can conceivably raise six times the amount authorized by voters. The result is an obligation at the ten-year maturity date of more than double the amount raised initially. To raise six times what has been authorized means an ultimate obligation of twelve times the authorization.

Debt limitations presumably are a function of the borrower's ability to repay; in the case at hand, that depends upon property tax rates and property values. Our example enables the borrower to incur debt far beyond its presumed ability to pay. The probability of default rises exponentially as we move in this direction and wishes of voters who approve bond issues are circumvented.

Currently, about 63 districts in Arizona, or 30 percent, use CABs. The bond payment schedule from FY 1996 to FY 2015 indicates $2.8 billion dollars of interest payments on a total

principal (summing outstanding principal each year) of $3.2 billion. This implies an 86 percent rate of interest! However, if we assume the actual interest rate on school bonds is 5 percent with the balance being principal including premium, interest payments are actually only $299 million with summed principal and premium of $5.7 billion. In effect, creative accounting has enabled school districts in Arizona to raise 177 percent of what they claim to owe (see Table 8-2).

This is dramatically illustrated in a number of districts. Kyrene Elementary District lists $55 million in principal and $289 million in interest although its debt authorization is $38.4 million. Mesa Unified has $199.8 million in principal and $91.5 million in interest with a debt authorization of $152 million. Tempe Union High School District lists $115 million in principal and $76 million in interest due, despite a debt limit of $60 million. Clearly, some districts in Arizona are abusing their borrowing authority.

Table 8-2 Calculation of True Principal from Arizona Bond Payment Schedule (FY 1996 to FY 2015)

YEAR	PRINCIPAL	INTEREST	TOTAL	ACTUAL INTEREST @ 5%	TRUE PRINCIPAL
1996	$200,246,489.	$236,430,676.	$436,677,165.	$21,833,858.	$414,843,307.
1997	188,053,918.	236,689,114.	424,743,032.	21,237,152.	403,505,880.
1998	173,855,564.	245,786,469.	419,642,033.	20,982,102.	398,659,931.
1999	173,006,623.	242,636,243.	415,642,866.	20,782,143.	394,860,723.
2000	183,476,317.	231,134,293.	414,610,610.	20,730,531.	393,880,080.
2001	166,573,272.	243,949,282.	410,522,554.	20,526,128.	389,996,426.
2002	158,597,016.	241,231,873.	399,828,889.	19,991,444.	379,837,445.
2003	191,452,769.	194,810,554.	386,263,323.	19,313,166.	366,950,157.
2004	201,685,179.	181,706,113.	383,391,292.	19,169,565.	364,221,727.
2005	203,735,751.	159,728,806.	363,464,557.	18,173,228.	345,291,329.
2006	207,901,336.	128,728,839.	336,630,175.	16,831,509.	319,798,666.
2007	170,107,989.	117,141,945.	287,249,934.	14,362,497.	272,887,437.
2008	173,173,000.	91,454,887.	264,627,887.	13,231,394.	251,396,493.
2009	174,023,000.	74,204,742.	248,227,742.	12,411,387.	235,816,355.
2010	169,566,000.	55,811,102.	225,377,102.	11,268,855.	214,108,247.
2011	135,335,000.	44,059,992.	179,394,992.	8,969,750.	170,425,242.
2012	133,015,000.	19,552,081.	152,567,081.	7,628,354.	144,938,727.
2013	118,225,000.	11,784,055.	130,009,055.	6,500,453.	123,508,602.
2014	84,565,000.	10,122,048.	94,687,048.	4,734,352.	89,952,696.
2015	8,685,000.	2,301,375.	10,986,375.	549,319.	10,437,056.
	3,215,279,223.	2,769,264,489.	5,984,543,712.	299,227,186.	5,685,316,526.
		86.1%		5.0%	176.8%

Leasing

Some school districts have attempted to avoid incurring debt by leasing their technology, particularly computers, rather than issuing bonds to purchase it. Indeed, this is becoming a more popular way of obtaining computers for the schools. Leasing has two benefits. First, it enables schools to purchase equipment before they have the full funding available. Rather than buying a few computers a month as the funds become available, schools can acquire computers for an entire school. For example, Apple Computer offers a dollar purchase option, where the schools lease computers for 12 to 24 months, and at the end of that period purchase the computers for a dollar each. Interest rates vary from 8 percent-13 percent for public schools. Leasing is less expensive only in that a large capital expense is not required at the start. Just as with leasing a car, however, monthly payments are higher. This is essentially a financing option. The second benefit of some leasing options is that they allow schools to maintain up-to-date equipment. Some enable periodic updating of equipment, and service contracts can often be negotiated with the lease. IBM Credit's Equity Lease program offers initial acquisition at fixed interest rates. After twelve months, schools have the option to use the equity they have accrued through lease payments to purchase some of their existing computers and add newer equipment for roughly the same monthly payments.

Leasing sounds like an attractive option for schools that lack the up-front capital, and is being used more than in the past. However, there are some cautions. Andy Rogers from the Los Angeles Unified School District cautions that "Kids beat up computers. What happens when the computers are not returned in great condition?" He adds, "I think there is a feeling that by leasing a computer, the school can remain on the 'cutting edge,' always with the most powerful systems. I do not think this is necessary in a school environment."[259] Without question, leasing is an option that schools and districts should look into, particularly as hardware manufacturers become more aggressive in seeking out the education market. The plans they offer are likely to become more competitive and offer schools more options.

Industry Taxes and Surcharges

In addition to the major revenue sources discussed above, several states have been experimenting with alternative sources, such as targeted industry taxes and surcharges. The logic behind these levies is: If schools were to begin making significant investments in education technology, the principal financial beneficiaries (putting aside the benefits to the individuals and the community) will be manufacturers of computer technology products and telecommunications companies. Schools will be not only purchasing their products but also creating new computer users who will be future customers. There appears to be some logic to taxing these industries. It might be easier to earmark the tax revenues, too, if the source is a beneficiary of the funded program.

Some states already have begun to impose taxes and surcharges on telecommunications providers and users. In Texas, the Telecommunications Infrastructure Fund receives an estimated $150 million per year from a tax on telecommunications companies. The Fund will be used to link all schools and libraries in the state to the Internet. Other states have opted for a user surcharge. For example, California's Public Utilities Commission established the California Teleconnect Fund, which provides $40 million per year in discounted telecommunications services for public schools and libraries. This fund receives its revenue from a 0.41 percent surcharge on most intrastate calls on users' phone bills. The Teleconnect Fund then subsidizes telecommunications discounts for schools and libraries. In Wisconsin, a 15-cent monthly surcharge on each telephone line is being proposed to fund various technology initiatives. These early levies on the technology industry may well augur a trend.

To date no state has attempted to tax the hardware or software industries. This version of our national excise tax proposal does not translate well to the state level. The main difficulty with taxing hardware and software products at the community or state level is that it makes these products more expensive, and there is little to discourage individuals or corporations from purchasing goods from out-of-state vendors. As noted earlier, there is an analogy to the cigarette tax here. Sellers of products within the state would be at a serious competitive disadvantage in this situation.

The price-based customer flight problem is minimal for products and services that are intrinsically local. Two examples are video rentals and Internet services. Missouri has had an earmarked tax on videotape rentals since 1988. This tax generates roughly $2 million per year, which has been used to purchase satellite dishes for schools, satellite course fees, and other educational items. Where a tax on computers might well motivate some Missourians to buy out of state, the amount of the videotape tax is very small relative to the cost of a road trip (two road trips, actually) to Illinois or Arkansas. Consequently, the number of rental customers crossing the border to escape the tax is minimal. Additionally, it is difficult to argue that this tax is particularly onerous. The people who rent the most are the people who pay the most. Though this might not be progressive the way a tax on opening-night Broadway show tickets might be—in Missouri at least—the videotape tax raises more revenue than a show would and generally spares the very poor. Finally, an entertainment tax can be appealing as a kind of sin tax. After all, we'd like to see kids spending less time idling in front of the TV and more time engaged in more demanding interactive pursuits. Certainly many teachers would say that they have to compete with the entertainment industry. If this is the case, why not even the playing field a little bit?

The pros of this type of tax are (1) it does not distort consumer demand for videos in the sense that consumers are not going to start renting their videos from neighboring states; and (2) video rentals are nonessential entertainment expenditures, and as such the tax on these items is not as regressive as a general sales tax. The higher rental costs might even cause some people to rent fewer videos and to read more!

A monthly surcharge on Internet service is another option that has yet to be taken by a state. Internet companies clearly will benefit from significant state expenditures on education technology. Though the cost of Internet service might rise due to a surcharge, the number of users has been increasing dramatically, so in the long run prices may not go up significantly.

Trade-off for Permissions
A handful of states have found ways to raise revenue by leveraging their power over the telecommunications and cable industries. The Texas Telecommunications Infrastructure Fund, mentioned above, was created as a trade-off for deregulation. In order to have deregulation at the state level approved, Texas telecommunications companies agreed to tax themselves. Now schools and libraries in the state will benefit from free wiring funded by these companies. Wisconsin has also created a trust fund, the "Advanced Telecommunications Foundation," but has asked, not mandated, that telecommunications companies contribute to the fund. The catch is that the state has set an endowment goal. If by a certain date that goal is not reached, the state has told the telecommunications companies that contributions will no longer be voluntary. If they want to maintain control, telecommunications companies in Wisconsin will have to be forthcoming with funding or risk being

taxed in the future. A final example is in Hawaii. The state used its regulatory power over the cable television industry to ensure that every school had a cable link. If the cable companies wanted to do business in Hawaii, wiring the schools was their entrance fee. Other regulatory permissions that states could use are taxes or fees on corporate mergers and on oil and mineral extraction. The problem with these permissions is that they are unrelated to the intended use of the funds.

Lottery Funds

Lottery funds have been used to fund education programs for several years. In the past, lotteries have been a source of funds for "education," although frequently the amount received has been less than what was expected. Table 8-3, a little old by now, provides data on the cumulative funds available to education from state lotteries. With all public funds, there are competitors for the use of the money. These funds must be dedicated to technology, not to education generally, to ensure their designated use.

A 1997 *USA Today* survey indicated ten states currently devote 100 percent of lottery proceeds to education, while four states devote some proceeds to education. This survey also indicated that there is a growing trend toward earmarking lottery funds for specific programs.[260]

Table 8-3   Lottery Funds for Education

STATE	CUMULATIVE PROFITS TO EDUCATION ($)	BEGAN	THROUGH	MONTHS	YEARS	AVERAGE ALLOCATION PER YEAR ($)	STATE GOVERNMENT EXPENDITURE ON EDUCATION ($)	LOTTERY/TOTAL EDUCATION EXPENDITURE (%)
California	6,626,000,000.	Oct 85	Jul 94	105	8.75	757,257,142.	28,285,000,000.	2.68
Florida	5,163,400,000.	Jan 88	Jul 94	72	6.00	860,566,666.	8,814,000,000.	9.76
Georgia	372,300,000.	Jun 93	Jul 94	12	1.00	372,300,000.	5,184,000,000.	7.18
Idaho	78,500,000.	Jul 89	Jul 94	60	5.00	15,700,000.	987,000,000.	1.59
Illinois	5,103,300,000.	Aug 74	Jul 94	239	19.92	256,189,759.	7,295,000,000.	3.51
Indiana	385,500,000.	Oct 89	Jul 94	57	4.75	81,157,894.	4,653,000,000.	1.74
Kentucky	214,000,000.	Apr 89	Jul 94	63	5.25	40,761,904.	3,572,000,000.	1.14
Louisiana	150,000,000.	Sep 91	Jul 94	34	2.83	53,003,533.	3,687,000,000.	1.44
Michigan	6,281,700,000.	Nov 72	Jul 94	260	27.67	227,022,045.	7,416,000,000.	3.06
Missouri	110,600,000.	Jan 86	Jul 94	102	8.5	13,011,764.	3,529,000,000.	0.37
Montana	41,500,000.	Jul 87	Jul 94	84	7.00	5,928,571.	771,000,000.	0.77
Nebraska	5,400,000.	Sep 93	Jul 94	10	0.83	6,506,024.	1,259,000,000.	0.52
New Hampshire	333,700,000.	Mar 64	Jul 94	364	30.33	11,002,307.	468,000,000.	2.35
New Jersey	6,926,400,000.	Dec 70	Jul 94	283	23.58	293,740,458.	7,018,000,000.	4.19
New York	9,760,000,000.	Jun 67	Jul 94	325	27.08	360,413,589.	17,972,000,000.	2.01
Ohio	5,563,400,000.	Aug 74	Jul 94	239	19.92	279,287,148.	8,489,000,000.	3.29
	$47,115,700,000.00					3,633,848,311.	109,399,000,000.	3.38

Source: The '95 *World Lottery Almanac,* U.S. Lotteries' Cumulative Profits by Program

Georgia, Missouri, Nebraska, Ohio, and West Virginia are among the states now earmarking the use of at least a portion of their lottery funds for education technology. Missouri's lottery has provided roughly $5 million since 1994 for this purpose.[261] In Nebraska, 12 percent of lottery proceeds, $7.3 million to date, are earmarked for the Education Innovation Fund, which includes funds for technology.[262] West Virginia has used lottery funds more extensively than any other state. The Basic Skills Computer Initiative was funded by dedicated lottery funds. Over $10 million per year in lottery funds has been raised for this program since it began.[263]

Of course, other states have received lottery funds for their technology programs indirectly when lottery receipts are placed in the general fund. Lotteries do have the potential to generate revenue for education technology; however, revenue from this source is variable from year to year. Lottery funds are not ideal sources of revenue for annual costs and are better used for one-time expenditures for infrastructure, pilot programs, planning grants, and the like. Because lottery funds are so variable, it is important that they do not take the place of existing funding. For example, in Florida, the share of the state contribution to education funding averaged 60 percent before the lottery was introduced in 1988. This share had sunk to 51 percent by 1993.[264] Thus we must be careful when using lottery funds.

Other Options

Some sin taxes are potential sources of revenue. Though casino gambling is not legal in many states, where it is, it has the potential to generate very large sums of money. For example, between 1995 and 1999, Indiana's technology program will receive an estimated $82 million from gaming revenues. Nevada funds most of its general education spending through gambling revenues. The option of gaming taxes is dependent on two main criteria: the legality of gambling in the state, and other claimants to the funds. In the sin tax category, cigarettes, cigars, and alcohol are also candidates, but they have many claimants on the funds. Moreover, the true purpose of a sin tax is to reduce the sinning, and if this is successful, revenue will decline!

As a rule, states have not been able to find a single earmarked source of revenue for educational technology that is capable of generating the necessary funding. States that have allocated significant resources to education technology have had to be creative in their funding mechanisms and rely on combinations of revenue sources. These sources range from traditional taxes and bonds to one-time monetary settlements from telephone company overcharges. Some of the more unusual things that have been suggested are taxes on tort settlements and entertainment venues, a limited-time increase in the gas tax, as well as personalized license plate fees. When deciding on a particular funding mechanism, states should keep in mind the ability to raise significant revenue as well as which revenue sources are most appropriate for particular uses. We maintain, however, that the ideal is a single earmarked source with adequate revenue potential.

Although there are few precedents for this in education, there are countless cases of successful earmarked levies (see Table 8-4). It seems that when a state or community is really serious about something, such as, say, professional sports, passing an earmarked tax is almost easy. Table 8-5 shows the total amount of public funds that have been allocated for stadiums and arenas around the nation. We hold out hope for the earmarked tax because we hold out hope that one day communities will value education as much as having six home football games a year!

Table 8-4   What Are Our Funding Priorities?

- Voters in Hillsborough County, Florida, have agreed to raise the local sales tax by half a cent for 30 years to build a new stadium for the Tampa Bay Buccaneers.
- Voters in six Colorado counties approved a .01% sales tax for 20 years to help build Coors Field.
- Comisky Park in Chicago was funded by legislation for a 2% hotel/motel tax in Chicago.
- Camden Yards in Baltimore is funded by the Maryland State Lottery.
- The Ballpark at Arlington, Texas, was paid for in part by a half-cent sales tax.
- Jacobs Field in Cleveland was financed largely by an alcohol and cigarette tax.
- A new baseball-only stadium in San Francisco will be helped by $10 million of city property tax money.
- A new stadium for the Detroit Tigers has funding from $40 million of Downtown Development Authority Bonds approved by Detroit voters and $55 million from Michigan from strategic funds (existing taxes on reservation casinos).
- An empty stadium in St. Petersburg, Florida, is being financed by tax dollars.
- Oakland and Alameda sold bonds to finance improvements in the Oakland Coliseum, California.
- The city and team will split the cost of Jacksonville, Florida, Municipal Stadium.
- The state of Missouri will pay $10 million a year for 30 years; the city of St. Louis and St. Louis county each pay $5 million per year for 30 years to build the Trans World Dome.
- The Carolina Panthers will get $55 million from the city, county, and state governments for acquiring and preparing the land for their stadium.
- The Houston Oilers will move to Nashville to a new stadium funded in part by a 3% water tax and by bonds.
- Maryland will finance a new stadium for the Ravens from public money and lottery sales.
- A new stadium in Landover, Maryland, will be funded by $70 million in state funds for roads and infrastructure.
- The Georgia Dome sold bond issues totaling $214 million, which will be repaid with dome earnings and a 21.2% hotel/motel tax.
- Hamilton County, Ohio, approved a half-cent sales tax increase to raise $35 million a year for a new stadium.
- New York State will cover $25 million, and the city of Buffalo and Erie County will put in $11 million to build a new stadium.
- The city of Anaheim built the Mighty Ducks arena.
- The city of Phoenix donated the land (approximately $12 million) and taxed rental cars and hotels/motels to provide an additional $35 million for the America West Center.
- Oakland city officials voted to issue joint bonds to reconstruct the Oakland arena (California).
- A half-cent sales tax was authorized by the Texas legislature and approved by voters for the Alamo Dome in San Antonio.
- Philadelphia lent $8.5 million and PA lent $20 million to build the Core States Center.
- Gund Arena was half paid by a county tax on alcohol and tobacco products; the balance was paid by a combination of public and private financing in Ohio.
- The city of San Jose sold public bonds for $136.6 million to build San Jose Arena (California).
- To finance the Ice Palace there were three public bond issues: one with Florida, one with Hillsborough County, and one with the city of Tampa.
- To build the Thomas and Mack Center there was a legislative bond issue—bonds were sold by the Federal Slot Machine Tax Rebate. Annual debt was paid for through a $250 annual tax on each slot machine in Nevada.

Table 8-5 Public Funds Allocated to Stadiums and Arenas

City / Football and Baseball	In Millions Spent ($)	Proposed ($)	Renovation ($)
St. Louis	280.0		
San Francisco	262.5		
Detroit	252.5		
Atlanta (Football)	214.0		
Seattle (Football)	212.5		
Seattle (Baseball)	192.0		
Charlotte	174.0		
Phoenix	166.5		
Milwaukee	155.0		
Chicago	150.0		
Raljon, MD	125.3		
Nashville	124.0		
Atlanta (Baseball)	121.3		
Denver	107.5		
Baltimore (Baseball)	105.0		
Baltimore (Football)	100.0		
Arlington, TX	85.5		
Cleveland	84.5		
Tampa Bay (Football)	84.0		
Minnesota		345.0	
Cincinnati		312.5	
Pittsburgh (Football)		196.0	
Pittsburgh (Baseball)		100.0	
Jacksonville			121.0
Oakland			100.0
Tampa Bay (Baseball)			65.0
Buffalo			60.0
Anaheim			50.0
San Diego			39.0
Hockey and Baseball			
Broward County, FL	212.0		
San Antonio	186.0		
Portland	131.0		
Atlanta	106.5		
Philadelphia	103.0		
Phoenix	88.0		
Indianapolis	87.5		
San Jose	81.3		
Boston	80.0		
Charlotte (Basketball)	77.5		
Cleveland	76.0		
Tampa Bay	69.5		
Buffalo	61.0		
Anaheim	60.0		
Minneapolis	52.0		
Los Angeles		125.0	
Charlotte (Hockey)		96.0	
Miami		82.5	
New York		80.0	
Seattle			110.0
Oakland			50.0
Pittsburgh			6.5
Totals	4,467.3	1,337.0	601.5
Grand Total	6,405.7		

allocation
and
implementation
issues

"Everything that can be invented has been invented."

— CHARLES H. DUELL, COMMISSIONER, U.S. OFFICE OF PATENTS, 1899

State or Local Control of School Technology Spending?

State planning to finance school technology must consider much more than how to pay for computers, software, and Internet connections in every school. Equally important as obtaining the hardware and software is getting highly competent professionals to utilize the technology effectively in their classrooms to enhance teaching and learning; training new teachers to use the technology properly; and providing in-service opportunities to experienced teachers. We need people to prepare new curriculum materials and software that can take optimum advantage of modern technology; and we need skilled technicians to support, maintain, and repair the technology used in schools. Any successful finance plan must include funds to pay for all of these people, or at least for the incremental costs of preparing them for the digital age.

In addition, certain activities must take place to ensure successful technology implementation and use, but these will not occur unless they are funded. These include: planning for the evolution of technology over time; selling the ideas of technology to those in the education system and gaining support for it from those outside; continually assessing and evaluating the impacts of new technology on the education system; and providing incentives for and rewards to those who get the whole thing right.

Most people will agree on the need for funding all of the above—and even more—but disagreement can arise about who should spend the money. As with most issues regarding the public schools, the debate over the wisdom of local versus central control arises. That is, given the need to hire staff, to train people, to provide support, to plan, to obtain buy-in and to evaluate progress, should each of these be undertaken separately by individual schools (or more likely by districts) or should certain aspects of these activities be the responsibility of the state (more specifically, the state Department of Education)?

Such decisions can be based upon a number of factors: efficiency, expertise, political philosophy, or legal/constitutional issues. We will briefly examine each of these factors.

1. Efficiency

Efficiency refers to the largest possible output for a given cost or, alternatively, the lowest possible cost for a given output. It can be achieved by getting the best prices, by making the most appropriate purchases, and by using available resources in the most effective means. Often the larger the order, the lower the price. This is an argument for developing the capacity to make large purchases at the state level to obtain quantity discounts. It might also be true that central purchasing would eliminate the need for purchasing offices at the district level, or at least the need for the person in a district who purchases technology.

On the other hand, large purchases may be possible only if all districts purchase the same configuration of technology. Because of diverse circumstances in various districts, some might want to purchase different items than would be dictated by a majority vote. Wealthy districts might want to take account of the fact that most of their students have access to computers at home. Rural districts might want to rely more on the Internet and distance learning and less on self-contained curriculum packages. What is saved in cost might be lost because standardization precludes the best use of resources in particular districts.

2. Expertise

A convincing argument might be made that the expertise necessary to implement an effective school technology plan could not possibly be available in every school district. The implication is that the required expertise is available or should be developed in one place (DOE) to serve as many districts as request assistance. This may be reasonable if the DOE has or can develop the capacity to serve the districts. Put aside the argument that it may be impossible for one central agency to serve the diverse needs of many districts. One solution to that is to maintain regional technical service centers. The questions are whether or not DOEs already have the technical expertise required, whether they have the ability to develop it if money were provided and, if so, would it be less expensive and more effective than having individual districts or small groups of districts develop the expertise themselves? Similarly, how many districts have the expertise needed, or do they even know what is required to do technology properly in their schools without advice and assistance from their regional office or the state?

We cannot assume that all state DOEs or their directors of technology are as competent as the best ones. Nor can we deny that in some cases bureaucratic rules, staff tenure, salary limits, and just plain ignorance will prevent DOEs from even developing the required capabilities. Will the same regulations hinder districts from developing their own expertise? Is the private sector more likely to provide assistance at the local or state level? To summarize, the decision to centralize or decentralize depends in part upon the relative ability of the state DOE, regional centers, and individual districts to recognize the need for and to acquire the expertise and support necessary to use technology effectively in the schools.

3. Political Philosophy

Even if quantity discounts and DOE experts were available to support centralization, some would argue that the best public policy will be made and the best public services will be provided only if done at the local level. They believe that local public schools exist to serve the needs of local youngsters and their families, and that distant bureaucrats in the state capital cannot correctly identify these needs. To the extent that wants and needs vary from district to district, an overall policy for all districts in the state will satisfy no particular district. Furthermore, oversight of spending and other activities is more effective if both those who provide the money and those who spend it are directly visible to each other. Hence, those advocating local control would argue that individual districts, with the help of their communities, are best qualified to make policy and to spend money. The contrasting images are flows from taxpayers to the state agency, then back to the local schools after the state takes its cut, versus a direct flow from taxpayers to their local schools.

On the other hand, there are philosophical arguments against local control and spending and in favor of state involvement. What if local districts are controlled by groups who are not looking out for the best interests of students? For example, districts with many retirees may vote against school funding because the majority of voters do not have children in school. Or the local board might be dominated by a fervent religious group that does not represent the more apathetic majority. Or what if what the locals believe is best for their children is in fact detrimental? Who is better able to decide what is best for kids in a district, parents and educators in the district or those in the state DOE? The "state versus local" philosophical choice often comes down to whether one believes a family and community knows what is best for its children or that a central office knows better.

4. Legal/Constitutional Issues

Regardless of efficiency, competency, or philosophical considerations, state constitutions and local laws can dictate the locus of control in education decision making and spending. When schools were funded solely or primarily from local property tax revenues, spending decisions were made at the local district level. Since the 1970s, the Serrano decision in California has been followed by similar decisions in other states. Such decisions argued that because of the huge variances in property values in different districts, property-poor districts would never be able to spend amounts on schooling that property-rich districts could. The property-poor districts would have to tax their (usually poor) residents at rates unfairly higher than the rates in districts with higher property values.

Since the courts asserted that equality of educational opportunity was a state responsibility, the state was responsible for equalizing spending per student across districts. This gave states a constitutional right and reason to become responsible for education spending, or at least for a part of it.

Some of the early results of such court decisions were funding equalization formulas wherein low-wealth districts received money from state general funds to bring their operating expenditures up to some percentage of the spending levels of wealthier districts. More recently, in a capital (facilities) equalization case in Arizona, the debate has shifted to whether the state's obligation is to have each district spend the same amount per student on facilities, or whether the state should specify facility standards and ensure that each district is in compliance. If the latter alternative prevails, the state DOE (or even the legislature) may have to specify standards not only for square feet per student, but also the number and type of computers in each school and classroom—to say nothing about number of students per Bunsen burner or carpet thickness in the classroom!

The Compromise

Clearly, the decision about the locus of control of school technology policy and spending is not an either/or decision—both the state and the local districts will play important roles. Some things can best be done at the state level and others at the district level. This, again, depends upon the factors discussed above and upon the characteristics of particular states.

Some districts' enrollments (e.g., New York City, Chicago, or Los Angeles) are larger than enrollments in many states. The diversity of needs within each district may be greater than that in whole states with smaller populations. To have the state DOE develop policies that satisfy both Los Angeles Unified and Hayward may be overly optimistic. In Arizona, Higley District has fewer than 300 students. To expect such a small district to have the capacity to develop and support its own technology plan may be even more fanciful. Small districts, however, might be able to collaborate with nearby districts with similar characteristics and needs to develop regional plans.

When districts are not able to provide all the planning, technical support, and professional development they require, there are other alternatives than relying on the state DOE. It may be that one district could develop in-service teacher training for a group of districts, while another specializes in providing technical support, another provides planning services, and still another does the purchasing. The central state authority might still be preferred, but other alternatives should be considered.

In efforts to secure the funds to get technology in America's public schools, the ultimate goal is to provide students with the best, most modern educational experience possible. Some potential supporters view any money that does not go directly to the classroom, or at least to the school building, as wasted. Certainly, any level above the school will require administrative overhead to provide its services. In some cases, it may be that the state is more likely to get money directly to the schools than is the district. Big city districts may require a greater administrative "cut" than the state would. The funds for training, technical support, planning, and evaluation should be allocated to the administrative unit that can provide goods and services to the schools in the most cost-effective manner while taking the smallest share of the funds for administrative costs. In some cases this may mean that money flows directly from the state to the schools (California's Digital

High School program does this). In other situations states can rely upon the districts to provide all the desired goods and services or to purchase them as needed. In still other situations the responsibilities might justifiably go to the state DOE.

What If There Is Not Enough Money?

Education technology is very expensive, and few states can find the funds to implement it all in one fell swoop. Thus, when there is not enough money to fully implement a comprehensive school-technology plan, the question becomes, how should a state allocate available funds? A little bit to all schools? A lot to some schools? The state of West Virginia decided that the best way to reform the entire system was to start in kindergarten and add one grade a year, focusing on drill and practice, and at the same time provide training for all elementary school teachers. Kentucky took a different approach, not focusing on one grade each year. Kentucky's technology plan is a component of the Kentucky Education Reform Act, which was enacted to address funding inequities among the state's schools. In Kentucky, technology funding has been allocated annually by district, based on average daily attendance (ADA), probably as a result of the state's history of funding inequities. South Carolina allocates funds for hardware using a socioeconomic status formula, and has separate pots of money for wiring and connectivity, and teacher grants. Each of these states has committed to bringing technology to their schools, but each has chosen a different allocation approach based on their specific financial, educational, and political requirements.

We have been working with a number of governors and education chiefs who are trying to determine what approach would best meet their needs. From our discussions with them and with many others across the country for whom the technology money questions have become complicated and vexing, we offer the following thoughts to guide decision making.

Factors Affecting Allocation Decisions

Allocation decisions depend upon a number of considerations. First, does a state have a special need that can be met by targeting its technology spending? In a state where the student population is geographically dispersed, a distance learning network provides comprehensive curricula to isolated schools. Georgia is at the forefront of the country in this technology with the deployment of its Integrated Services Digital Network (ISDN). In 1993, the state established distance learning via video telecommunications systems that allows every elementary and high school in the state to receive a multitude of educational services. Says Governor Zell Miller, "Many rural school systems simply do not have the critical mass of students or the tax base to be able to offer enrichment courses like calculus, physics or foreign languages. Distance learning will hook together classrooms around the state. It can put a teacher in dozens of places at the same time."[265] In rural south central Colorado, many children live on farms and are home schooled. The Center Consolidated School District offers Internet courses so that these children can continue to take classes offered by district teachers and local community college professors. "We know we're going to lose a lot of kids at age 16, so we have to provide services beyond the typical K-12 education," says superintendent Gary Kidd.[266]

States with high student dropout rates might benefit from a technology program that excites high-risk students in ways that more traditional teaching cannot. Florida is one state often mentioned for its high dropout rate. The technology program at Vero Beach High School in Florida increased the retention rate for at-risk students from 60 percent to 80 percent. The computer-based class-room was originally intended to remove difficult students from the main classrooms but, surprisingly, these students realized that school and learning could be engaging and as a result increased their levels of achievement. East Bakersfield High School in Bakersfield, California, the majority of whose students are considered at-risk, has also found that technology-based instruction has a dramatic impact on its dropout rate. Emphasizing the school-to-work transition, the curriculum uses technology in five career tracks that students might want to pursue: (1) science, technology, engineering, and manufacturing; (2) health careers; (3) communications and graphic arts; (4) human and government services; (5) and business and entrepreneurship. The results have been a lower dropout rate and an increase in graduates' success at finding work.[267]

Thomas Stevens, executive director of the Denver Public Schools' technology department, convinced the school board and the bond review committee that buying computers was not the place to start. His plan was to invest in the infrastructure for technology and teacher training, before any computers were purchased. Stevens said, "All technology goes out of date."

A second consideration is whether spending patterns enable a state to get more bang for its bucks through quantity discounts or through the leveraging of its funds. A state that gives companies the opportunity to bid competitively for the state's technology infrastructure will find that it will incur a significant cost saving by not purchasing similar products from several companies. In Kentucky's technology plan, large savings were made due to a plan of open architecture, uniform standards, and competitive acquisitions. Open architecture required connectivity among various system elements and, therefore, enabled districts to use the technology in the form most appropriate for their needs. Uniform standards for hardware and some software, however, allowed compatibility to be established among schools and districts as well as with the state department of education. Competitive acquisition allowed the state to get large cost breaks from technology vendors. As part of the competitive acquisitions process, the Department of Education experienced a "prefeeding frenzy" where vendors from across the country lobbied to influence the Master Plan in their direction. This frenzy produced a great deal of savings. Roughly 10 percent of the $600 million allocated was saved due to the competitive prices offered by businesses.

When the city of Denver passed a $24 million bond issue in 1990 to equip classrooms for the information age, the plan was to spend $16 million for Apple IIe computer labs and $8 million for a new telephone system. Before the money was spent, however, Thomas Stevens, executive director of the Denver Public Schools' technology department, convinced the school board and the bond review committee that buying computers was not the place to start. His plan was to invest in the infrastructure for technology and teacher training, before any computers were purchased. Stevens said, "All technology goes out of date. Our thinking was if we invested in training and people and the plumbing—the way to connect us all together—then we would have something that would last beyond 20 years."[268] According to Stevens, the district's inefficient use of telecommunications services was amounting to a significant waste in fees for various telephone and information lines. By upgrading the telecommunications infrastructure and not leasing multiple lines from the local phone company, the district will save $640,000 per year. This investment is expected to pay for itself in four years. Based on the district's particular situation, the choice to spend limited funds on infrastructure and training will save the district a significant amount down the line. And quite significantly, too, Denver's public schools have not spent limited resources on Apple IIe computers.

Training teachers before computer purchases are made can also be a wise implementation choice. In the Denver Public Schools District as well as in the state of West Virginia, teachers were trained prior to their being expected to use technology in their classrooms. The training allowed teachers to feel comfortable with the new tool. Further, it encouraged enthusiasm for technology, which teachers then took back to their school sites. In Denver, in addition to 30 hours of training, teachers were given a computer to take home so they could familiarize themselves with the computers. Thomas Stevens explained this decision simply: "You can't teach with the technology unless you feel comfortable with it."[269]

A third issue of consideration is that it is important to acknowledge that particular approaches garner strong political support for future education technology spending. For example, Denver Public Schools' plan to give each teacher a computer to take home, in addition to training, ensured more effective uses of technology and thereby won the teachers' support for future fund-raising. Many policy makers and educators understandably would like to make sure that technology does have an impact before they authorize funds for large technology expenditures. Leaders in Boston are preparing to bring technology to their classrooms but caution, "A good idea can turn into a dumb one in a matter of months. It is, therefore, critical that...school districts think before they act."[270] Model schools are one way to facilitate this. In Boston these are called "Lighthouse Schools." Their purpose is to "provide other school systems with opportunities to test new products and even provide teachers with a chance to test-drive software and hardware to determine if they do, in fact, make teaching easier and more productive."[271] This type of program reassures politicians that technology will be tested, and money spent carefully.

Bay Vista Elementary, a model school, is located in a working-class neighborhood in the West. Eighty-nine percent of the students enrolled are minorities and 25 percent are eligible for free or reduced-price lunches. Most of the students' parents are employed with the industries related to the nearby airport. Bay Vista Elementary School sounds like an average school in an average town. However, when you look closely, you will find that a typical classroom lesson integrates the chalkboard to write down concepts; images and video clips from a laser disc to illustrate concepts; a micro/macro video projection system for students to make presentations; and access to computers using their "mobile labs"—Macintosh computers on wheeled carts—for students to research topics and develop their projects. If you look even more closely you will find, in one fifth-grade class, students working on multimedia science and language art presentations using word processing programs and other graphic interface software. While half of the students collaborate in small groups at the computers, the other students work individually at their desks.

In its Model Technology Schools Self Study, Bay Vista documented improved achievement in science on several state skills test and increased motivation of their students: Nine students won awards in the county science fair, which no students even had entered in previous years. Students that were surveyed thought that technology had improved their problem-solving, writing, and reading skills. Other students noted that their grades improved, they enjoyed school more, and felt that they took more interest in their own learning.[272]

Bay Vista Elementary received its first computer in 1979, when the school received Chapter 2 funds after applying for a grant. Impressed, the school administration set a goal of attaining a computer for every student. After all the teachers actively began to use computers, Bay Vista successfully competed for a state Level II Model Technology Schools grant to fund their present program. Bay Vista's leadership has encouraged other schools to attempt to capture the necessary funding to attain similar results from their students. As a model school, Bay Vista has demonstrated to politicians, administrators, and teachers what can be done with technology, and the positive outcomes that can result. Other schools will also benefit from their experiences. Seeing the demonstrated success of a school such as Bay Vista Elementary, politicians are more likely to support further spending on education technology.

Another important area from which to gain support is the business community. If technology is implemented in a way that provides skilled workers for a state's businesses, their direct contribution to school technology and its support for public fund-raising efforts can be enhanced. Contributions from the private sector are often in the high schools and take the form of school-to-work programs utilizing technology in collaboration with local business. Ford Motor Company, concerned that high school graduates will not have the basic and technical skills that the company will require to produce cars successfully for the next century, has begun to work with schools. Currently, Ford is spending its own money to create programs for high school students in which they learn the basics of manufacturing systems and processes, quantitative literacy, computer technology, and specialized science and math operations. If the company is concerned enough to pay for this type of program, it might support a similar program that is publicly funded. On one hand, why not get others to share the cost through taxes? On the other, when done privately, Ford can limit its costs and stop the program whenever it decides to do so. Thus, spending that most clearly and quickly demonstrates the effectiveness of school technology, such as model schools or high schools that can quickly provide more skilled labor, is the most powerful argument for more resources.

Equity or Merit?
The first question that those who make allocation decisions must address is equity or merit—which should take precedence when distributing funds for school technology? Allocation on a per student basis across the state enables every school to receive its "fair share" of available funds. Taxes are paid in every school district; shouldn't every school benefit from their use? Though allocation by enrollment is most equitable, this method of distribution may spread limited resources too thin to have any significant impact. If every classroom gets a single computer, the benefits from having a critical mass of computers in each classroom will not materialize. In California, $2 billion can equip every school with computers and pay for connectivity, but there would be no funds left for teacher training or technical support. That same $2 billion could provide every high school in the state with computers, audio and video technology, teacher training, and technical support. Without the teacher training and technical support, it is unlikely that voters will see much payoff from technology spending and consequently will be unwilling to spend more in the future. Kentucky has, in fact, run into this problem.

In 1985, a lawsuit was filed by 66 property-poor Kentucky school districts seeking equal resources for equity in education. The result was a Kentucky Supreme Court decree that Kentucky's whole system of public schools was unconstitutional. Out of this lawsuit came the Kentucky Education Reform Act of 1990, a comprehensive reform package to address financial inequities and years of educational inequities. Part of this plan was to bring technology to every school, with at least one workstation for every six students, and at least one teacher workstation for every classroom. Because of the state's history of funding inequities, funds were provided annually to districts based on average daily attendance. The problem is, given only a little funding each year, schools have not accomplished very much and thus have created doubt in legislators that technology will have an impact. This in turn has resulted in reduced funding each year. Of the $280 million that was to have been spent by October 1995, only $137 million had actually been spent. That was less than 50 percent of the planned funding. As it currently stands, few schools will reach the goal of one computer for every six students, and positive results will be sparse. Legislators will continue to doubt the value of technology, and hence to reduce its funding in the absence of these positive results.[273]

It is often suggested that limited funds could be well spent on computer labs. This suggestion should be rejected out of hand. Many schools with computer labs for a decade or more have had no commensurate improvement in student outcomes. Thomas Stevens, of Denver, describes how computer labs were traditionally run by a "computer nerd," and "teachers marched their students down there once or twice a week for a class in computers.... Most teachers were happy, because they did not have to figure out how to teach with computers, and the computer lab instructors controlled equipment purchases."[274] Labs may teach students how to use technology but they rarely enable the integration of technology into instruction and allow students to use technology for all subjects —which is what we intend.

A school with computers could benefit greatly from funds for Internet access or for development of sophisticated course software. Generally, a school with no technology would not be able to accomplish as much. Wealthier schools or districts (which probably already have some technology) can afford to hire grant writers to make the most plausible case for more funds.

Under a competitive-grant program, schools that can demonstrate that they will make the most effective use of technology will receive the most funds. There is a strong argument for providing funds to these schools first. Schools with a demonstrated interest in technology use (through application for scarce federal, state, and private funds), and schools that have teachers using technology are schools most likely to provide a supportive environment.

At Alexandria Street Elementary School, in a stressful urban neighborhood in Los Angeles, teachers realized that technology met a need presented by a student body that spoke seventeen different primary languages. Educators at Alexandria clearly identified the need as a problem in their students' ability to write proficiently in English. The small cadre of interested teachers was able to write grants successfully and purchase computers. These teachers were clear on what their need for technology was, how they would use it and, most important, they had a strong interest in using it.

In these circumstances, where teachers are ready to use technology, the school will be in a good position to compete for grants, and technology can then have a significant impact. These schools are likely to be the ones that already have some technology and that can leverage new money. To illustrate, a school with computers could benefit greatly from funds for Internet access or for development of sophisticated course software. Generally, a school with no technology would not be able to accomplish as much. Wealthier schools or districts (which probably already have some technology) can afford to hire grant writers to make the most plausible case for more funds. This would be expected in wealthier communities like Beverly Hills. Poorer schools are then at a competitive disadvantage, creating a "have and have-not" situation.

On the other hand, poorer schools often have a greater ability to purchase technology by using their Title I compensatory-education funds. Schools serving a middle-class population are the most likely to suffer. Joe Ferrell, who works for Redondo Beach Unified School District, noted that "wealthy schools could get parents to donate computers while schools in poorer neighborhoods could qualify for federal grants."[275] It is at middle-income schools such as his that funding for technology is most limited. But a competitive process would make funds more available to those schools than a grant based on socioeconomic status. In either case, an allocation by demonstrated commitment tends to make "the rich" richer, but will provide funds to schools that are most likely to produce positive results.

Allocation by Socioeconomic Status

Although high socioeconomic status schools may be more effective in competing for technology funds, research implies that their students might not benefit from technology as much as educationally disadvantaged students. Technology has a particular advantage in this student population, where traditional teaching methods, fear of teachers, or the pace of the class all may cause students to be unresponsive. Computer-based instruction has produced significant achievement gains for this group. Technology is perceived by students to be less threatening than traditional instruction; it provides extensive drill and practice with immediate feedback; it enables individualized diagnostics; and it allows students to work at a pace that meets their needs. Going beyond drill and practice, Union City, New Jersey, an urban district with a large number of educationally disadvantaged students, used technology in support of the district's curriculum changes. The results were dramatic. Passing rates for the elementary grades went from the 30 to 35 percent range to between 70 and 80 percent after the implementation of technology. The marginal benefit of providing funding for a district such as Union City surely exceeds the benefit to a less educationally disadvantaged district.

South Carolina has decided to address the needs of low-income schools without denying funding to other districts. It has two concurrent initiatives. The first provides funding for wiring, connectivity, and teacher training. The second is for hardware purchases. Funding for hardware is allocated by a socioeconomic status formula. This formula is based on the number of children in grades K-3 on free lunch. This ensures that those districts that have the greatest financial need will be given more funds to purchase hardware. All schools, on the other hand, are eligible for wiring, connectivity, and teacher training grants.

There is one other point to keep in mind when considering allocation by socioeconomic status. Though many schools serving low-income populations have been able to purchase technology using federal funds, we have to remember that these funds are generally for compensatory education. The funding is supposed to make up for other funding inequities at the state and local levels. Having used federal funds to purchase 28 computers and 20 printers for his school, Marina Middle School Principal John Michaelson commented, "That means we have to go without something else. But we need to have [technology] now. Otherwise I think we're shirking in our duty to prepare children."[276] Schools like Marina Middle School, in San Francisco, have chosen to make technology a priority, but they should not be penalized for this.

Allocation to Selected Districts or Schools

Based on effectiveness criteria, then, a state should prefer allocation by socioeconomic status or by competitive grants, rather than by enrollment. Both merit-based allocation and socioeconomic-status-based allocation, however, only benefit a segment of the taxpaying population. Recognition of this has led some states to consider allocating funds sequentially to districts. Such a plan begs the question of which districts should be first in line for technology funds. If eligibility depends upon ability to use the money most effectively, we are back to a merit-based system at the district rather than the school level. Low-socioeconomic status districts or low-achieving districts might make more sense—with a caution to avoid allocation to districts based on political grounds.

By implementing technology one district at a time, there may be savings, particularly for wiring and infrastructure costs. For instance, purchasing one T1 line per district and sharing an Internet connection among schools is more cost-effective than providing an independent connection for each school. In addition, district needs will tend to be part of a comprehensive plan allowing for quantity discounts. In addition to cost savings, implementation at a district level has educational benefits. These plans allow for an overall technology plan in support of curriculum changes—changes that are from grade to grade and school to school. District implementation also allows for greater efficiency in administration.

If resources cannot fully fund technology in all district schools, model schools might be an effective way to demonstrate the impact of education technology. These models can also rally public support for larger and broader financial support. With continuing support and significant dissemination, carefully selected model schools provide evidence that technology improves learning, as Bay Vista Elementary was able to do. This would help other schools and community members understand technology and make decisions about how to use it in schools. Unfortunately, model schools may benefit the "haves" more than the "have-nots," or at least some schools rather than all of them. This is so because the least expensive place to build a model school is where there is already some technology available.

If resources cannot fully fund technology in all district schools, model schools might be an effective way to demonstrate the impact of education technology. These models can also rally public support for larger and broader financial support.

One Grade at a Time

If everything can't be done at once, some states implement technology one (or several) grades at a time. This can start at the beginning of elementary school, the first year of high school, or even in the twelfth grade. Each such case presents opportunities for cost savings from large purchases of grade-specific software, curriculum development, and teacher training. As we mentioned at the beginning of this chapter, West Virginia chose this approach. As of this writing, over $54 million has been spent on basic skills/computer education in West Virginia. All K-5 classrooms and many in grades 6, 7, and 8 are equipped with four computers and a trained teacher to enhance basic skills. The West Virginia Department of Education credits computers in the classrooms, new curricula, and teacher training with significant improvements in CTBS scores. Students spend at least 90 minutes a week working on the computers. Nearly 18,000 student workstations are in use and over 12,000 educators, representing all 55 counties in West Virginia, have been trained. Internet use in 667 schools in West Virginia is being supported by Bell Atlantic, and by the end of 1997, all schools in the state should be on-line. Now that every school is or will be connected, the state is working to connect every classroom. There are already 215 home pages for specific schools. This approach has a political advantage over a district-by-district allocation in that every school with the targeted grade gets some resources.

By starting with the lowest elementary grades and adding a grade or two each year, the first set of students will have access to technology throughout their K-12 experience. Younger students are able to learn new technologies more easily and will not need to adjust to a new way of learning midway through their school years. It is probably the case that technology will have a greater impact on these young learners. The early foundation they receive in basic and technological skills will be critical for them to be prepared for the work force and continue lifelong learning.

Intel, a major producer of computer microprocessors, has found it necessary to work with vocational institutes and universities to create training programs to provide the company with qualified employees. They found that classes were not as full as they would have hoped. Richard Draper, a spokesman for Intel, explained that "students were not qualified [for specific programs], and our employee pool was shrinking. So now we are starting at the kindergarten level to get kids to pursue the math and communication skills they need."[277] Intel's realization was that a long-term investment needs to be made, starting in the elementary grades, in order to create a continuing stream of qualified labor.

Another benefit is that students and their parents will create a demand for funds to continue implementing technology in successive grades, because they recognize its effectiveness. They will not accept a sudden end to learning with technology when a student reaches a particular grade. Dr. Ginger Hovenic, principal of Clear View Elementary School in Chula Vista, California, has seen this happen. Clear View Elementary is located eight miles from the Mexican border and serves a largely low-income population, of which 68 percent of the students do not speak English. According to Dr. Hovenic, "Because of what they have been exposed to at Clear View, [children who graduate from our elementary school] are pushing the bar at middle school... . They don't want to sit in rows and read books. They want to talk about it, give their opinion, produce things. Now they are having the same effect in high school."[278]

The downside to this option is obvious: Children already in high grades will not receive the benefits of a technology-rich education. Further, support from the business community will be scant when the promised labor-market benefits of technology-literate graduates are twelve or more years away.

Implementing technology first in high schools puts limited resources into students that are closer to entering the labor market. Business is more likely to support a program that provides more skilled labor *in the short term*. As we mentioned in Chapter 6, California's Governor Wilson chose to introduce a "Digital High School" initiative that would equip each of the state's high schools with modern technology. This plan was readily supported by California's Business Roundtable. Moreover, if high schools today have more technology than elementary schools do, new funds could be better leveraged there. The key obstacle here is the way high schools are organized. Fifty-minute class periods attended by different groups of students precludes many of the benefits that technology can provide, such as integrated instruction across disciplines and cooperative learning. But this also means that a greater number of students might be able to benefit from a limited number of computers and trained teachers.

Allocation by Subject Matter

A final option is allocation by subject matter. This option makes the most sense when combined with some sort of allocation by grade level. For example, a state could decide to fund technology for all high school math classes. The advantage of this method is that it tells software developers where the investment is going to be made. They in turn will focus their software development on those subjects where there will be the greatest demand. When California and Texas, the two biggest textbook buyers in the country, began to use "new math," publishers responded by rewriting many of the standard textbooks to conform to the new approaches. High-quality software for education is not that readily available. If software publishers knew that there would be a demand for their product, they would be more likely to invest in its development. In addition, teacher training could be directed toward this area. This would mean fewer teachers would have to be trained in the beginning, and their training could be in greater depth, which would probably be more effective than had they received more generalized training.

Like allocation by grade level, this method has the advantage that every school teaching that subject will benefit. All students who take that particular subject will have access to technology. In other words, every school district will benefit, which is good because citizens in every district will be asked to help pay. The disadvantages are that this method does not work particularly well for elementary schools where children remain in the same classroom throughout the day. Additionally, this method does not encourage integrated instruction across disciplines.

Summary of Allocation Issues

Limited funds should not be distributed to all classrooms by enrollment. Giving every school a little money will not enable them to do anything meaningful, and classroom technology will fail. Counting on incremental funding each year, as Kentucky did, is likely to leave most schools far short of their technology goals. Although such an allocation is the automatic suggestion of many politicians who do not want to favor one area over another, it is the least effective path.

Competitive grants, by themselves, should be ruled out because they are not equitable. The public will not generally support grants that benefit only some schools or districts, perhaps schools outside many taxpayers' districts. Competitive grants in conjunction with other grants—by socioeconomic status, for example, or by district allocation—might still be an option. Although we preclude model schools financed by the state for the same reasons, this does not rule out such models financed at the local level.

This leaves us with implementation by district, grade level, or subject matter. If politically feasible, implementation by district would be our first choice. Funds would be provided based on a plan demonstrating that the district was prepared to use the funds effectively. Within the district, emphasis could then be placed on implementation at particular grade levels. In order to maintain broad-based support, however, grade-level or subject matter implementation might be more likely to occur.

From an educational standpoint, technology implementation starting in kindergarten or first grade makes most sense. Yet from a political perspective, if business support is important for additional funding, consideration should be given to starting in the ninth or tenth grade. An obvious compromise would be to start simultaneously in grades 1 and 10, rather than funding two elementary grades each year. Finally, if money is not available one whole grade level in a year, implementing technology for one or more subjects in that grade level would reduce costs, or funds should go first to the lowest socioeconomic status schools in the selected grade. This will bring these schools up to par, in terms of technology, with better endowed schools. There is evidence that educationally disadvantaged students will demonstrate the greatest gains from their technology-rich education.

We have drawn some broad conclusions about how to allocate scarce resources for technology in the schools, but every state must consider its unique circumstances before selecting a particular path. Each state must make short-run choices to maximize the likelihood that adequate funds will be available over time in order to ensure full implementation of technology and the benefits that will result.

A logical approach to implementing technology on a statewide basis is to begin with the infrastructure, then teacher training (or simultaneously with the wiring), and finally hardware and software purchases.

Implementation Issues

Once funds have been allocated, there is the issue of what should be done first. Should every classroom be given a computer first? Should each school set up a computer lab? Or should teachers be sent for training before any equipment is purchased? We have learned two lessons in our research of schools that have had success with technology. First, putting a computer in a classroom does not drive change, nor does it increase student learning in and of itself. The way the computer and other technologies are used in the classroom *by the teacher* determine how much pedagogical value they will have. Second, one of the greatest benefits of modern computer technology is the ability it provides to access current information such as the Pathfinder mission's Mars images, and communication with individuals around the world. These benefits are available only if the computers are wired for Internet access.

Given these lessons, a logical approach to implementing technology on a statewide basis is to begin with the infrastructure, then teacher training (or simultaneously with the wiring), and finally hardware and software purchases. The computers are not being used to their full potential without wiring to connect them to wide area networks. Without trained teachers, the technology is being wasted. Wiring is not something that is going to become obsolete as rapidly as the hardware and software. If you purchase a computer first, by the time you have the wiring in place, the computer might be very outdated.

Next, trained teachers are absolutely essential for the proper use of technology. Teachers can begin to learn technology in classes or if they are provided with a computer that they can take home. Professor Paul Resta of the University of Texas at Austin's College of Education commented that providing teachers with their own computers is costly but effective. "If you can first make the technology accessible to the teachers, then they're more receptive and enthusiastic and more likely to incorporate it into the curriculum," he says.[279] By the time teachers have access to computers in their own classrooms, they will be comfortable with them, and ready to begin integrating the computers into their curriculum. Teacher training, like wiring, is not something that is likely to become outdated as fast as hardware and software. The computer skills that teachers receive will only build upon their foundation of knowledge in this area. Teachers really need to be allowed time to become familiar with the technology. We don't want to be spending huge sums of money on equipment that teachers find unfamiliar, or are resistant to using.

Our recommendation is to build on the infrastructure—wiring and teacher training—before making mass purchases of equipment. Teachers should have computers before the students do, so they can play with them and learn. Additionally, incremental purchases in the beginning will allow teachers and administrators to experiment with different products before making schoolwide commitments. This will help them determine what purchases will best meet their needs.

conclusion

"The future ain't what it used to be."

— YOGI BERRA

No previous technological innovation has had a significant impact on the public schools, whether that innovation was radio, film, or television. This does not surprise us, because these technologies were theoretically or pedagogically unsound and usually were implemented improperly. Schools operate today in pretty much the same way as they have for a century, and prior technology has not changed them. The model is that a teacher lectures a class of between 20 and 40 students using a blackboard and a textbook; every attempt to alter this general model has failed.

So why then are we bullish on school technology generally, and a $50 billion initiative in particular? Our enthusiasm is not based upon the "glitz" of some of the pilot programs now in place, although the glitz factor is what has convinced many supporters of educational technology. Even though a classroom with Internet access can dial up paintings from the Louvre and see them in full color with commentary, one might be skeptical about whether or not such an activity will improve student learning in the long run, particularly without a teacher who will adapt the curriculum to take full advantage of this opportunity. Some may assume such improvement on faith, but we maintain that a classroom full of computers is useful only to the extent that the technology is used appropriately. There is no more reason to believe that technology inputs alone will improve student outcomes than there is to believe that a teacher with a legislatively mandated degree or with 60 ad hoc credit hours beyond the masters will do more for students than a more highly motivated teacher with minimum credentials. The resources available must be utilized properly.

Technology can affect and enhance many of the instructional innovations—such as cooperative learning, self-paced learning, and individualized instruction—that have been shown to improve student achievement. Technology in the classroom is likely to motivate students further who are so enamored of similar technology in their nonschool lives. Technology has the *potential* to force changes in the organization of schools, for example to break down the system of talking heads in 50-minute segments, which we believe will improve teaching. Access to experts and materials not available in traditional classrooms or school libraries could stimulate student interests in subjects now considered dry and boring. Students could pursue in depth their own interests in ways not feasible when all students must depend upon a teacher and a textbook as the sole sources of information. By challenging the traditional structure of education and by promoting a system in which the teacher will be judged on the basis of a specific skill set, technology may even lay some of the foundation for further reforms. There are, of course, myriad decisions that must be made in order to *do* technology properly. To do this, it is important that we all gain a basic grasp of the issues surrounding education technology. We should understand what the critics are saying and be prepared to dismantle their arguments. If we are going to overcome the politics of education, it is essential that we know how to make believers out of technology skeptics.

There is the potential for students themselves to become more sophisticated consumers of education, even without the intervention of their parents. Who better to explain why technology is critical to the future of education? Today's youngsters are thought to be among the most adroit users of computers and other technology, certainly more so than most parents. The typical student is more comfortable with and less intimidated by technology than are many teachers. Indeed, some think teachers will resist technology because it puts them in a position of having less expertise than their students. But much of the technology experience held by youngsters is with gimmicky and often mind-numbing games. The question is whether this experience can be translated into utilizing technology in new and creative ways to solve problems. If so, technology's effects on students will be enhanced.

Education technology *can* have an impact on the way that our children learn, and it *can* improve their motivation, critical thinking, and their grasp of basic skills. Combined with serious reform efforts, this powerful new medium will put learning into the hands of the students, so that their curiosity does not hit a brick wall when there is no adult around to answer questions. The question is how we are going to get it into our schools. The process of changing or creating policy always involves interest groups—their incentives and their politics. A policy to obtain technology for schools is no exception. Through our discussion, six identifiable interest groups have emerged. They are: the general public, the education establishment, college and university teacher education programs, the technology industry, business in general, and government. Each has an interest in obtaining technology for our schools; however, within and between groups there are differing opinions as to the best way of accomplishing this goal, and tendencies to pass the buck and not take a leadership role. Every one of these groups should be taking a leadership role. These roles vary based on the individual group's goals, but each has significant power within its control to make education technology a reality for our public schools.

There is a chain of interrelated incentives and self-interest that if properly organized by each interest group will have the combined effect of bringing technology and real change to our schools. This chain reaction begins with the general public. In 1997, when asked to rate the quality of the education students receive in the public schools today, 60 percent of respondents from the general public rated school quality between "poor" and "just fair."[280] Clearly the public feels that schools need significant improvement. Rather than bemoaning the state of our schools, though, the public needs to be more active in its involvement. Parents should be critical of how their children are being taught, and investigate whether or not they are learning to their full potential. If this isn't happening, parents need to talk to the teachers regularly and they need to be willing to go to the principal and voice their discontent with teachers who are not performing. Most important, parents need to be persistent and not let up until they see changes being made. Four in five Americans say "knowing how to use computers and up-to-date technology will be very important for young people to get ahead in life."[281] Given that parents see the value of technology in their children's lives, it is their responsibility to push to make it available at their children's schools. As daunting as this may seem, history shows that it is possible for parents to organize a powerful lobby to advocate for children. Special education as we know it today is due in great part to the concerted efforts of parents in the 1950s (see the Special Education case study). The great success of a small group of parents in obtaining funding and other support for children with mental and physical handicaps reinforces our opinion that a small group—provided it is committed and vocal—can move the education establishment. Indeed, a parents' technology lobby could go on to effect changes in other facets of education.

The great success of a small group of parents in obtaining funding and other support for children with mental and physical handicaps reinforces our opinion that a small group—provided it is committed and vocal—can move the education establishment.

If parents create a drive to have technology in their children's schools, one institutional change that might be moved forward more quickly is the opportunity for parents to choose the appropriate schools for their children, that is, to exercise some type of school choice. One of the arguments against even public school choice holds that parents are not capable of distinguishing among schools to determine the best ones for their children. Whether that point is correct or not, as schools implement technology, the ability to distinguish among schools should improve. To the extent that technology facilitates communication between the school and the home, parents will have more information. This is particularly true if schools provide relevant and useful information to parents through the network. At a minimum, the different uses of technology in different schools may be more observable than, say, the performance of individual teachers in the current environment. Mere availability of technology does not assure higher quality education; however, if technology is used appropriately, that fact might be one criterion parents use to select schools for their children.

By providing easily observable distinctions among schools for parents and by enabling judgments by the students themselves, technology may provide a means for parents to make informed choices of appropriate schools. This could provide the impetus for the implementation of choice plans around the country. By facilitating both choice and merit pay, technology could aid significantly in changes in the incentive systems in public schools while improving teaching and learning in their own right.

The public can also play a role in eliminating three major barriers. The public must have a realistic perspective of what technology can do for student learning and how long it will take to see significant improvements and, most important, understand that we are broadening our definition of student learning and achievement. Technology will not spur dramatic changes in schools that are fundamentally dysfunctional. The school's administration and teachers must have sound educational goals determined before they can use technology effectively. Once teachers know what their learning goals are, they can begin to figure out how technology can facilitate those goals. It is also unlikely that technology will produce dramatic achievement improvements in the first year or two after implementation. How can it? The teachers need to have time to learn and experiment before major benefits will be passed on to the students. Many schools have seen immediate improvements in student motivation, attitudes toward learning, better attendance, and better behavior. Unfortunately, these are not measures that the public or their government representatives use to determine the success of a program. To cut off funding for a program because it has not produced dramatic gains in student achievement in the first year is a waste of everyone's investment. From the outset, the public should be willing to invest in a longer-term plan, and rely on various means of assessment along the way, such as attendance, motivation, and dropout rates.

Along with this change in perspective, the first thing that parents must do is to organize themselves, and in a clear united voice make it known to their local school teachers and administration that technology is a priority for them. If parents do not make it a priority, there is no real incentive for the school administration to make it a priority. This leads us to the second interest group, the education establishment.

The education establishment wields tremendous power over government. The combined lobbying expenditure of the National Education Association (NEA) and the American Federation of Teachers (AFT) is over $1 billion dollars annually. That level of funding gives the teachers unions a significant voice. What they lack, however, is the public's faith. It is this lack of faith that stands in the way of one of the union's biggest goals—more funding for education. The public no longer believes that spending more on education matters—at least at a state or national level. On the other hand, at some level it is clear that many parents believe that more money does matter. If they didn't, we would not see affluent schools raising significant funds from parents. At a nonlocal level, though, the public has lost faith that this money will ever make it into the classroom. As a result, it is difficult to get public support for increased spending on education. Perhaps if the public felt that the education establishment was more responsive to its needs, it would support higher levels of funding for education. We believe it is the role of the education establishment to take a lead, individually and collectively, in using technology and demonstrating its value to the public. The unions should be willing to encourage the use of technology by rewarding those teachers who have made the effort to learn how to use it.

Along with demonstrating the use of technology, teachers can play an important role in educating the general public about the value of technology, and broadening its perspective of educational achievement. Artistic ability and cooperative and creative problem solving are often difficult-to-measure indicators of student achievement. Standardized tests cannot be our only indicator. Many teachers are concerned about using technology in their classrooms because much of that learning is not reflected in standardized achievement tests. Again, individual teachers as well as the teachers' unions must find ways to educate the public about the various types of learning and achievement that exist.

It is possible that saturation of technology in the public schools will have a significant impact on promoting more global changes in schools that many, particularly economists, believe are the *sine qua non* of real school improvement. An example is technology's potential role in introducing merit pay.

There is a strong sense that teaching, and hence learning, would be improved if teachers had an incentive to do a better job. As things now stand, why should a teacher revise curricula, alter teaching methods, or work harder in other ways if there is no reward for doing so? Yet if such changes resulted in students' learning more, shouldn't the teachers who achieve this growth be rewarded for doing so? We acknowledge there is a host of arguments against such a system; key among them being the question how to measure "merit." Although there are reasonable responses to each objection, technology could play an important role in addressing the problem of measuring merit.

With technology available to all teachers, one of three things may happen. Some teachers might be so threatened, they would leave teaching. That might not be a bad result. Others might be encouraged to join or remain in the profession because of the increased professionalism, challenge, and collegiality of teaching that will come from the use of technology. Of those who stay, some might embrace technology and others might ignore it. Were this to occur, it could be argued that teachers who seriously utilize technology—that is, modify curricula, change teaching style, take in-service training, reorganize their classrooms, and so forth—would be given some sort of salary supplement. We are *not* saying that teachers who are not comfortable with technology are necessarily bad (or worse) teachers compared to those who do use it. Rather, we are assuming that appropriate use of technology is a desirable trait that should be rewarded. Those who eschew technology would have to demonstrate their effectiveness in order to receive a similar salary increase. Thus we have an *objective* measure of merit as we define it, and the burden of proof is shifted to nontechnology-using teachers to prove they deserve similar increases. As nontech teachers endeavor to demonstrate their effectiveness without technology, inevitably they will begin to look at student outcomes. As a result, a more comprehensive system of identifying merit could evolve. Further, as departed teachers are replaced, pro-technology teachers could be recruited in their place. As salaries of new teachers will be lower than the salaries of those who leave, resources might be found *in the current salary pool* to supplement the salaries of those using technology. Having said this, we should reiterate that careful measures must be developed to evaluate the technology-using teacher. Simply sitting children down in front of a "drill and kill" program is not necessarily a pedagogical improvement.

Most schools of education are lacking the up-to-date equipment and the funding to train their faculty to use modern technology and modify their classroom lessons to incorporate technology.

Besides the possible facilitation of pay for productivity, or at least rewards for utilizing new technology in classrooms, there are other ways that technology could improve the quality of the teaching force. Technology requires a new, publicly recognizable skill from teachers. Those who have it will bring a more positive image to the profession. Opportunities for alternative careers as a result of their new, marketable skill will grow, and so teachers will have expanded career opportunities if they later decide they want to leave education. The use of computers will make teachers more productive, particularly in terms of classroom management (recording grades and attendance, for example) and greater productivity is a reason for higher salaries. In addition, teachers who use technology will be less isolated than has been the case traditionally. These factors are likely to attract a larger and more able pool of applicants for teaching jobs. If so, schools could become more selective in their hiring, and then offer salaries based on characteristics of teachers that have been shown to be associated with greater student achievement (e.g., teacher scores on standardized tests rather than years of experience or degree credits). If the teaching profession attracts higher-quality people, these new entrants are likely to be more receptive to a pay structure that rewards their success.

The education establishment can also drive change by having superintendents and principals make it a policy to hire new teachers that are able to use technology in their teaching. Until they start demanding technologically proficient teachers, schools of education have no major incentive to integrate technology into their teacher-training programs.

Teacher-education programs have no major incentives to make their faculty learn how to use technology in their own teaching. Without the faculty's demonstrating the use of technology in their own courses, it is unlikely that their students will learn how to use it before they are on their own in a classroom. Teacher-education programs also lack many of the necessary resources to equip their schools with modern equipment that faculty and students can work on. What can some of the other groups do to alter this situation? First, as we've already mentioned, our public school administrators need to be more selective when hiring new teachers. If the public schools demand technologically proficient teachers, teacher-education programs will have to respond to this market by changing their programs to remain competitive with other teacher-education schools. Students who want to ensure that they can get a teaching job when they complete their schooling will begin to seek out those schools that have integrated technology into their programs and have successfully trained new teachers to use technology in their own classrooms. This will take new resources. Most schools of education are lacking the up-to-date equipment and the funding to train their faculty to use modern technology and modify their classroom lessons to incorporate technology. Industry and the state and federal governments, as well as the teachers' unions, could take a greater role here in ensuring that teacher education programs are given the resources they need to update their programs.

The technology industry's main concern is profits. There appears to be some interest in education as consumers of technology, but no major efforts have been made to win over this market. Perhaps there has been a conscious decision on the part of most technology companies to avoid the education market because it is too bureaucratic. In any case, there is a great opportunity for the technology industry to make users and believers out of our nation's future teachers. These companies should be putting as much energy into teacher-education programs as they do in K-12, and both could use greater commitment. As we have already mentioned, teacher-education programs have been neglected by the technology industry partly because they lack the same public relations value as K-12 schools. Most of these businesses do not seem to realize that there is an incredible opportunity to influence how all future teachers are going to think about technology and the extent to which technology will be used in their personal and professional lives. With a majority of our teachers retiring in the next decade, teacher-education programs are now training the teachers that will be in our schools for the next 40 years. This is a chance to make sure that teachers of the next generation will not just be used to technology, but that they will believe it is an integral part of education. A little foresight and daring could go a long way.

Traditionally the technology industry has taken the stance that it is their role to donate some equipment and software, and perhaps wiring.

Traditionally the technology industry has taken the stance that it is their role to donate some equipment and software, and perhaps wiring. However, there is a big hump to get over to make technology an integral part of education. More innovation and training are absolutely critical. As we saw in the example of IBM's contributions to pre-service education programs, the equipment was a generous gesture, but educators need a significant amount of training and on-hand support if they are going to be truly comfortable using computers. And this is only the first step. Major innovations in the *use* of technology in education still need to be made. Rather than saying "We'll provide you with the equipment, but you need to figure out what to do with it," businesses should invest in understanding and developing educational uses for technology. The widespread use of technology in our schools may very well not happen unless some pretty bold steps are taken.

If this is a market that business really wants, they need to be bolder, perhaps contribute more for training, hire teachers to work with them. At the 1997 Milken National Education Conference (MEA), Bert Roberts, chairman of MCI, remarked, "Have we worked with the educators to find out what they need? Maybe this huge teacher market that is supposedly out there, but not buying, is not buying for a reason. Nobody's asked them what they want."[282] To go after this market more aggressively, corporations should not only offer to donate equipment and services, they should also aggressively seek out schools to take them up on their offers. These schools mean future customers.

At the 1997 MEA Conference, representatives from the technology industry had the opportunity to interact with educators and state superintendents of education. A senior representative of Intel Corp. announced his shock and disappointment that in the four months since Intel had offered schools 100,000 free Pentium motherboards only 10,000 had been claimed. To make it worse, those 10,000 were claimed by schools in the Silicon Valley where Intel is based. When the attendees were asked if they had heard of this offer, few hands were raised. This was a generous offer indeed, but it highlights the fact that schools need more than pieces of high-tech hardware. They need expertise, vision, and know-how. They also need education, so they'll know that "motherboard" is not a swear word!

At the 1997 MEA Conference, representatives from the technology industry had the opportunity to interact with educators and state superintendents of education. A senior representative of Intel Corp. announced his shock and disappointment that in the four months since Intel had offered schools 100,000 free Pentium motherboards only 10,000 had been claimed.

We've established that most of the funding for a nationwide technology initiative will need to come from public coffers. What should *not* be handed down from government officials is the plan. Indeed, technology companies would be wise to offer themselves in the role of visionaries, advisors, and trainers. This would win the support of overwhelmed and beleaguered teachers, it would allow industry an opportunity to shape its future role in education, and it would lessen the likelihood that federal and state authorities will attempt to centrally direct the nature and use of technology in education.

Business in general needs skilled workers. They must be willing to support public funding—even a tax. From our experiences with the California Business Roundtable, business has shown a lot of concern, and has done a lot of talking, but they still have not put their money where their mouth is. This needs to change.

Government's role should be to provide funding but to resist the urge to hand down sweeping edicts. It must use its bully pulpit to spur industry on, scold the teachers' unions when they drag their collective feet, and to fire the public imagination. Indeed, the federal government is critically important as a leader. Technology holds out the promise of giving us a leg up on the rest of the world, as it did when it landed a man on the moon. The premiere high-tech nation should lead the world in high-tech education, and ensure itself continued hegemony as the world's computing superpower. In brief, government should promote a brave vision, and our leaders must have the courage to challenge the populace with a grand goal. They must also have the character to stay above the fray rather than getting mired down in an attempt to direct the details. In the United States we can have a shared goal, but there is no one-size-fits-all plan; we are far too diverse a country in terms of politics, wealth, beliefs, and priorities. States and local communities will have to determine their needs, and find an appropriate funding option. There is no doubt that educational technology will be a profitable investment and a great national achievement.

The integration of technology into education will suffer some fits and starts, but we must remember that this is the nature of innovation and discovery. It will take years to reinvent education, and it is critical that we not allow slow starts, wrong turns, or temporary inequities to shake our resolve. Says Microsoft CEO Bill Gates, "When books first came out, not everybody was literate, so books at first did create a gap between the literate and the illiterate. Were books a bad thing? Should we have blocked their use? Probably not... . But over a long period of time, the notion of universal literacy and access to libraries, funded by local government and philanthropy, got pretty well established. Today, the kids who are willing to go down to the library can get plenty of books. The same thing is happening now with computers."[283] Suffice it to say that unless parents, educators, college faculties, businesses, and government show courage, foresight, and commitment, a comprehensive technology program will never become a reality. Country, corporations, families, educators, it's up to you.

Top 10 Reasons *Not* to Put Technology into the Schools, but...
There are myriad decisions that must be made in order to *do* technology properly. At every stage, political considerations play a role. If we are going to overcome the politics, it is essential that we make believers out of the skeptics. What are some of their criticisms? Here's a list that we call the Top Ten Reasons *Not* to Put Technology into the Schools, but...

10. **I learned fine without technology when I was in school, but...**
    - Back then, teachers' only responsibility was to teach, rather than to serve the function of social workers.
    - In today's information-rich society, no one person can provide information on the full range of topics that might interest a student. The Internet will provide students with other resources and experts so that the teacher is not the sole source of information in the classroom.
    - People lived fine before the lightbulb, automobile, airplane, and stereo, but no one argues that we should have eschewed the introduction of these technologies.

9. **Forget technology; focus on basic skills, but...**
    - Technology helps improve students' basic skills through self-directed drill and practice, by facilitating writing and rewriting, and by making all learning more interesting and challenging.

8. **Instead of spending money on technology we should raise teacher salaries, reduce class sizes, or impose standards, but...**
    - Institutional barriers (union pay scales, tenure, entrenched bureaucrats) and public skepticism of most new initiatives make the availability of money for solving these problems difficult, if not impossible. Money for technology may be a different story because technology has been seen as valuable in other settings.

7. **It will fail, just as instructional television did, but...**
    - Instructional television was a passive form of instruction; computers are interactive. Before VCRs, programs were limited in diversity and constrained by the time they were to be aired. Networked computers will provide students with unlimited sources of information, and they will be able to use them whenever they have access to the computer.
    - We must learn from the instructional television experience. Make sure teachers are part of the process of implementing technology. Don't *impose* modern technology from above; train teachers to use it, and provide technical support.

6. **There is no evidence that technology works either, but...**
    - The lack of broad-based evidence is due to the fact that properly implemented technology has never been tried on a large scale.
    - Where it has been implemented properly (e.g., Union City, New Jersey), there is evidence of improved student outcomes.
    - There *is* theoretical evidence that it works: Technology has been shown to enable constructivist learning—the idea that we learn through the interaction with content, rather than by memorization, which is known to improve student learning.

5. **When teachers want technology, it will come on its own, but...**
    - There are many things teachers want that they do not get, particularly because often the public believes, rightly or wrongly, that teachers want what is best for them, rather than

what is best for their students.

4. **Teachers' unions will never allow the massive infusion of technology, but...**
   - Unions *are* willing to accept technology *if* it is accompanied by training and *if* technology does not displace teachers, which it will not do.
   - Statements by union leaders indicate their belief that technology, used properly, can be an important educational tool, but that educators must guide its uses rather than being slaves to it.

3. **Wait a year for more powerful machines. This year's technology will be outmoded by the time it arrives in the classroom, but...**
   - This argument could be made against ever purchasing any high-tech product, including the automobile.
   - Just because marginally better products come on the market next year does not mean this year's stuff is no longer useful. Computers with currently available power and with networking and multimedia capabilities will still be useful in the schools five years hence.

2. **We will never get the required funding, but...**
   - This is simply a matter of public will. If policy makers were convinced that their constituencies wanted school technology, and that they were willing to pay for it, they would find ways to raise the money.
   - If the public were convinced that technology would improve the schools significantly, and that new taxes would go for the intended purposes, they would support public funding. For example, money has been found for public roads, for prisons, and for police, not to mention football stadiums.

1. **We could do better things with the money, but...**
   - We must ask the counterfactual question: Without technology, what new money will be made available to the schools? Not very much, particularly given the huge amounts of money that have been thrown at the schools in recent decades without much evidence of increased student learning.

WHEN VOICES FOR EDUCATION WERE HEARD: SPECIAL EDUCATION

Compared to the influence of the highway lobby, a powerful advocacy effort for technology in the schools appears to be in the formative stage. Is there something about education per se that may inhibit a strong, successful lobbying effort, or is it the particular issue of educational technology and the particular time and environment we are in that seem to make the present cause a difficult one? A look at the history of efforts to obtain funding and other support for special education—for educating the physically handicapped and those with learning disabilities—may help answer this question.

A Brief History of Special Education

In the United States, prior to the 1850s, there were few, if any, services available to mentally retarded children and their families. While there were some public institutions for deaf, mute, and blind individuals, no similar services existed for the mentally retarded. It was not until the independent successes of H. B. Wilbur and Samuel Howe in demonstrating the ability of these individuals to benefit from instruction that the United States opened its first public facility for the training of mentally retarded individuals. With the opening of that first institution in 1850, an era of institutionalization began. For the following 50 years, the number of institutions and the number of individuals they served expanded with the support of the public. Though originally intended to provide educa-

tion and training that would allow mentally retarded individuals to return to the outside community, after the initial years, children who entered institutions remained there. The result was more institutions, overcrowding, a shift from rehabilitation to custodial care, and a loss of public support.[284]

Special education classes around the turn of the century were not used as a method of reintegrating institutionalized individuals into society, but as a way of segregating difficult, low functioning, and immigrant children from the regular classrooms, and as a transition for mentally retarded children before being institutionalized.[285] The feeling at that time was that IQ scores for mentally retarded individuals were not improving regardless of the quality of the institutions that they were in. This in turn led to a belief that these individuals were incapable of adjusting to life outside of an institution. In the 1920s, a different type of study was conducted that changed the earlier views about mentally retarded persons. Grace Fernald, a leader in the field, conducted a study of the status of 646 mentally retarded children released from the Waverly Institution.[286] The results showed that over half of them "had made at least a fair adjustment to life outside the institution."[287]

The finding that mentally retarded individuals could benefit from instruction and that many could be reintegrated into the community created a change in the role of both institutions and special education classes. With long wait lists and overcrowding, the need for care and training outside of the institutions was clear. Public support for special education classes as a way of training mentally retarded individuals within the community grew. Between 1910 and 1930, enrollments in public schools and the number of different special education classes that were offered grew rapidly. Beginning in the 1940s some state legislatures began to appropriate funds for public school programs for the mentally retarded. Unfortunately, this funding and the need for more classes grew far more quickly than new special education teachers could be trained. The resulting teacher shortage meant that many poorer states were temporarily priced out of the market.[288]

Following World War II, the continuing overcrowding and poor conditions in institutions created an even greater demand for services within the community. Parents with mentally retarded children were told that the institutions had three-and four-year-long wait lists. Special education classes in schools were also limited. Children with IQs below 50 were not being accepted. Taxpaying parents were frustrated that they could not find care for their children in the institutions or in the schools. A growing feeling that institutions were inhumane and kept children isolated from their families was also emerging. These mounting pressures led more states to appropriate funds for special education programs in the public schools and led parents to band together.[289]

During the 1950s, parents of mentally retarded children became an important legislative force. Frustrated at the limited services for their children and the dismal quality of care that was available at the state institutions, parents joined together to found the National Association for Retarded Children. The association pushed for higher quality care within institutions and for more services for their children within the community. Position statements such as the 1953 "Educational Bill of Rights for the Retarded Child" proclaimed that each mentally retarded child was entitled to a "program of education and training suited to his particular needs." As a lobby for the rights of mentally retarded individuals, the association gained public support and received legal and financial assistance from state and federal sources. Parent groups also served to educate legislators about the needs of retarded individuals and the problems related to meeting those needs.[290]

With increasing enrollment and a greater variety of special education classes being offered, the demand for teachers trained in special education was high. Unfortunately, there were only a few colleges preparing teachers for this field. Part of this problem was the lack of funding for specialized teacher training. To remedy the situation, in 1955, Congress passed P.L. 83-531, which appropriated $1 million for educational research, of which $675,000 was earmarked for research in the education of the mentally retarded. This earmarking of funds had several critics, both in general education and in other fields of special education that subsequently received less funding. As a result, the categorical funding for mental retardation was removed two years later. The funding for research in mental retardation diminished each year after that until 1963, when it reached zero. In 1958 P.L. 85-926 was passed, appropriating $1 million to higher education institutions and state education agencies to encourage the preparation of personnel in the field of mental retardation. From 1958 to 1976, the number of institutions offering programs in special education grew from less than 40 to more than 400.[291]

The 1950s were also a time of growing recognition of the rights of disabled persons to a suitable education. The presence of many disabled World War I veterans who were visibly contributing to society led to a greater public understanding and acceptance that disabled individuals were capable of supporting themselves and contributing to their communities. Within the public school system, there was

also growing recognition that most mentally disabled students could be trained to support themselves upon leaving school. The use of special education classes for these individuals had also received wide public support. The same understanding of the rights of mentally disabled individuals in the community extended into the institutions and highlighted the need for standards. In 1959, a report on institutional standards was published by the American Association on Mental Deficiency (AAMD). This report did not seem to have much effect. As late as 1966, the per capita expenditure for mentally disabled persons in institutions was less than $5 a day.[292]

The rapid growth in the number of special education students continued into the next decades. A polio epidemic in the 1950s and a rubella epidemic in the 1960s added to this growing population. Additionally, advances in medicine meant that more disabled children were surviving. These changes between 1948 and 1968 resulted in growth of the special education population from 1.2 to 4.5 percent of the total K-12 enrollment. Public Law 85-926 was passed in 1959 to provide educational institutions and state educational agencies with funds to train personnel in the field of mental retardation to meet the needs of the rapidly growing special education population. The expansion of that population continued until 1972, when mental retardation was redefined from those with an

IQ below 85 (1 standard deviation below the mean) to those individuals with an IQ that was 2 standard deviations below the mean. This procedural stroke eliminated 80 percent of the mentally retarded population.[293]

The civil rights movement and the general egalitarian climate of the 1960s led several deprived and oppressed groups such as African-Americans, Chicanos, and the disabled to become more vocal about their rights. Parents of seemingly normal children who were not learning for various reasons and were unrecognized by existing labels began to organize under such names as the Society for Brain-Injured Children or the Society for the Perceptually Disabled. On a national level, these organizations grouped under the title of the Association for Children with Learning Disabilities.[294] "Learning disabilities became a general term for a heterogeneous group of disabilities of varying degrees of severity which are, however, similar in that they seem to stem from intrinsic cognitive or perceptual difficulties interfering with a child's learning."[295]

Photographs published in *Look* magazine showing the horrors and inhumane conditions of institutions rallied public support for change at institutional level. The Supreme Court decision in *Brown v. Board of Education* (1954) led educators, parents, and professionals to question the merits of segregated special education classes.[296] The 1960 election of John F. Kennedy, who had a retarded sister, also brought to special education an important advocate at the top of the federal government. With the public calling for change and an ally in the White House, it was an opportune moment in history to pass legislation to benefit exceptional individuals.

Soon after taking office, President Kennedy created the President's Panel on Mental Retardation. After months of research and deliberation, the final report of the panel identified three major needs in the area of mental retardation. These were "research, a system of service to provide a 'continuum of care,' and social action to prevent mental retardation."[297] The resulting legislation was the Mental Retardation Facilities and Community Health Centers Construction Act of 1963 (P.L. 88-164). This bill broadened earlier legislation to include research and training not only for mentally disabled children, but for those who were hard of hearing, deaf, speech-impaired, visually disabled, seriously emotionally disturbed, crippled, or had other health impairments. Congress provided an appropriation of $14 million, which was doubled the following year. Another significant aspect of the bill was that it provided for a Division of Disabled Children and Youth within the U.S. Office of Education. Due to a White House reorganization effort, the Division was abolished only eighteen months after its creation. Despite this reorganization, Congress continued to demonstrate its interest in supporting efforts to help the disabled. A series of bills were passed that provided funds for special education, extended the legislation for captioned films for the deaf to other media, provided more research funds for mental health, and created the Bureau of Education for the Disabled. Serving as a rallying point in government for those concerned with the education of the disabled, the bureau was also a source of financial risk capital to fund creative programming in the education of children with special needs.[298]

The availability of funds for special education in the 1960s allowed schools to raise the eligibility requirement for special education classes from an IQ of 70 to 78. In 1962, the American Association on Mental Deficiency formally defined mild mental retardation as an IQ of 84 or 85 and below. Both newly defined groups were readily accepted by the schools. Special education classes were advocated by the regular classroom teachers because it allowed them to remove students who were difficult for various reasons. Along with children with behavioral and learning problems, it was found that special education classes had a disproportionate number of minority children. Many of these children had low IQs as a result of language and cultural differences rather than learning disabilities.[299]

Parents of both the minority and nonminority children who were placed in special education classes began to challenge the schools in court. The Supreme Court decision in Brown vs. Board of Education (racially segregated classrooms could not be separate but equal) was in line with the thoughts of special educators and parents. Several lawsuits were brought against the states and school districts claiming that the rights of mentally disabled children were being violated. Most cases focused on five major points: "That tests were inappropriate, that parental involvement was lacking, that special education itself was inadequate, that placement was inadequate, and that placement stigmatized children."[300] All of these points emphasized the fact that children in special education classes were not receiving an adequate education. In *Wolf v. Legislature of the State of Utah* (1969), the first case to challenge the right of mentally retarded individuals to a free and appropriate education, the court ruled that "Segregation, even though perhaps well intentioned, under the apparent sanction of the law and state authority has a tendency to retard the educational and mental development of the children."[301, 302]

Although the Utah case was an important beginning, two landmark cases determined the course of special education. The first was a class action suit, the *Pennsylvania Association for Retarded Citizens* (PARC) *v.*

the *Commonwealth of Pennsylvania et al.* (1971). The decision in this case overruled a state law that enabled schools to deny admission to students who were considered "uneducable" or "untrainable." Based on extensive expert testimony, the court's finding was that mentally retarded individuals benefited from education, and as such were entitled to it. In addition to clarifying the rights of mentally retarded individuals to an appropriate education, the court also found that "placement in a regular public school class is preferable to placement in a special public school class, and placement in a special public school class is preferable to placement in any other type of program of education and training."[303] The second landmark case was *Mills v. the Board of Education* (1972). The ruling in this case expanded on the PARC decision to include all children who were thought to suffer from a mental, behavioral, emotional, or physical disability. The decisions in these two landmark cases accomplished two things. First, the right of all children, regardless of their disability, to receive a free and appropriate education was established. Second, the concept of mainstreaming and the "least restrictive environment" was given the endorsement of the judicial system.[304]

The concept of mainstreaming was derived from the principle of normalization, which essentially advocates that mentally retarded and other disabled individuals model the daily patterns and conditions of the normal mainstream society. Within the school system, this principle translates to the integration of disabled students, whenever possible, into regular classes, supplemented by special educational services tailored to the individual needs of each child.[305]

Reasons for Growth and Change

What precipitated the massive increase in special education in this country following World War II? Just as the presence of World War I veterans had helped to change the public's views about disabled individuals, the over 3 million exceptional individuals who participated in the war effort by performing necessary tasks had a positive effect on the public's perception. Additionally, the devastation of the war created a humanitarian desire in U.S. citizens to aid individuals with physical and mental disabilities. Several states led the way by passing laws that funded and helped to organize special education programs in the public school systems.[306]

Another driving force behind special education programs was the parent movement. The overcrowding in the institutions and the rejection by the public schools left many parents with no alternative services for their children with special needs. Frustrated that their taxes were funding these two public agencies, yet they were receiving few or no services, parents joined together to create a powerful lobby.[307]

The shift from segregated to integrated placement within mainstream classrooms was largely due to the growth of research that showed little difference in academic achievement between special education students in separate classes and similar students in regular classrooms. In addition, special needs students who were placed in regular classrooms had greater advancements in their social skills than peers in segregated classrooms. An influential article by L. M. Dunn[308] argued that segregated classrooms and the labels given to children within those classes stigmatized special needs students. Special education teachers, he argued, had proven to be ineffective and ill prepared to deal with these students. Additionally, concerns for minority children who were being inappropriately labeled and removed from regular classrooms led educators to the conclusion that homogenous diagnostic categories did not exist for all special needs children. An emphasis on individual needs was stressed instead. Fueled by this research, emerging legislation and litigation supported the movement toward integration.[309]

The federal government's involvement with the integration movement began in 1965 with the Elementary and Secondary Education Act. The bill and its amendments served to create the Bureau of Education for the Disabled, provide funding, and put into law due process protections for special needs children. The funding and other forms of support for the education of special needs children was continued on into the 1970s. Compliance with these new laws was minimal. Many schools continued to claim that many special needs students were uneducable, and that there was not enough funding to provide the additional services for them.

In response to the continued failure of many schools to provide an appropriate education for children with special needs, Public Law 94-142, the Education for All Disabled Children Act, was signed into law by President Gerald R. Ford in November 1975. The new law mandated that schools provide an appropriate education for children in the least restrictive environment. Children with mental disabilities could no longer be denied admission to public schools. Schools were also required to provide the necessary services to enable physically disabled students to attend school. Additionally, individualized educational plans and culturally fair testing were mandated. The permissive nature of previous laws was corrected, forcing each state into compliance.[310]

The new law represented the culmination of many years of activism on behalf of physically and intellectually disabled children. Impassioned parents and educators were able to achieve greatly increased enrollment among the special needs population and were able to integrate this group into the educational mainstream to a remarkable degree. By 1984 the fraction of special needs children receiving their education in separate schools had fallen below 7 percent. Further, the federal government estimated that in 1982 over 90 percent of the special needs children in the country were receiving an appropriate education, as compared to less than 25 percent in the early sixties. But even these figures understate the power of organized groups to refocus the attention of the educational system and to force it to serve special needs. Champions of the seriously disabled were so successful in their campaign that advocates of more mildly challenged children began to play off the earlier successes and were able to channel substantial resources to another group of inadequately served children with special needs.[311]

By the 1980s activists had profoundly changed the educational landscape. Integrated schools were handling students of wide ranging abilities, from the severely disabled to students with mild learning disorders. Not only were traditional schools made aware of the special needs of certain students, but they were compelled to cater to them. More generally the evolution of our approach to the education of the special needs population demonstrated the ability of vocal groups to bend the system to their will.

Funding for Special Education

The costs associated with the growth of special education have been large. Figures from the U.S. Department of Education indicate that in 1977, the year following passage of P.L. 94-142, total expenditures for special education were estimated to be $12.9 billion in current dollars or $33.5 billion in 1996 dollars. These rose to $76 billion in 1996.[312] (Table 10-1). Figures 10-1 and 10-2 show the continuous increase in total special education funding since the 1960s and the growth in federal funding, albeit with some ups and downs in the 1980s.

Education is primarily a responsibility of the states, and so it is not surprising that the bulk of the financing comes from state and local sources. Federal funds have risen from $419 million in 1977 to $3.5 billion for 1996 in current dollars. Between 1975 and 1980 the federal appropriation for special education rose from $151 million to $822 million. This demonstrates how federal funding grew after the enactment of P.L. 94-142. Federal money has provided between 3.24 percent of total expenditures (1977) and 4.85 percent (1980), with the federal share in 1996 estimated to be 4.62 percent (Table 10-1).

The special education lobby worked at both the federal and the state/local levels. Much of their effort resulted in very large nonfederal allocations. However, the importance of federal support lies not only in its funding but also in its mandating that certain activities are to be paid for by the states. Circumstances would likely be similar if funding for educational technology were to become a top priority. It is likely that federal funds would provide seed money and perhaps encourage states to match federal funds on a greater than one-to-one basis. The relative distribution of funding responsibilities among federal, state, and local governments in the case of special education emphasizes the need for all levels of government to be convinced of the efficacy of technology for the schools.

The Power of Parents

The past 50 years have seen monumental changes in the organization of and funding for special education. These resulted from the dissatisfaction of parents of handicapped children and the confluence of support from state officials, special education experts in higher education, K-12 educators and, finally, the federal government. As an aside, it is probably more than coincidental that President John F. Kennedy and later Vice President Hubert H. Humphrey had personal, family experience with a special education child. Special education prospered greatly during their administrations.

Although we have seen little agitation for school technology by parents, the case of special education was very different. Our brief

history of the evolution of special education underlines the leadership role played by parents. Parents of handicapped children often feel victimized, angry, and frustrated at not being able to help their offspring. They are often heavily dependent upon the schools to deal with their children. They demonstrate a passion for their cause that is rarely matched by other parents.

These attitudes were made clear during the attempt by UCLA and its chancellor, Charles E. Young, to close the Fernald School at the end of the 1986 school year. That school was a research and educational program that served 65 to 75 special education students and had been operating for 65 years. University officials decided that too little academic research was being conducted at Fernald and it was not contributing to the university's teaching program. Closure was said to allow funds formerly allocated to Fernald to be used for an expanded research program on childhood disabilities in the UCLA psychology department.

After the announcement of the school's closing, "all hell broke loose." A group called Friends of Fernald was formed to ask that the school remain open. A state Department of Education consultant on special education said that the closure would be "a tremendous loss." Fernald officials defended their school and research program. Parents argued that comparable programs were not available elsewhere. The school was called an irreplaceable resource. Letters were sent to university and elected officials—students even wrote to Nancy Reagan.

Friends of Fernald then held a "Save Fernald" rally, with everyone wearing buttons proclaiming their goal. They went to the University of California Regents requesting that Chancellor Young be overruled, but were rebuffed. The state legislature passed a resolution asking the chancellor and regents to reconsider their decision. The parent group went to the regents again, this time accompanied by the president of the California Association for Neurologically Handicapped Children. The regents again upheld Chancellor Young, but the university president suggested looking for another site for the school.

Then the California Association of the Physically Handicapped demonstrated at UCLA to protest members' "extreme dissatisfaction" with university enrollment and hiring practices. The protest was cosponsored by the Los Angeles City Council on Disabilities. The groups alleged that UCLA had violated a 1979 federal requirement by failing to appoint a "compliance officer" to oversee programs for the handicapped, and the group filed a federal civil rights complaint with the U.S. Department of Education. These groups got state legislators and the American Civil Liberties Union involved.

A couple of months later, seven parents of Fernald students filed a lawsuit charging Chancellor Young and the regents with discrimination against disabled children in closing the school. They claimed the closure violated the constitutional and civil rights of all the students. The suit asked for unspecified damages and an injunction forcing the chancellor to reopen the school. Parents argued that children were traumatized and that they could not find alternative schools. The judge ordered Fernald parents to post a $650,000 bond and the university to hold hearings.

The parents then attempted to eliminate the cost-saving argument by convincing actors Paul Newman and Joanne Woodward to pay the school's operating expenses for a year, estimated to be $100,000. The chancellor refused the offer.

The judge in the lawsuit signed an injunction ordering the university to open the school for fall classes, but a week later the university appealed that decision. Finally, the university agreed to keep the school open for one more year. Parents then appealed to the Los Angeles School Board to find a way to keep the school going. The Fernald School finally

case study

closed at the end of the 1986-87 academic year, one year after it was originally scheduled to close. In July of 1989, a parent of a former Fernald student was still writing letters to the *Los Angeles Times* bemoaning the school's fate.

of "true believers," the engineers, provided the impetus for road and highway building. Then the users of roads and highways, automobile and truck drivers came on board. In the case of special education, parents who would use the services for their children were

In the case of special education, parents who would use the services for their children were the prime movers. They were supported by a number of groups of "true believers" who would benefit from having better-quality special education only by having jobs in that field.

This describes only one case, but it illustrates the resources that can be brought to bear on behalf of special education students when a passionate issue arises. A small group of parents managed to involve the state legislature, the judicial system, the University of California Board of Regents, the ACLU, groups of advocates for the handicapped, the local school board (although the school was not part of the board's district), and even two Hollywood stars in a cause for only 70 children. Parents of handicapped children clearly are a potent advocacy group.

Lessons for Educational Technology
In a previous chapter, we noted that a group

the prime movers. They were supported by a number of groups of "true believers" who would benefit from having better-quality special education only by having jobs in that field. These groups included researchers in higher education, as well as those administering special education programs (research, teacher preparation, and the schooling itself) in state and federal government agencies. In special education there does not seem to be a group analogous to the profit-making companies who could sell products and services to this sector.

Perhaps most striking is the fact that K-12 educators jumped on the special education bandwagon enthusiastically. They saw special education as a source of new funding (which perhaps could be commingled with other funds for the enrichment of all schooling). They saw increased demand for teachers and other educational staff as classes were smaller for special education students and special laboratories were added. They saw special education classes as opportunities to meet students' needs in ways that were not possible in regular classrooms, and perhaps to get their most troublesome pupils out of their classrooms, either permanently or for part of the day. Perhaps most important, teachers realized that advances in special education enabled them and their colleagues to serve better a group of clearly disadvantaged and deserving students. Special education's growth was seen as an opportunity.

A successful lobby on behalf of an educational issue can be mounted. To do so on behalf of getting technology into our schools poses some challenges. First, how can we get a critical mass of parents to take up the cause with the fervor possessed by parents of special education children? But perhaps of greater importance to the success of getting technology in America's classrooms is the development of a teacher-led lobby.

Table 10-1 Expenditures for Special Education

YEAR	ESTIMATED TOTAL SPECIAL EDUCATION EXPENDITURES IN CURRENT $	FEDERAL ON-BUDGET FUNDS FOR SPECIAL EDUCATION IN CURRENT $	ESTIMATED TOTAL SPECIAL EDUCATION EXPENDITURES IN 596	FEDERAL ON-BUDGET FUNDS FOR SPECIAL EDUCATION IN 96$	TOTAL LESS FEDERAL IN 96$	FEDERAL % OF TOTAL USING 96$
1966	1,148,014	26,897*	5,559,391	130,252	5,429,139	2.34
1967	1,425,266	39,945	6,695,336	187,648	6,507,688	2.80
1968	1,736,957	52,993	7,831,281	238,928	7,592,353	3.05
1969	2,097,496	66,042	8,967,226	282,342	8,684,884	3.15
1970	2,498,426	79,090	10,103,171	319,825	9,783,345	3.17
1971	2,901,110	93,521	11,239,116	362,307	10,876,809	3.22
1972	3,982,031	107,952	14,946,905	405,206	14,541,699	2.71
1973	5,278,957	122,382	18,654,694	432,473	18,222,221	2.32
1974	7,026,580	136,813	22,362,483	435,416	21,927,067	1.95
1975	8,939,328	151,244	26,070,272	441,081	25,629,190	1.69
1976	10,799,055	285,351	29,778,061	786,846	28,991,215	2.64
1977	12,933,349	419,457	33,485,850	1,086,020	32,399,829	3.24
1978	14,723,854	553,564	35,432,096	1,332,119	34,099,977	3.76
1979	17,199,180	687,670	37,170,129	1,486,164	35,683,965	4.00
1980	19,968,818	821,777	38,023,150	1,564,767	36,458,382	4.12
1981	22,552,457	1,035,353	38,927,179	1,787,094	37,140,084	4.59
1982	24,442,127	1,141,444	39,740,619	1,855,881	37,884,737	4.67
1983	26,573,674	1,289,710	41,861,541	2,031,682	39,829,859	4.85
1984	29,006,905	952,778	43,803,497	1,438,796	42,364,701	3.28
1985	31,811,685	1,017,964	46,387,113	1,484,373	44,902,740	3.20
1986	34,026,867	1,627,894	48,711,819	2,330,443	46,381,376	4.78
1987	36,990,770	1,339,241	51,090,245	1,849,709	49,240,536	3.62
1988	40,104,404	1,465,985	53,190,033	1,944,320	51,245,713	3.66
1989	45,033,386	1,880,751	56,981,760	2,379,757	54,602,003	4.18
1990	49,802,083	1,616,623	59,785,362	1,940,690	57,844,672	3.25
1991	53,392,261	2,174,358	61,506,944	2,504,822	59,002,122	4.07
1992	56,755,709	2,243,338	63,470,925	2,508,765	60,962,160	3.95
1993	60,307,559	2,564,070	65,482,740	2,784,101	62,698,639	4.25
1994	64,570,405	2,980,328	68,360,976	3,155,287	65,205,689	4.62
1995	68,538,044	3,177,000	70,561,805	3,270,809	67,290,996	4.64
1996	75,983,973	3,511,000	75,983,973	3,511,000	72,472,973	4.62

Figure 10-1 Spending on Special Education

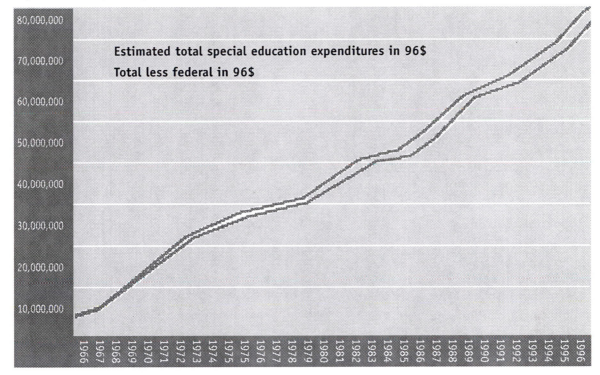

Estimated total special education expenditures in 96$
Total less federal in 96$

Figure 10-2 Federal on-budget funds for special education

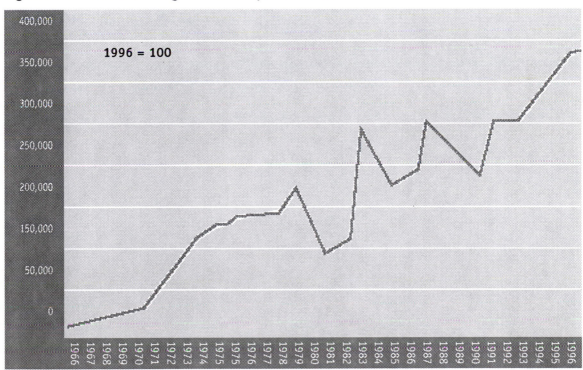

1996 = 100

The Model to Estimate Gains in Labor Market Productivity

CALCULATING THE VALUE OF A 5 PERCENT INCREASE IN
WORKER PRODUCTIVITY DUE TO EDUCATION TECHNOLOGY

We estimate the distribution of educational attainment (eight years of education, some high school, a high school degree, some college, an associate degree, or at least a college degree) for each member of single-year age groups when they reach each year between 16 and 30 using the data on educational attainment of all individuals who are currently between 16 and 30 (Table A-1). We assume 0-year-olds will have the same educational distribution when they are 16 as current 16-year-olds, and the same educational level at 17 as current 17-year-olds. Similarly, we assume the attainment of 1-year-olds at 16 equals the attainment of those currently 16 years old, and so forth.

As Table A-1 indicates, educational attainment generally increases with age and stabilizes in the late twenties, implying that a substantial number of individuals increase their education until their mid-twenties and then move permanently into the labor force full-time by age 30. Before age 30, some people will have finished school and entered the labor force on a full-time basis, but others will still be in school and be working either part-time or not at all.

We then assume that after age 30, there is no further increase in educational attainment. When each age group now between 0 and 14 reaches 30 and over, it is assigned the average educational distribution of those currently 30-45, and this does not change (Table A-2). We've selected the 30- to 45-year-old group because to go any farther back (i.e., to look at educational attainment of people older than 45) would be unrealistic, given the growth in educational attainment over time. Because we assume that in the future, people 30 years of age or older will have the same educational distribution as current 30- to 45-year-olds, we apply the average education attainment level of current 30- to 45-year-olds to each age cohort between 0 and 14 to allocate those of a particular age across educational attainment levels once they reach age 30. Although the proportion of, say, those currently three years of age who ultimately complete college may be higher or lower than the proportion of, say, current 12-year-olds who do so, we assume that on average the proportion of all age cohorts currently 0 to 14 that complete college by age 30 will be the same as the average of those who are currently 30 to 45.

Historically, there has been an upward trend in educational attainment of successive age cohorts.[313] Furthermore, the relative growth rate of post-secondary graduates has fluctuated over the past 40 years. With the entrance of the highly educated baby boomers into the labor force and the resulting decline in the relative wages of college graduates, there was a decline in the relative growth rate of college graduates entering the labor force for successive cohorts until the late 1970s. Since then, there has been an upward trend in the relative growth rate of college graduates. It is likely that a static distribution of educational attainment biases downward our estimates of the educational distribution for children currently aged 14 or less. That is, our estimates of absolute levels of productivity gains are too low because we assume the work force of the future is no more educated on average than the current 30-to 45-year-old labor force is. Our downward bias would have been even greater had we included people over the age of 45.

Once we determine the number of each age cohort entering the labor force at various ages with varying amounts of schooling, we make some assumptions about earnings levels by educational attainment. Prior to age 30, a number of factors that are not related to marginal productivity explain average earnings, as people move between school and the labor force and may work either full-time, part-time, or not at all. Many are still adding to their productivity by obtaining more schooling. Because only a fraction of those younger than age 30 work, we attribute to all people now 0-14 when they reach age 16 the average earnings of all people now age 16, including those working part-time or not working because they are in school, unemployed, or out of the labor force. We do the same for those currently 0-14 when they reach age 17, and so on; that is, we use average earnings of current 17-year-olds as a measure of earnings of future 17-year-olds. People who are not working are included in the average to adjust for people still in school, unemployed, or out of the labor force. Future earning streams are identical to those of individuals currently ages 16 to 30 at each level of educational attainment.

After age 30, we assume no more education was obtained and all individuals were fully employed. From age 31 on, we assume that individual incomes grow at a rate of 2 percent per year until age 55, after which time earnings remain constant until retirement at age 65. We do not allow for growth of labor productivity above 2 percent for anyone. It is not inconceivable that technology-rich education will lead to greater productivity gains than have been observed in recent years. By assuming all workers retire at age 65, we ignore the fact that many people continue to work well beyond age 65. These steps provide us with estimates of lifetime earning streams for those who are currently 0 to 14 years of age depending on their age-education cohort, assuming no change in schooling attainment (see Table A-3).

We then assume that the incomes, or at least the productivity, of those with a high school degree or more would increase by 5 percent due to the skills acquired from exposure to modern technology in school; for example, the purchasing power of the annual salary of the technology-rich high school graduate would be 5 percent higher in the future than that of someone having the same number of years of education but without using technology. We do not consider the labor market benefits obtained by those who drop out of high school before receiving their diplomas. However, it may be precisely those individuals who will benefit most even though they learn to use technology during fewer years in school. This possibly is a major downward bias in our estimate. On one hand, one potential benefit of technology-rich schools is that they might keep students in school longer. If so, more labor force participants will fall into categories where the absolute value of their productivity gain is higher. On the other hand, we assume an increase of 5 percent in the earning of even the most educated workers. However, many of these already are using computers at work; thus their earnings probably already reflect some premium. Table A-4 shows the earnings premiums for individuals by age and educational attainment. If the increased supply of workers who attended schools that use technology reduces the wage premium even to zero, we still can consider the assumed premium to reflect the increased productivity resulting from improved education.

We then assume that the incomes, or at least the productivity, of those with a high school degree or more would increase by 5 percent due to the skills acquired from exposure to modern technology in school; for example, the purchasing power of the annual salary of the technology-rich high school graduate would be 5 percent higher in the future than that of someone having the same number of years of education but without using technology.

The next step is to calculate the total premiums for all those currently 0 years of age when they are 16, when they are 17, and so on. The total lifetime premiums for all members of a particular age cohort now between ages 0 and 14 depend upon the total number of people in that age cohort, their distribution by educational attainment, and the current earnings of people in the corresponding age-education cohort. To accomplish this, we multiply the total number of people of a particular age (from the right hand column of Table A-2) by their levels of educational attainment for each year (in Table A-1). The resulting columns are then multiplied by the corresponding columns of wage premiums in Table A-4. The result is a matrix of total wage premiums of current 0-year-olds as they progress from age 16 to age 65 for each level of educational attainment that a 0-year-old might achieve. We then add the total premiums for 0-year-olds across educational attainment levels separately for each age.

Since those currently 0 years of age will not be 16 until 16 years from now, we must reduce the sum of premiums at age 16 to its present value and do the same for premiums of current 0-year-olds at every subsequent age. We discount these premiums over the work life by 10 percent per year, which is a reasonable estimate of the total real return of investment in the U.S. economy (private returns plus tax payments)(Table A-5). This is the appropriate way to calculate the present value of government (as opposed to private) spending. We follow this same procedure for those currently 1 year of age, 2, 3, etc. In effect, what this yields for people of a particular age is a current-year value of the total premiums due to technology in the schools (see Table A-5).

In summary, then, the purpose of this exercise has been to determine the present value of the extra labor force productivity achieved by all those currently between the ages of 0 and 14 who will attend technology-rich schools. To do this, we first determined the ultimate educational achievement levels of each person currently 0 to 14 years of age by assuming that their levels of educational achievement will be similar to the levels of educational achievement of the population currently aged 16 to 30. For individuals older than 30, we assumed educational levels equivalent to those now aged 30 to 45 years. Next we impute the lifetime earning streams of those currently 0-14 by assuming they will be equal in real terms to the earning streams of those currently aged 16 to 30 during that period of their lives, and then assuming that their real wages will increase by 2 percent a year between the ages of 30 and 55 and remain constant between the ages of 55 and 65 when they retire. The productivity premium is then calculated to be 5 percent of their income streams, over their work life, which is then reduced to present value.

RELATING OUR ESTIMATED PRODUCTIVITY LOSS TO TODAY'S $25 BILLION ANNUAL LOSS TO BUSINESS BECAUSE OF POOR WORK AND LOW PRODUCTIVITY

We assume that the $25 billion loss to American business because of poor work performance and low productivity is due to inadequate education of the labor force and that our 0- to 14-year-old group would be educated well enough to reduce their contribution to that loss to zero. If the total labor force were educated in technology-rich schools, there would be no productivity loss at all, but since our 0- to 14-year-olds constitute only a portion of the total labor force, we save only that proportion of lost productivity. In 1998, some fraction of those 14 years of age in 1996 would enter the labor force and would constitute 93 percent of the total labor force. In 1999, some of those who were 13 years of age in 1996 would enter, and also the share of 14-year-olds (1996) in the labor force would increase to the 17-year-old share, bringing the total of our 0- to 14-year-old age group as a share of the labor force to 2.23 percent. We can determine the share in the labor force of each particular age group 16 and older by looking at the Current Population Survey. Sixteen years from now, those 14 in 1996 will turn 30 and represent 2.61 percent of the labor force. The labor force share peaks at 3.02 percent at age 35. Sixteen years from now, no more 16-year-olds from our group will enter the labor force because the youngest of that group will already be 16. Thus, from the sixteenth year on, we subtract an additional group's share from the total (in year 17 there are no 16-year-olds or 17-year-olds from our group working). We now have calculated the share of the labor force from each year between the time our 14-year-olds begin to enter the labor force and the time that age cohort retires.

At first glance, these shares might be thought to represent the share of lost productivity saved because of a better-educated workforce. However, it is obvious that working 16-year-olds contribute much less to aggregate productivity than do older workers at the peak of their performance. If productivity can be represented by earnings, 16-year-olds earn only 6.12 percent of the average salaries of all workers 16-65, whereas 49-year-olds earn 43 percent more than the average.

We used these shares of the average wage by age to adjust the share of the labor force of each age group. For example, the 16-year-old share becomes 6.12 percent of .93 percent, or .06 percent, and the 49-year-old share becomes 143.02 percent of 2.35 percent or 3.36 percent. Thus, we determine the weighted share of the labor force between 1998 (when the oldest members of our 0-14 group can begin work) and 2047 (when this same group retires). We determine the savings out of the annual $25 billion productivity loss by multiplying the weighted share of the labor force composed by our 0-14 1-year-old group trained in technology-rich schools by $25 billion for each year.

The sum of these savings is conservative because it stops when the oldest members of our groups retire even though younger members are still employed; it ignores savings from better-trained people not yet born in 1996 entering the labor market; and it assumes all workers retire at age 65, not later.

Table A-1 Distribution of Educational Attainment by Age

CURRENT AGE	8TH GRADE OR LESS	SOME HIGH SCHOOL, NO DEGREE	HIGH SCHOOL GRADUATE	COLLEGE, NO DEGREE	ASSOCIATE DEGREE	BACHELORS, MASTERS, OR DOCTORATE	TOTAL
16	10.20%	89.29%	0.39%	0.12%	0.00%	0.00%	100.00%
17	2.82%	94.45%	2.05%	0.65%	0.00%	0.02%	100.00%
18	2.87%	61.60%	21.12%	14.22%	0.16%	0.03%	100.00%
19	3.37%	21.44%	36.43%	38.10%	0.58%	0.09%	100.00%
20	3.08%	13.68%	32.68%	47.92%	2.32%	0.32%	100.00%
21	3.49%	11.89%	31.99%	46.79%	4.70%	1.15%	100.00%
22	4.21%	10.66%	32.40%	37.41%	6.30%	9.01%	100.00%
23	4.38%	10.32%	29.99%	29.89%	7.21%	18.21%	100.00%
24	4.62%	9.85%	31.50%	24.72%	6.95%	22.36%	100.00%
25	4.32%	9.80%	29.95%	23.04%	8.17%	24.72%	100.00%
26	4.25%	9.59%	31.84%	21.39%	7.26%	25.67%	100.00%
27	4.72%	9.02%	31.98%	20.37%	7.62%	26.29%	100.00%
28	4.91%	9.22%	32.26%	19.73%	9.45%	24.44%	100.00%
29	4.68%	9.12%	31.44%	19.42%	8.77%	26.57%	100.00%
30	4.94%	8.86%	32.78%	19.56%	9.23%	24.64%	100.00%
30-45	4.75%	7.84%	33.47%	18.64%	9.01%	26.29%	100.00%

Source: CPS March 1995 and 1996; based on combined two-year survey of 123,872 satisfying the age requirements

Table A-2   Educational Attainment of Current 0-Year-Olds from 16 to 65

0 YEAR OLD AT AGE	8TH GRADE OR LESS	SOME HIGH SCHOOL, NO DEGREE	HIGH SCHOOL GRADUATE	COLLEGE, NO DEGREE	ASSOCIATE DEGREE	BACHELORS, MASTERS OR DOCTORATE	TOTAL
16	398	3481	15	5	0	0	3898
17	110	3682	80	25	0	1	3898
18	112	2401	823	554	6	1	3898
19	131	836	1420	1485	22	3	3898
20	120	533	1274	1868	90	13	3898
21	136	463	1247	1824	183	45	3898
22	164	416	1263	1458	246	351	3898
23	171	402	1169	1165	281	710	3898
24	180	384	1228	964	271	872	3898
25	168	382	1168	898	318	964	3898
26	166	374	1241	834	283	1001	3898
27	184	352	1247	794	297	1025	3898
28	192	359	1257	769	368	953	3898
29	182	355	1226	757	342	1036	3898
30	192	345	1278	763	360	960	3898
31	185	305	1305	727	351	1025	3898
32	185	305	1305	727	351	1025	3898
33	185	305	1305	727	351	1025	3898
34	185	305	1305	727	351	1025	3898
35	185	305	1305	727	351	1025	3898
36	185	305	1305	727	351	1025	3898
37	185	305	1305	727	351	1025	3898
38	185	305	1305	727	351	1025	3898
39	185	305	1305	727	351	1025	3898
40	185	305	1305	727	351	1025	3898
41	185	305	1305	727	351	1025	3898
42	185	305	1305	727	351	1025	3898
43	185	305	1305	727	351	1025	3898
44	185	305	1305	727	351	1025	3898
45	185	305	1305	727	351	1025	3898
46	185	305	1305	727	351	1025	3898
8	185	305	1305	727	351	1025	3898
49	185	305	1305	727	351	1025	3898
50	185	305	1305	727	351	1025	3898
51	185	305	1305	727	351	1025	3898
52	185	305	1305	727	351	1025	3898
53	185	305	1305	727	351	1025	3898
54	185	305	1305	727	351	1025	3898
55	185	305	1305	727	351	1025	3898
56	185	305	1305	727	351	1025	3898
57	185	305	1305	727	351	1025	3898
58	185	305	1305	727	351	1025	3898
59	185	305	1305	727	351	1025	3898
60	185	305	1305	727	351	1025	3898
61	185	305	1305	727	351	1025	3898
62	185	305	1305	727	351	1025	3898
63	185	305	1305	727	351	1025	3898
64	185	305	1305	727	351	1025	3898
65	185	305	1305	727	351	1025	3898

Table A-3

Expected Maximum Educational Attainment (by Age 31) of Current Population (000) Age 0-14

People Currently Age	8th Grade or Less	Some High School, No Degree	High School Graduate	College, No Degree	Associate Degree Bachelors,	Masters, or Doctorate	Total
16	10.20%	89.29%	0.39%	0.12%	0.00%	0.00%	100.00%
17	2.82%	94.45%	2.05%	0.65%	0.00%	0.02%	100.00%
18	2.87%	61.60%	21.12%	14.22%	0.16%	0.03%	100.00%
19	3.37%	21.44%	36.43%	38.10%	0.58%	0.09%	100.00%
20	3.08%	13.68%	32.68%	47.92%	2.32%	0.32%	100.00%
21	3.49%	11.89%	31.99%	46.79%	4.70%	1.15%	100.00%
22	4.21%	10.66%	32.40%	37.41%	6.30%	9.01%	100.00%
23	4.38%	10.32%	29.99%	29.89%	7.21%	18.21%	100.00%
24	4.62%	9.85%	31.50%	24.72%	6.95%	22.36%	100.00%
25	4.32%	9.80%	29.95%	23.04%	8.17%	24.72%	100.00%
26	4.25%	9.59%	31.84%	21.39%	7.26%	25.67%	100.00%
27	4.72%	9.02%	31.98%	20.37%	7.62%	26.29%	100.00%
28	4.91%	9.22%	32.26%	19.73%	9.45%	24.44%	100.00%
29	4.68%	9.12%	31.44%	19.42%	8.77%	26.57%	100.00%
30	4.94%	8.86%	32.78%	19.56%	9.23%	24.64%	100.00%
30-45	4.75%	7.84%	33.47%	18.64%	9.01%	26.29%	100.00%

Source: CPS, March 1995, 1996

Note: 1) Based on distribution of educational attainment of survey participants 31 to 45 years old

Table A-4

Estimated Average Annual Labor Income (96 $) by Age and Educational Attainment for People Currently 0-14 years old

WHEN THEY REACH AGE	8TH GRADE OR LESS	SOME HIGH SCHOOL, NO DEGREE	HIGH SCHOOL GRADUATE	COLLEGE, NO DEGREE	ASSOCIATE DEGREE	BACHELORS, MASTERS OR DOCTORATE	DISCOUNT RATE 10% ANNUALLY
16	$512	$654	$2,262	$663	$0	$0	1.0000
17	$1,501	$1,389	$2,430	$2,495	$0	$530	0.9091
18	$3,336	$2,188	$4,356	$3,024	$1,237	$0	0.8264
19	$3,046	$3,433	$5,901	$4,417	$5,716	$17,399	0.7513
20	$4,846	$4,157	$8,751	$5,435	$8,381	$8,556	0.6830
21	$5,555	$6,174	$10,259	$6,902	$9,264	$9,606	0.6209
22	$5,608	$6,263	$10,856	$8,584	$11,657	$9,846	0.5645
23	$7,574	$7,378	$11,889	$10,712	$14,176	$14,125	0.5132
24	$6,868	$8,020	$13,339	$12,685	$15,192	$18,316	0.4665
25	$6,792	$8,690	$14,202	$15,346	$18,013	$21,522	0.4241
26	$6,986	$9,206	$15,586	$17,069	$17,912	$23,213	0.3855
27	$7,829	$8,041	$15,873	$17,488	$19,915	$26,549	0.3505
28	$8,306	$10,451	$16,741	$17,817	$21,639	$29,543	0.3186
29	$9,623	$10,778	$16,737	$19,248	$21,317	$30,514	0.2897
30	$9,476	$10,244	$17,172	$20,264	$21,949	$32,702	0.2633
31	$17,522	$20,671	$25,970	$28,237	$29,353	$43,820	0.2394
32	$17,872	$21,085	$26,490	$28,802	$29,940	$44,696	0.2176

Table A-4   continued

WHEN THEY REACH AGE	8TH GRADE OR LESS	SOME HIGH SCHOOL, NO DEGREE	HIGH SCHOOL GRADUATE	COLLEGE, NO DEGREE	ASSOCIATE DEGREE	BACHELORS, MASTERS OR DOCTORATE	DISCOUNT RATE 10% ANNUALLY
33	$18,230	$21,507	$27,019	$29,378	$30,539	$45,590	0.1978
34	$18,594	$21,937	$27,560	$29,965	$31,150	$46,502	0.1799
35	$18,966	$22,375	$28,111	$30,565	$31,773	$47,432	0.1635
36	$19,346	$22,823	$28,673	$31,176	$32,408	$48,381	0.1486
37	$19,732	$23,279	$29,247	$31,800	$33,056	$49,348	0.1351
38	$20,127	$23,745	$29,832	$32,436	$33,718	$50,335	0.1228
39	$20,530	$24,220	$30,428	$33,084	$34,392	$51,342	0.1117
40	$20,940	$24,704	$31,037	33,746	$35,080	$52,369	0.1015
41	$21,359	$25,198	$31,657	$34,421	$35,781	$53,416	0.0923
42	$21,786	$25,702	$32,291	$35,109	$36,497	$54,485	0.0839
43	$22,222	$26,216	$32,936	$35,811	$37,227	$55,574	0.0763
44	$22,666	$26,741	$33,595	$36,528	$37,971	$56,686	0.0693
45	$23,120	$27,275	$34,267	$37,258	$38,731	$57,819	0.0630
46	$23,582	$27,821	$34,952	$38,003	$39,505	$58,976	0.0573
47	$24,054	$28,377	$35,651	$38,763	$40,296	$60,155	0.0521
48	$24,535	$28,945	$36,364	$39,539	$41,102	$61,358	0.0474
49	$25,026	$29,524	$37,092	$40,330	$41,924	$62,586	0.0431
50	$25,526	$30,114	$37,834	$41,136	$42,762	$63,837	0.0391
51	$26,037	$30,717	$38,590	$41,959	$43,617	$65,114	0.0356
52	$26,557	$31,331	$39,362	$42,798	$44,490	$66,416	0.0323
53	$27,088	$31,958	$40,149	$43,654	$45,379	$67,745	0.0294
54	$27,630	$32,597	$40,952	$44,527	$46,287	$69,100	0.0267
55	$28,183	$33,249	$41,771	$45,418	$47,213	$70,482	0.0243
56	$28,183	$33,249	$41,771	$45,418	$47,213	$70,482	0.0221
57	$28,183	$33,249	$41,771	$45,418	$47,213	$70,482	0.0201
58	$28,183	$33,249	$41,771	$45,418	$47,213	$70,482	0.0183
59	$28,183	$33,249	$41,771	$45,418	$47,213	$70,482	0.0166
60	$28,183	$33,249	$41,771	$45,418	$47,213	$70,482	0.0151
61	$28,183	$33,249	$41,771	$45,418	$47,213	$70,482	0.0137
62	$28,183	$33,249	$41,771	$45,418	$47,213	$70,482	0.0125
63	$28,183	$33,249	$41,771	$45,418	$47,213	$70,482	0.0113
64	$28,183	$33,249	$41,771	$45,418	$47,213	$70,482	0.0103
65	$28,183	$33,249	$41,771	$45,418	$47,213	$70,482	0.0094

Source: CPS-March 1995, 1996

Notes:

1. Age 16-30 values are calculated from previous year annual income of all survey participants belonging to the relevant age-education cohorts.

2. Age 31 values are mean annual labor income (1996 dollars for survey participants with full-time and full-year employment in 1994 or 1995).

3. Age 32-55 values are 2 percent more than previous annual income.

4. Age 56-65 values are same as age 55 income.

5. CPS earnings values have been adjusted to real 1996 dollars with the Consumer Price Index for Urban Areas.

Table A-5

Average Annual Labor Income Premium (96 $) from Schooling Using Technology by Age and Educational Attainment

AGE	8TH GRADE OR LESS	SOME HIGH SCHOOL, NO DEGREE	HIGH SCHOOL GRADUATE	COLLEGE, NO DEGREE	ASSOCIATE DEGREE	BACHELORS, MASTERS OR DOCTORATE	DISCOUNT RATE 10% ANNUALLY
16	$26	$33	$113	$33	$0	$0	1.00
17	$75	$69	$122	$125	$0	$27	0.9091
18	$167	$109	$218	$151	$62	$0	0.8264
19	$152	$172	$295	$221	$286	$870	0.7513
20	$242	$208	$438	$272	$419	$428	0.6830
21	$278	$309	$513	$345	$463	$480	0.6209
22	$280	$313	$543	$429	$583	$492	0.5645
23	$379	$369	$594	$536	$709	$706	0.5132
24	$343	$401	$667	$634	$760	$916	0.4665
25	$340	$435	$710	$767	$901	$1,076	0.4241
26	$349	$460	$779	$853	$896	$1,161	0.3855
27	$391	$402	$794	$874	$996	$1,327	0.3505
28	$415	$523	$837	$891	$1,082	$1,477	0.3186
29	$481	$539	$837	$962	$1,066	$1,526	0.2897
30	$474	$512	$859	$1,013	$1,097	$1,635	0.2633
31	$876	$1,034	$1,299	$1,412	$1,468	$2,191	0.2394
32	$894	$1,054	$1,324	$1,440	$1,497	$2,235	0.2176
33	$911	$1,075	$1,351	$1,469	$1,527	$2,280	0.1978
34	$930	$1,097	$1,378	$1,498	$1,557	$2,325	0.1799
35	$948	$1,119	$1,406	$1,528	$1,589	$2,372	0.1635
36	$967	$1,141	$1,434	$1,559	$1,620	$2,419	0.1486
37	$987	$1,164	$1,462	$1,590	$1,653	$2,467	0.1351
38	$1,006	$1,187	$1,492	$1,622	$1,686	$2,517	0.1228
39	$1,026	$1,211	$1,521	$1,654	$1,720	$2,567	0.1117
40	$1,047	$1,235	$1,552	$1,687	$1,754	$2,618	0.1015
41	$1,068	$1,260	$1,583	$1,721	$1,789	$2,671	0.0923
42	$1,089	$1,285	$1,615	$1,755	$1,825	$2,724	0.0839
43	$1,111	$1,311	$1,647	$1,791	$1,861	$2,779	0.0763
44	$1,133	$1,337	$1,680	$1,826	$1,899	$2,834	0.0693
45	$1,156	$1,364	$1,713	$1,863	$1,937	$2,891	0.0630
46	$1,179	$1,391	$1,748	$1,900	$1,975	$2,949	0.0573
47	$1,203	$1,419	$1,783	$1,938	$2,015	$3,008	0.0521
48	$1,227	$1,447	$1,818	$1,977	$2,055	$3,068	0.0474
49	$1,251	$1,476	$1,855	$2,016	$2,096	$3,129	0.0431
50	$1,276	$1,506	$1,892	$2,057	$2,138	$3,192	0.0391
51	$1,302	$1,536	$1,930	$2,098	$2,181	$3,256	0.0356
52	$1,328	$1,567	$1,968	$2,140	$2,224	$3,321	0.0323
53	$1,354	$1,598	$2,007	$2,183	$2,269	$3,387	0.0294
54	$1,382	$1,630	$2,048	$2,226	$2,314	$3,455	0.0267
55	$1,409	$1,662	$2,089	$2,271	$2,361	$3,524	0.0243
56	$1,409	$1,662	$2,089	$2,271	$2,361	$3,524	0.0221
57	$1,409	$1,662	$2,089	$2,271	$2,361	$3,524	0.0201
58	$1,409	$1,662	$2,089	$2,271	$2,361	$3,524	0.0183
59	$1,409	$1,662	$2,089	$2,271	$2,361	$3,524	0.0166
60	$1,409	$1,662	$2,089	$2,271	$2,361	$3,524	0.0151
61	$1,409	$1,662	$2,089	$2,271	$2,361	$3,524	0.0137
62	$1,409	$1,662	$2,089	$2,271	$2,361	$3,524	0.0125
63	$1,409	$1,662	$2,089	$2,271	$2,361	$3,524	0.0113
64	$1,409	$1,662	$2,089	$2,271	$2,361	$3,524	0.0103
65	$1,409	$1,662	$2,089	$2,271	$2,361	$3,524	0.0094

Source: CPS-March 1995, 1996

Note:1) Estimates are 5 percent of corresponding annual labor income, Table A-4

Table A-6

Net Present Value of Lifetime Earnings Premium from Computer Use for the 1996 Population Aged 0-14 by Maximum Level of Educational Attainment (96 $000)

AGE	8TH GRADE OR LESS	SOME HIGH SCHOOL, NO DEGREE	HIGH SCHOOL GRADUATE	COLLEGE, NO DEGREE	ASSOCIATE DEGREE	BACHELORS, MASTERS OR DOCTORATE	TOTAL FOR HIGH SCHOOL GRADUATE AND HIGHER
0	$178,116	$514,289	$2,069,659	$1,429,964	$562,662	$2,228,854	$6,291,140
1	$202,516	$584,741	$2,353,180	$1,625,853	$639,741	$2,534,182	$7,152,956
2	$221,390	$639,236	$2,572,484	$1,777,374	$699,361	$2,770,355	$7,819,575
3	$243,958	$704,399	$2,834,721	$1,958,558	$770,654	$3,052,763	$8,616,697
4	$274,899	$793,739	$3,194,250	$2,206,964	$868,396	$3,439,947	$9,709,557
5	$315,414	$910,720	$3,665,019	$2,532,226	$996,381	$3,946,927	$11,140,552
6	$333,989	$964,352	$3,880,851	$2,681,348	$1,055,057	$4,179,359	$11,796,614
7	$353,288	$1,020,077	$4,105,107	$2,836,290	$1,116,024	$4,420,865	$12,478,286
8	$375,428	$1,084,004	$4,362,371	$3,014,038	$1,185,964	$4,697,917	$13,260,291
9	$426,657	$1,231,921	$4,957,634	$3,425,316	$1,347,794	$5,338,967	$15,069,711
10	$465,290	$1,343,469	$5,406,538	$3,735,472	$1,469,834	$5,822,401	$16,434,245
11	$511,715	$1,477,517	$5,945,986	$4,108,186	$1,616,490	$6,403,342	$18,074,004
12	$547,124	$1,579,756	$6,357,429	$4,392,459	$1,728,345	$6,846,432	$19,324,664
13	$619,652	$1,789,172	$7,200,182	$4,974,732	$1,957,458	$7,754,009	$21,886,382
14	$666,551	$1,924,584	$7,745,125	$5,351,243	$2,105,608	$8,340,868	$23,542,844
TOTAL			$66,650,537	$46,050,022	$18,119,768	$71,777,190	$202,597,518

Source: CPS—March 1995, 1996

bibliography

American Electronics Association National Infrastructure Taskforce (1995). *Building the National Information Infrastructure in K-12 Education: A Comprehensive Survey of Attitude Towards Linking Both Sides of the Desk.* Washington, D.C.: American Electronics Association.

Ashworth, Kenneth H. *American Higher Education in Decline.* College Station: Texas A&M University Press, 1979.

Bailey and E. Mosher (1968). "ESEA: The Office of Education Administers a Law," in Yudof, M., Kirp, D., et al. (1982), *Educational Policy and the Law, Second Edition.* McCutchan Publishing Corporation, Berkeley, Calif. p. 651.

Baker, Charles. "As you were saying...Get it right on classroom computers." *Boston Herald,* Dec. 7, 1996.

Baker, E. L., and O'Neil, H. F., Jr. (Eds.) (1994). *Technology Assessment in Education and Training.* Hillsdale, N.J.: Lawrence Erlbaum Associates.

Bangert-Drowns, R. L., Kulik, J. A., and Kulik, C. - L. C. (1985) Effectiveness of computer-based education in secondary schools. *Journal of Computer-Based Instruction,* 12, 59-68.

Barksdale, Joye. Harvard Ed School Gives Itself a D- in Technology. *Electronic Learning,* Exclusive Reports, 1996-1997. Http://place.scholastic.com/el/exclusive/harvard496.htm.

Becker, Ann DeVaney (1987) "Instructional Television and the Talking Head." *Educational Technology,* 27(10), 35-40.

Becker, H. J. (1990) *Computer Use in United States Schools: 1989.* An initial report of U. S. participation in the I.E.A. Computers in Education Survey. New York: Johns Hopkins University.

Bitter, Gary G., and Pryor, Brandt W. *The National Study of IBM's Teacher Preparation with Technology Grant Program,* Arizona State University, Technology Based Learning and Research. Tempe: Arizona State University, 1994, p. 13.

Brock, P. A. (1994) *Educational Technology in the Classroom.* New Jersey: Educational Technology Publications.

California Department of Education. *Connect, Compute, and Compete.* Sacramento, Calif., 1996.

Carroll, S. R. "Preparing for the 21st century business-education partnership launches students into real world." *Chicago Tribune,* April 7, 1996.

Cassirer, Henry R. (1960) *Television Teaching Today.* UNESCO, Paris.

Chandrasekaran, Rajiv. "Group Urges New Technology Education Programs," *Washington Post,* December 18, 1996, p. C14.

Chase, Bob. Remarks by: "The New NEA: Reinventing Teacher Unions for a New Era." Before the National Press Club, February 5, 1997. Washington, D.C.

Children's Partnership (1995). America's children and the information superhighway: A briefing book and national action agenda. Santa Monica, Calif.: Children's Partnership.

Clark, R. E. (1985) "Evidence for confounding in computer-based instruction studies: Analyzing the meta-analyses." *Educational Communication and Technology Journal,* 33(4), 249-62.

Clark, R., and Salomon, G. (1986) "Media in Teaching," in M. Wittrock (Ed.), *Handbook of Research on Teaching (Ed. 3).* New York: Macmillan.

Clark, R. E., and Surgrue, B. M. (1988) "Research on instructional media, 1978-1988," in D. Ely (Ed.), *Educational Media and Technology Yearbook,* Vol. 14, 19-36. Denver, Colo.: Libraries Unlimited, Inc.

Cognition & Technology Group at Vanderbilt (1990). "Anchored Instruction and its Relationship to Situated Cognition." *Educational Researcher,* 19(6), 2-10.

Colvin, Richard Lee. "Online school is no longer a lonely outpost." *Los Angeles Times,* February 12, 1996.

Committee for Economic Development (April 1995). Connecting Students to the Future: A Technology Strategy for Improving Mathematics and Science Education. Unpublished draft.

Conference Board (1994). Business and Education: Dynamic Partners, Garone, S. J. (Ed.). New York: The Conference Board, Inc.

Council of Economic Advisors. *Economic Indicators.* Washington, D.C.: Council of Economic Advisors, Feb. 1997.

Cuban, Larry (1986). *Teachers and Machines: The Classroom Use of Technology Since 1920.* New York: Teachers College Press.

Dexter, L. (1987) *How Organizations Are Represented in Washington: Toward a Broader Understanding of the Seeking of Influence and of Patterns of Representation.* Lanham, Md.: University Press of America.

DiNardo, John E. and Pischke, J. "The Returns to Computer Use Revisited: Have Pencils Changed the Wage Structure Too?" *Quarterly Journal of Economics,* February 1997, 291-303.

Dirr, P. and Pedone, R. (January 1978) "A national report on the use of instructional television." *AV Instruction,* 11-13.

Dunn, L. M. (1968) "Special education for the mentally retarded—Is much of it justifiable?" *Exceptional Children,* 35, 5-22.

Ellis, Thomas. "Class Size." ERIC Clearinghouse on Educational Management, 1984.

Fagnano, C. L. and Droege, K., prod., Golway, J. dir. *Expanding Classroom, Shrinking World.* Videotape, 20 min., 1995; Milken Family Foundation, Santa Monica.

Finch, Christopher (1992). *Highways to Heaven.* New York: Harper Collins Publishers.

Finn, C. E. (1993) "Whither Education Reform?" in C. Fagnano and K. N. Hughes (Eds.) Making Schools Work (pp. 17-29). San Francisco: Westview Press.

Fiore, F. and Hook, J. "Clinton Signs Aid Bill; California to Get $2.4 Billion." *Los Angeles Times,* June 13, 1997.

Fletcher, J. D. (1990) Effectiveness and cost of interactive videodisc instruction in defense training and education. Alexandria, Va.: Institute for Defense Analysis.

Ford Foundation (1961). *Teaching by Television.*

Friedman, Milton. "The Social Responsibility of Business Is to Increase Its Profits." *New York Times Magazine,* September 1979.

Gale Research, Inc. (1994) *Gale Book of Averages.* Kathleen Droste (Ed.).

Gates, Bill. *The Road Ahead.* New York: Viking, 1995.

Goddard, Stephen B. (1994) *Getting There: The Epic Struggle between Road and Rail in the American Century.* New York: Basic Books.

Gottlieb, Alan. "DPS launches 'high-tech' high." *Denver Post,* October 7, 1996.

Green, K. C. (1995) Campus Computing 1994. Los Angeles: Technology, Teaching and Scholarship Project.

Hanushek, E. A. (1994) Making Schools Work. Washington D.C.: Brookings Institution, 1994.

Harmon, Amy. "High-Tech Barn-Raising Shows Disparity of Schools." *Los Angeles Times,* March 9, 1996.

Hartford Courant. "School to work: Business leaders, educators heed the call of a changing workplace." Business Weekly, April 25, 1994, 1.

Hartley, J. (1966) *New Education,* 2(1), 4-page reprint of article.

Havemen, R. and Wolfe, B. (1984) "Schooling and economic well-being: The role of nonmarket effects," *Journal of Human Resources,* Vol. XIX, No. 3.

Hawkins, Christy. "Strides in Technology," *Dallas Morning News,* Northeast Tarrant County. November 30, 1996, 1N.

Heller Associates, Nelson B. "Failure for Technology or a Matter of Inappropriate Expectations?" *The Heller Report.* Highland Park, Ill. March 1995, 3.

Honey, M., and Henriquez, A. (1993) *Telecommunications and K-12 Educators: Findings from a National Survey.* New York: Center for Technology in Education, Bank Street College of Education.

Hood, P. (March 1994) Don't Leave Schools Behind. *New Media,* 8.

Information Access Company. "Partners in transition; business and education." Vol. 48; no.11, 6-32, 1994.

International Society for the Accreditation of Technology in Education, Accreditation Committee, Eugene, Oreg., 1992.

Jamison, D., Suppes, P., and Wells, S. (1974) "The Effectiveness of Alternative Instructional Media: A Survey." *Review of Educational Research,* 44, 1-68.

Kahn, Ronald C. (1982) *Political Change in America: Highway Politics and Reactive Policymaking,* in *Public Values & Private Power in American Politics,* Greenstone, D. J. (Ed.). Chicago: University of Chicago Press, 139-172.

Katz, L., and Murphy, K. (February 1992) "Changes in Relative Wages, 1963-1987." *Quarterly Journal of Economics.*

Keltner, Brent, and Ross, Randy. *The Cost of School-Based Educational Technology Programs.* Santa Monica, Calif., RAND, 1996.

Kirk, Samuel A. (1978) The Federal Role in Special Education: Historical Perspectives. *UCLA Educator,* 20(2), 5-11.

Kirk, Samuel A., with editors Harris, Gail A., and Kirk, Winifred D. (1993) *The Foundations of Special Education: Selected Papers and Speeches of Samuel A. Kirk.* Virginia: Council for Exceptional Children.

Knowlton, J. Q. (1964) "A conceptual scheme for audiovisual field." *Bulletin of the School of Education,* Indiana University, 40(3), 1-44.

Koenig, John. "School-business team working in Seminole," *Orlando Sentinel,* January 19, 1997, Business, H1.

Kowsky, Kim. "A lesson in giving." *Los Angeles Times,* August 3, 1995, B4.

Kreuger, A. B. (February 1993) "How computers have changed the wage structure: evidence from microdata 1988-1989." *Quarterly Journal of Economics,* 1993, 33-60.

Kulik, C. C., and Kulik, J. A. (1991) "Effectiveness of Computer-Based Instruction: An Updated Analysis." *Computers in Human Behavior,* 7, 75-94.

Kulik, J., Kulik, C. C., and Bangert-Drowns, R. (1985) "Effectiveness of Computer-Based Education in Elementary Schools." *Computers in Human Behavior,* 1(1), 59-74.

Kulik, J., Bangert R., & Williams, G. (1983) "Effects of Computer-Based Teaching on Secondary Students." *Journal of Educational Psychology,* 75(1), 19-26.

Lawton, Millicent (1995). "Students fall short in NAEP geography test." *Education Week,* October 25, 1995.

Lehrer, R., Erickson, J., and Connell, T. (1992) *Assessing Knowledge Design.* Paper presented at the annual meeting of the American Educational Research Association, San Francisco.

Maloy, Richard. "A Law That Changed America: The GI Bill Was a Lucky Accident." *Washington Post,* June 24, 1994.

McKinsey & Co. *Connecting K-12 Schools to the Information Superhighway.* Palo Alto, Calif.: McKinsey & Co., 1996.

Means, B., et al. (1993) *Using Technology to Support Education Reform.* Office of Educational Research and Improvement, Washington, D.C., U.S. Government Printing Office. ED 364 220.

Means, Barbara, and Olson, Kerry. *Technology's Role in Education Reform, Findings from a National Study of Innovating Schools.* U.S. Department of Education, September 1995.

Melton, L. J. (1966) A Rational Approach to Highway Finance. *Land Economics,* 42(1), 130-134.

Meyers, H. G. (1987) Displacement Effects of Federal Highway Grants. *National Tax Journal,* 40(2), 221-236.

Microsoft. *Educators see a dramatic transformation in learning when students use technology to learn Anytime, Anywhere.* Microsoft Press Release. http://www.microsoft.com/corpinfo/press/1997/Apr97/anytime.htm.

Milken Exchange on Education Technology: Public Opinion Survey. *"Preparing Our Young People for a Changing World."* Presented at the 1997 Milken Family Foundation National Conference. 1997.

Milken Institute. *Survey of Technology in the Public Schools.* Santa Monica, Calif.: Milken Institute, 1994.

Moore, M. T., Strand, E. W., Schwartz, M., and Braddock, M. *Patterns in Special Education Service Delivery and Cost.* Washington, D.C.: Decision Resources Corporation, 1988.

Nasser, Haya El. "More Lottery Funds Headed for Education." *USA Today.* February 18, 1997.

National Association of State Directors of Teacher Certification (NASDTEC). *The NASDTEC Manual 1996-1997.* Theodore E. Andrews (Ed.). Iowa: Kendall/Hunt Publishing Company.

National Center for Education Statistics (NCES). *Digest of Education Statistics, 1996.* Washington, D.C.: U.S. Government Printing Office. 1996.

National Center for Education Statistics (NCES). *Third International Mathematics and Science Study (TIMSS). Pursuing Excellence: A Study of U.S. Eighth-Grade Mathematics and Science Teaching, Learning, Curriculum, and Achievement in International Context,* Washington, D.C.: U.S. Government Printing Office. 1996. http://www.ed.gov/NCES/timss/report/97255-04.htm.

National Center for Education Statistics (NCES). *Findings from the Condition of Education, 194, High School Students Ten Years After 'A Nation at Risk,'* Washington, D.C.: U.S. Government Printing Office. 1995.

National Center for Education Statistics (NCES). *Projections of Education Statistics to 2006.* Washington, D.C.: Department of Education. 1996.

Niemiec, R. P., and Walberg, H. J. (1985) "Computers and achievement in the elementary schools." *Journal of Educational Computing Research,* 1(4), 435-440.

Office of Management and Budget (OMB), *FY 98 Federal Budget.* Washington D.C.: OMB, 1997.

Papert, Seymour. *The Children's Machine.* New York: Basic Books, 1993.

Paul, Paula. Education: "New Mexico's 'hiring highway' is full of potholes. Business had better be concerned." *New Mexico Business Journal,* March 1996, Vol. 20, No.3, 11.

Pellegrino, J. W., Hickey, D., Heath, A., Rewey, K., and Vye, N. J. (1992) *Assessing the Outcomes of an Innovative Instructional Program: The 1990-1991 Implementation of the "Adventures of Jasper Woodbury."* Nashville, Tenn.: Learning Technology Center, Vanderbilt University.

Ponessa, Jeanne. "Chain of Blame," *Education Week,* May 22, 1996.

Pinkerton, James. "Learn to Earn is the New Mantra," *Los Angeles Times,* April 7, 1996, 1.

Quality Education Data. *Technology in Public Schools,* 15th ed. Denver, Colo.: Quality Education Data, 1996.

Ramirez, A. (March 1994) "Reluctant Partners." *Basic Education,* 38(7).

Reeves, Richard. "50 Years Ago, Man-Made Miracle Changed America." *Baltimore Sun,* September 12, 1995.

Reich, R. B. (1991) *The Work of Nations: Preparing Ourselves for 21st-Century Capitalism.* New York: A. A. Knopf.

Reich, R. B., interview by John Ydstie. "The growing inequality of incomes in America," part 1, NPR Morning Edition, February 27, 1996.

Repp, Alan C. (1983) *Teaching the Mentally Retarded.* Englewood Cliffs, N. J.: Prentice-Hall, Inc.

Riel, M. (1989) "The Impact of Computers in Classrooms." *Journal of Research on Computing in Education,* 22(2), 180-89.

Roblyer, M. D., Castine, W. H., King, F. J. (1988) *Assessing the Impact of Computer-Based Instruction: A Review of Recent Research.* Computers in the Schools Volume 5, Numbers 3/4. New York: Hawthorne Press. Rogers, E. M. (1986). Communication Technology: the New Media in Society. New York: Free Press.

Rose, M. H. (1979) *Interstate: Express Highway Politics, 1941-1956.* Lawrence: Regents Press of Kansas.

Rothenberg, Leon (1978). "Energy Taxation for Highway Financing." *National Tax Journal,* V. 31 (3), pp. 285-290.

Rothstein, R., and McKnight, L. (1995) Technology and Cost Models of K-12 Schools on the National Information Infrastructure. Unpublished manuscript. MIT Research Program on Communications Policy.

Ryan, A. W. (1991) "Meta-analysis of achievement effects of microcomputer applications in elementary schools." *Educational Administration Quarterly,* 27(2), 161-84.

Saettler, Paul (1990). *The Evolution of American Educational Technology.* Colorado: Libraries Unlimited, Inc.

Salomon, G., and Clark, R. E. (1977) "Reexamining the Methodology of Research on Media and Technology in Education. *Review of Education Research,* 47(1), 99-120.

Samson, G. E., Niemiec, R., Weinstein, T., and Walberg, H. J. (Summer, 1986) "Effects of Computer-Based Instruction on Secondary School Achievement: A Quantitative Synthesis. *AEDS Journal,* 312-26.

Scheerenberger, R. C. (1987) *A History of Mental Retardation: A Quarter Century of Promise.* Brookes Publishing Co., Baltimore.

Scheuer, Hon. James H. Report titled *"A Cost-Benefits Analysis of Government Investment in Post-Secondary Education Under the World War II GI Bill."* Hearing before the Subcommittee on Education and Health of the Joint Economic Committee, Congress of the United States, 101st Session, February 26, 1990.

Scott, Jonathan. "The New Look in Manufacturing." *Memphis Business Journal,* March 11, 1996.

Segal, T., Del Valle, C., et al. "Saving Our Schools." *Business Week,* September 14, 1992.

Siegel, Jessica. "The State of Teacher Training: A model staff development program in North Carolina." *Electronic Learning,* May/June 1995.

Sipchen, Bob, and Lindsay, John. "Bill Gates Charts 'The Road Ahead.'" *Los Angeles Times,* December 5, 1996, E1.

Sivin-Kachala, J., and Bialo, E. R. (1994) *Report on the Effectiveness of Technology in Schools 1990-1994.* Software Publishers Association, Washington, D.C.

Smith, Adam. *An Inquiry into the Nature and Causes of the Wealth of Nations,* Book IV, Chapter 11, 423. Modern Library Edition, New York, 1937.

Sommerfield, Meg. "Who's Responsible? Taking Sides on Remedial Classes," *Education Week,* April 12, 1995.

Software Publishers Association (July 1994). SPA K-12 Education Market Report. Washington, D.C.

Tejada, Carlos. "Technology (A Special Report): A Lot to Learn." *Wall Street Journal,* November 13, 1995.

Thompson, Ann D., Simonson, Michael R., and Hargrave, Constance P. (1992) *Educational Technology: A Review of the Research, Revised Edition.* Association for Educational Communications and Technology, Washington, D.C.

Tyor, Peter L., and Bell, Leland V. (1984) *Caring for the Retarded in America: A History.* Connecticut: Greenwood Press.

Tyler, Bus. "Salute to the GI Bill...and Electing a Future." Ethnic NewsWatch, July 8, 1994.

U.S. Bureau of the Census. *1950 Census of the Population: Characteristics of the Population,* Table 3.

U.S. Bureau of the Census. *1970 Census of the Population: Characteristics of the Population,* Table 221.

U.S. Bureau of the Census. *1980 Census of the Population: Detailed Population Characteristics,* Table 278.

U.S. Bureau of the Census. *Statistical Abstract of the U.S.: 116th edition.* Washington, D.C., 1996.

U.S. Bureau of the Census. *1990 Census of the Population: Supplementary Reports, Detailed Occupation and Other Characteristics from the EEO File for the United States,* Table 2.

U.S. Congress, Office of Technology Assessment (1995). *Teachers and Technology: Making the Connection,* OTA-EHR-616. Washington, D.C.: Government Printing Office.

U.S. Department of Commerce. *KickStart Initiative.* United States Advisory Council on the National Information Infrastructure. Department of Commerce, Washington, D.C., 1996.

U.S. Department of Education. *Impact of Education Recessions on Selected Programs.* Washington, D.C.: Government Printing Office. April 18, 1995.

U.S. Department of Education. *Education Statistics 1995: Educational Outcomes.* Washington, D.C.: Government Printing Office, 1996.

U.S. Department of Education. *"Findings from the condition of education, 194, high school students ten years after 'A Nation at Risk.'"* Washington, D.C.: Government Printing Office, 1995.

U.S. Department of Education. *Getting America's Students Ready for the 21st Century: Meeting the Technology Literacy Challenge.* Washington, D.C.: Department of Education, 1996.

U.S. Department of Education. *Resource Guide to Federal Funding for Technology in Education.* Washington, D.C.: Department of Education, 1997.

U.S. Department of Veterans Affairs, "GI Bill." *Strategic Review.* Veterans Benefits Administration Education Service, Washington, D.C.: March 1997.

U.S. General Accounting Office. School Facilities: America's Schools Not Designed or Equipped for 21st Century. GAO/HEHS-95-95. Washington, D.C., 1995.

Viadero, Debra. "Less Is More." *Education Week,* July 12, 1995, 33-35.

Wagner, Venise. "Cutting-edge classrooms; S.F. hosts program where kids use computers right from start." *San Francisco Examiner,* October 8, 1995.

Weeden, Curtis G. "How Much Should a Company Give?" *Los Angeles Times* (op-ed), May 30, 1995, B5.

Weick, K. E. "Small Wins: Redefining the Scale of Social Problems." *American Psychologist,* 1984, 39(1), 40-49.

Weiner, Roberta, and Hume, Maggie (1987). *...And Education for All.* Public Policy and Handicapped Children. Education Research Group, Capitol Publications, Inc., Virginia.

West, P. "Airwave Auction Should Fund School Wiring, F.C.C. Head Says." *Education Week,* Nov. 9, 1994.

West, P. "Kentucky Needs More Money for Technology, Panel Urges." *Education Week,* Oct. 4, 1995.

Winzer, Margaret A. (1993) *The History of Special Education: From Isolation to Integration.* Gallaudet University Press, Washington, D.C.

Wynn, R., and Wynn, J. (1988) *American Education, Ninth Edition.* Harper & Row, Publishers, New York, 416.

Zeiger, Dinah. "DPS gets wired for the future techno loop to link all classrooms." *Denver Post,* Feb. 20, 1994, A section, A-01.

Zellermayer, M., Salomon, G., Globerson, T., and Givon, H. (1991) "Enhancing writing-related metacognitions through a computerized writing partner." *American Educational Research Journal,* 28(2), 373-91.

Zigler, Edward, Hodapp, Robert M., and Edison, Mark R. (1990) "From theory to practice in the care and education of mentally retarded individuals." *American Journal on Mental Retardation,* 90(1), 1-12.

endnotes

CHAPTER 1

1. NCES. Available: http://www.ed.gov/NCES/timss/report/97255-04.htm. 1996.

2. NCES, *Digest of Education Statistics,* 1994, Tables 388–396.

3. Lawton, 1995.

4. "Round Table: A Discussion of Poverty in the Valley." Compiled by David E. Brady, Donna Mungen, Lucille Renwick and Stephanie Stassel. *Los Angeles Times,* June 12, 1996.

5. Sommerfeld, 1995.

6. Jeanne Ponessa, "Chain of Blame," *Education Week on the Web,* May 22, 1996.

7. U.S. Department of Education, *Education Statistics,* 1995.

8. U.S. Department of Education, National Center for Education Statistics: *National Adult Literacy Survey.* Washington, D.C.: Government Printing Office, 1992.

9. NCES, *Findings from the Condition of Education,* 1995.

10. U.S. Bureau of the Census, *1990 Census of the Population,* Table 2.

11. *Statistical Abstract of the United States,* 1996, Table 637.

12. There may be a ray of hope in this regard, as expressed by the National Education Association's new president, Bob Chase, in a speech before the National Press Club, February 5, 1997, in Washington. Chase asserted, "...America's public schools do not exist for teachers and other employees. They do not exist to provide us with jobs and salaries. Schools *do* exist *for the children*—to give students the very best...beginning with a quality teacher in every classroom... . If a teacher is not measuring up in the classroom...if there is a bad teacher in one of our schools—then *we* must do something about it."

    Chase recommends intervention "to help veteran teachers whose skills need sharpening...in roughly 10 percent of the cases...*members of our union* [should] take the lead in counseling a problem teacher to leave the profession...and, if necessary, they recommend dismissal."

    Whether this will ever happen, if union members are the ones empowered to get rid of colleagues, may be questionable. But at least the intent of the union president is in the right direction. Remarks by Bob Chase, President, National Education Association.

13. Ellis, "Class Size," ERIC Clearinghouse on Education, 1984.

14. Viadero, 1995, p. 33-35.

15. Noteworthy in this general lack of systematic evaluation is the absence of such evaluation under-taken by the Coalition of Essential Schools (Theodore Sizer's "schools within schools" movement). In a December 18, 1994 article, *The Wall Street Journal* reported,"...even Coalition officials conceded they...haven't tried to determine comprehensively whether Coalition students are learning more.."

16. Commitee for Economic Development,1995, p.36.

17. Ibid.

CHAPTER 2

18. Papert, 1993.

19. Colvin, Richard Lee. *Los Angeles Times*, Metro, Part B, p.2. October 31, 1995.

20. Gates, 1995.

21. Microsoft. Available: http://www.microsoft.com/corpinfo/press/1997/Apr97/anytime.htm. 1997.

22. Thompson, Simonson, and Hargrave, 1992.

23. Clark and Surgrue, 1988.

24. Rogers, 1986.

25. Thompson, Simonson, and Hargrave, 1992.

26. Hartley, 1966; Knowlton, 1964; Salomon and Clark, 1977.

27. Clark and Salomon, 1986.

28. Thompson, Simonson, and Hargrave, 1992, p. 17.

29. Becker, 1990.

30. Jamison, Suppes, and Wells, 1974.

31. Roblyer, M. D., *Learning and Leading with Technology*. "Is research giving us the answers (and the questions) we need." Vol. 24, n. 1, 1996.

32. Kulik, Kulik, and Bangert-Drowns, 1985; Clark, 1985: Kulik and Kulik, 1991; Ryan, 1991.

33. Meta-analysis is a method of assessing the impact of a treatment across many different studies using a common measurement scale called effect size (Sivin-Kachala and Bialo, 1994). Meta-analysis allows researchers to synthesize the findings of many studies into a single result. Although meta-analysis can provide an effective method of summarizing a great deal of research, it also has its flaws. In particular, meta-analysis often includes studies spanning many years, so the data are not necessarily current; it often does not account for the magnitude of relations in each study; and it can be biased toward studies that have been published as compared to dissertation research or other analyses that have not. On the other hand, if unpublished work is included, there is no screening for differences in quality of various studies.

   By definition, meta-analysis summarizes previous research. As a result, there is often a long lapse of time between the earliest studies reviewed and the publication of the meta-analysis. In some instances, this lag time does not have a significant impact. For example, it does not affect studies in which the variables have remained fairly standard over time. This is not the case with technology.

34. Kulik, Bangert and Williams, 1983.

35. Kulik, Kulik, and Bangert-Drowns, 1985.

36. Bangert-Drowns, Kulik and Kulik, 1985; Samson et al., 1986.

37. Niemiec and Walberg, 1985.

38. Clark, 1985.

39. Ibid.

40. Fletcher, 1990.

41. Riel, 1989.

42. Ibid.

43. Zellermayer et al., 1991.

44. Because different technologies are often combined, it is difficult to offer a single description of hypermedia. Thompson, Simonson, and Hargrave (1992, p. 52) describe hypermedia by the two Greek words from which it stems: "Hyper means nonlinear or random, and media refers to information represented in many formats."

45. Cognition and Technology Group, 1990.

46. Lehrer, Erickson, and Connell, 1992.

[47] However, the issue of study controls is prevalent in these studies. Because of the combined nature of hypermedia, it is difficult to attribute academic gains to specific technologies.

[48.] Cognition and Technology Group, 1990.

[49.] Pellegrino et al., 1992.

[50.] Dwyer, David; Ringstaff, Cathy; and Sandholtz, Judith (1992). Teacher beliefs and practices, part I: Patterns of change. Apple Classrooms of Tomorrow Research Report Number 8. http://www.research.apple.com/go/ACOT/full/acotRpt08full.html.

[51.] Saettler, 1990, p. 401; Cassirer, 1960, pp. 26-29.

[52.] Saettler, 1990, p. 366.

[53.] Ibid., p. 369.

[54.] Cuban, 1986, p. 29; Cassirer, 1960, pp. 53-54.

[55.] Cassirer, 1960, p. 29; Cuban, 1986, p. 33; Saettler, 1990, p. 368.

[56.] Ford Foundation, 1961, p. 5.

[57.] Cassirer, 1960, p. 30.

[58.] Cassirer, 1960, p. 30; Saettler, 1990, p. 368.

[59.] Cassirer, 1960, p. 30-31, 34.

[60.] Becker, 1987, p. 35.

[61.] Cassirer, 1960, pp. 31-32; Cuban, 1986, p. 34.

[62.] Cuban, 1986, p. 34.

[63.] Cassirer, 1960, p. 59.

[64.] Cited in Cuban, 1986, p. 39; cited in Saettler, 1990, p. 403.

[65.] Dirr and Pedone, 1978.

[66.] Cuban, 1986, p. 40.

[67.] Cuban, 1986.

68. Cuban, 1986, pp. 41-47.

69. Cuban, 1986, p. 48; Saettler, 1990, p. 488.

70. Becker, 1987, p. 36.

71. Sputnik came to be regarded as a symbol of the consequences of lax educational standards. Americans believed that Sputnik occurred before an American launching not just because the Russians had succeeded in scientific discovery, but because U.S. schools had failed. U.S. foundations and institutes responded by issuing reports on the pursuit of both excellence and equality. The reports were to no effect, but they do illustrate our hope that society can be renewed through "improved" education. Further, that quality of high schools could be raised through the development of advanced academic courses.

72. Becker, 1987.

73. Ibid., p. 37.

74. Becker, 1987; Finn, 1993.

75. Sputnik also greatly increased the National Science Foundation's role in high school curriculum reform, particularly as that agency greatly expanded its programs in math, biology, chemistry, and social science after Sputnik.

76. Cassirer, 1960, p. 21.

77. Cuban, 1986, p. 55.

78. Cassirer, 1960, p. 54.

79. Cuban, 1986, p. 58.

80. Cuban, 1986.

81. Saettler, 1990, pp. 401-402.

82. Ibid., p. 405.

83. Dirr and Pedone, 1978, p. 12.

84. Ibid.

85. Cuban, 1986, pp. 52-54.

86. Becker, 1987, pp. 35-40.

87. Cuban, 1986, pp.52-54; Becker; Saettler.

88. Dirr and Pedone, 1978, p. 12.

89. Since lessons or exercises provided through computer network technology can be downloaded and saved, the timing problem is less of an issue in this case.

90. Dirr and Pedone, 1978, p. 12.

CHAPTER 3

91. U.S. Bureau of the Census, *Current Population Survey*, March 1968-1996.

92. Pinkerton, 1996, p. 1.

93. *Hartford Courant*, April 25, 1994, *Business Weekly*, p. 1.

94. Reich, February 27, 1996.

95. Children's Partnership, 1995.

96. Scott, 1996.

97. Chandrasekaran, 1996, p. C14.

98. *Hartford Courant*, April 25, 1994, *Business Weekly*, p. 1.

99. *1995 Survey of Small and Mid-Sized Businesses,* Arthur Andersen Enterprise Group and National Small Business United.

100. "The Poor Need High Tech," *Los Angeles Times,* May 20, 1996.

101. Al Shanker, National Center on the Educational Quality of the Workforce, "The Other Shoe: Education's Contribution to the Productivity of Establishments," advertisement, *New York Times,* May 5, 1996.

102. *Gale Book of Averages,* 1994.

103. Ibid.

104. U.S. Bureau of the Census, 1996.

105. Haveman and Wolfe, 1984.

106. Ibid.

107. Hanushek, 1994.

108. Krueger, 1993.

109. The reader who has followed Krueger's work and the debate that derived from it knows his 15 per cent figure has been criticized; however, we have seen Krueger's response to the criticism and believe that his result remains valid. (See DiNardo and Pischke, 1997.)

110. We are ignoring the effects of possible differences in demand and supply elasticities.

111. Reich, 1991.

112. U.S. Bureau of the Census, *Current Population Survey*, March 1996.

113. Scheuer, 1990.

114. "50 Years of the GI Bill; A new social order and college, too." *The Record*, June 23, 1994.

115. U.S. Department of Veterans Affairs, 1997.

116. Ibid.

117. Ibid.

118. Ibid.

119. Tyler, 1994.

120. Scheuer, 1990.

121. Ibid.

122. Ashworth, 1979.

123. Reeves, 1995.

124. Maloy, 1994.

125. Brent Keltner and Randy Ross. *The Cost of School-Based Educational Technology Programs.* Santa Monica, Calif.:RAND, 1996; McKinsey & Co. *Connecting K-12 Schools to the Information Superhighway.* Palo Alto, Calif.: McKinsey & Co., 1996.

126. We assume a 4 percent decline in the cost of computer hardware, based on an estimate by McKinsey & Co.

127. Based on average enrollment per school per state, and national average class size of 25 students. These averages were derived from figures provided by the National Center for Education Statistics (NCES), *Digest of Education Statistics.* Washington, D.C.: Department of Education, 1996.

128. Based on projected enrollment figures from NCES, *Projections of Education Statistics to 2006.* Washington, D.C.: Department of Education, 1996.

129. For example, assume there are 100 schools in a model that allows for one district for every ten schools. In calculating the number of technical support personnel required, allowing for one full-time employee in each district, our 100 schools would require a total of 10 full-time employees. However, if in another more-disaggregated model we found that each district had five schools, making 20 districts in all, 20 full-time employees would be required.

130. Quality Education Data, *Technology in Public Schools,* 15th ed. Denver, Colo.: Quality Education Data, 1996.

131. Based on expenditures for public elementary and secondary schools: NCES, *Digest of Education Statistics;* 1996; Council of Economic Advisors, *Economic Indicators.* Washington, D.C.: Council of Economic Advisors, Feb. 1997; and Office of Management and Budget (OMB), *FY 98 Federal Budget.* Washington D.C.: OMB, 1997.

132. Based on informal survey and interviews conducted by American Association of School Administrators, August 1996.

133. Milken Institute for Job & Capital Formation, *Survey of Technology in the Public Schools.* Santa Monica, Calif.: Milken Institute, 1994.

134. This can be demonstrated by looking at the seven states that appear already to have acquired the highest percentages of what we calculate they need (all more than 25 percent). Iowa requires a total of $547.8 million and has spent $520.7 million. Some of this funding has been to support educational television. Delaware needs $62.3 million and Utah needs $119.3 million, the smallest two amounts of the seven states. They have received 46.7 percent and 25.6 percent, respectively, by getting some allocation over each of the past few years. On the other hand, Florida appears to have received 73 percent of its need of $900.5 million, but 74 percent of that was received *before* 1994, and probably for a plan that is now out of date. From our 1994 survey we found that most states had put resources into computer labs, but few had begun to integrate technology into the

curriculum. Similarly, Ohio, which appears to have received 35.1 percent of its need of $819.6 million, received $300 million before 1994, and $95 million came from bonds that probably are to be used for nontechnology-related construction as well as for technology itself. Mississippi, which has met 44.6 percent of its need of $283 million, has received $95 million of these funds before 1994 and $60 million from bonds. Thus, of the total spent, 48 percent in Ohio and 55 percent in Mississippi can be only loosely related to the current technology plan. Finally, Texas, which has "received" 49.4 percent of its $1.7 billion need, will get 70 percent or $1.2 billion in the uncertain future. Those states that appear to have received the highest share of their needed school technology funding usually are in that position because of early, now mostly outdated spending; reliance on bonding which may or may not be exclusively for technology; or hoped-for funding in the future.

135. The correlation between the completion rate from QED data and the percentage of required expenditures made or planned is .33.

136. Surveys and telephone interviews that we have conducted, as well as estimates by McKinsey & Co. and others, lead us to believe that the contribution of the private sector has been somewhere between 7 and 10 percent. The assumption of a continued 10 percent contribution as more money is spent is generous, but also considers telecommunications discounts that are likely to be provided in the future.

137. Lewis Solmon and Kalyani Chirra, "When Enough Is Not Enough: Allocating Scarce Resources for School Technology," *Education Week,* October 9, 1996.

CHAPTER 5

138. A recent survey of K-12 education, conducted by the American Electronics Association (1995), underlines that teacher training is a key to linking the classroom to technology. Eighty percent of respondents indicated that training educators in the use and application of technology is a key to overcoming roadblocks in providing access to technology in the classroom.

139. Teacher's College; SUNY Geneseo; Bank Street; Cal State Northridge; Arizona State University; University of Massachusetts; University of California, Berkeley; University of Washington; University of Georgia; Michigan State University; Clark Atlanta; Emory; University of Nebraska, Lincoln; University of Texas, Austin.

140. The Heller Report, March 1995, p. 3.

141. U.S. Congress, Office of Technology Assessment (OTA), 1995.

142. Ibid.

143. Barksdale, 1997.

144. Green, 1995.

145. U.S. Congress, OTA, 1995.

146. Ibid.

147. Ibid.

148. National Association of State Directors of Teacher Education and Certification, *Manual on Certification and Preparation of Educational Personnel in the United States and Canada,* 1996-1997.

149. Ibid.

150. Barksdale, 1997.

151. U.S. Congress, OTA, 1995. State of Michigan, 87th Legislature, Enrolled House Bill No. 5121, sec. 1531b, December 31, 1993.

152. U.S. Congress, OTA, 1995.

153. International Society for the Accreditation of Technology in Education, Accreditation Committee, Eugene, Oreg., 1992.

154. U.S. Congress, OTA, 1995.

155. Ibid.

156. Barksdale, 1997.

157. Bitter and Pryor, 1994, p. 13.

158. Five Trends Your Job Depends On (1997). *Electronic Learning on the Web.* http://place.scholastic.com/el/exclusive/fivetrends/pro.htm.

159. Ibid.

160. NCES, Digest of Education Statistics, 1996.

161. Milken Exchange on Education Technology, Public Opinion Survey, 1997.

162. Tejada, 1995.

163. McKinsey & Co., 1996, p. 40.

164. NCES, 1994.

165. Gottlieb, 1996.

166. Siegel, 1995.

167. The State of Washington requires that all new teaching and administration credential holders must take 150 class hours of continuing education each five years. For those teachers and administrators that received their credential prior to this requirement, continuing education courses allow them to advance on the salary schedule.

168. NASDTEC, 1996-97.

169. QED. *Educational Technology Trends,* 9th Edition. 1997.

170. Milken Exchange on Education Technology, Public Opinion Survey, 1997.

171. Siegel, 1995.

CHAPTER 6

172. Smith, 1937.

173. Friedman, 1979.

174. "Industry Report," conducted by Lakewood Research, 58. *Training Magazine,* October 1996.

175. Walsh, Mark, "Businesses' Enthusiasm for Reform Seen Flagging." *Education Week,* June 14, 1995.

176. Segal, T., Del Valle, C. et al., 1992.

177. The Conference Board, 1994, p. 10.

178. Weeden, 1995, p. B5.

179. "Head of School-Improvement Group Resigns." *New York Times,* February 21, 1993, Sec. 1, p. 22.

180. Turner, Alison. "Dade schools in talks with teaching gurus." *South Florida Business Journal,* March 10, 1995, Sec. A, p. 3.

181. Colvin, 1996.

182. Segal, T., Del Valle, C., et al., 1992.

183. Koenig, 1997.

184. Corley, Asta, "Getting Students on Line," *Anchorage Daily News,* January 12, 1997.

185. MCI, *The Promise of Technology* (1997). Company brochure.

186. Harmon, 1996.

187. Ibid.

188. Available: http://www.ustc.org/press-rel.html.

189. Colvin, 1996.

190. "How Four Districts Work Their Business Partnerships." Electronic Learning. http://place.scholastic.com/el/exclusive/states1195.htm

191. Ibid.

192. Available: www.detwiler.org/intro.html

193. Hawkins, 1996.

194. Carroll, 1996.

195. Information Access Company. "Partners in transition; business and education," 1994.

196. Available: Electronic Learning: Exclusive Reports. "How Four Districts Work Their Business Partnerships." http://place.scholastic.com/el/exclusive/states/195.htm.

197. Ibid.

198. Carroll, 1996.

199. MCI, *The Promise of Technology* (1997). Company brochure.

200. California Department of Education, 1996.

201. PR Newswire Association. "Pennsylvania Lt. Gov. Schweiker Unveils Public-Private Partnership to Bring Technology to Schools." December 16, 1996.

202. Weick, 1984.

203. Ramirez, 1994.

CHAPTER 7

204. Bailey and E. Mosher, 1968.

205. Ibid.

206. Wynn, R., and Wynn, J., 1988.

207. Wynn and Wynn, 1988; Bailey and Mosher, 1968.

208. Wynn and Wynn, 1988.

209. Ibid., p. 653.

210. An Open Letter by FCC Chairman Reed Hundt and Education Secretary Richard Riley. "The Benefits of Education Technology for Education." http://www.fcc.gov/learnnet/letter.html.

211. U.S. Department of Education, 1997. *Resource Guide to Federal Funding for Technology in Education.*

212. Ibid.

213. U.S. Department of Education, 1996. *Getting America's Students Ready for the 21st Century: Meeting the Technology Literacy Challenge.*

214. Ibid., p. 5.

215. Ibid.; Department of Education Press Releases: (1) *Washington Receives Award from Technology Literacy Challenge Fund.* February 25, 1997, http://www.ed.gov/PressReleases/02-1997/tech-wa.html. (2) *Clinton Announces Alaska Receives Grant from Technology Literacy Challenge Fund.* April 19, 1997, http://www.ed.gov/PressReleases/04-1997/tech-ak.html; (3) *Clinton Announces Connecticut Receives Grant from Technology Literacy Challenge Fund.* April 19, 1997, http://www.ed.gov/PressReleases/04-1997/tech-ct.html; (4) *New Mexico Among First to Receive Technology Literacy Challenge Fund.* http://www.ed.gov/PressReleases/02-1997/tech-nm.html.

216. U.S. Department of Education, 1997. *Resource Guide to Federal Funding for Technology in Education.*

217. Available: www.benton.org.

218. FCC communications office, telephone interview by the coauthor.

219. Available: www.fcc.gov/learnet/#sites.

220. Federal Communication Commission Press Report No. CC 97-24, May 7, 1997.

221. EdLiNC Special Report. Vol. 1, No. 1, May 1997.

222. Based on numbers from McKinsey & Co. (1996).

223. In 1994, sales of personal computer applications software in the U.S. and Canada were $7.38 billion. Sales of PCs reached $50 billion in the U.S. Thus, the $50 billion total for the U.S. may be low,

particularly given high year-to-year growth rates of sales of both hardware and software.[Source: (Hardware figures) Apt Data Services, March 24, 1995; Software, 46; (Software figures) Software Publisher's Association 3/95].

224. Fiore, F., and Hook, J., 1997.

225. U.S. Department of Education, 1995.

226. U.S. Department of Education, Budget Office, telephone interview by the coauthor.

227. Bear, Stearns & Co. Inc., compiled from their data.

228. *American School & University Magazine;* 20th Annual Education Construction Survey, 1994.

229. Stephen B. Goddard, *Getting There,* 1994.

230. Seely, Bruce. *Building the American Highway System.* Philadephia: Temple University Press, 1987, p. 12.

231. Goddard, 1994, p. 44; Seely, 1987, p. 12.

232. Seely, 1987, p. 12.

233. Ibid.

234. Ibid., p. 13.

235. Ibid., p. 4.

236. Goddard, 1994, p. 53; Rose, 1979, p. 8.

237. Goddard, 1994, pp. 57-58.

238. Ibid., pp. 59-60.

239. Franklin Roosevelt proposed that Washington buy a two-mile strip of land coast to coast, snake a highway through the middle of it, and sell the newly valuable adjacent land to developers attracted by the highway's proximity. This violated the U.S. concept of private property and appeared to be use of arbitrary authority. The idea, although it resurfaced several times, was ultimately abandoned.

240. Goddard, 1994, pp. 155-156.

241. Ibid., pp. 156-157; Rose, 1979, pp. 5-8.

242. Goddard, 1994, p. 183.

243. Finch, 1992, pp. 225-26.

244. Goddard, 1994, pp. 185-94.

245. Ibid.

246. Rothenberg, 1978.

247. These new standards did not have an effect until the early 1980s. It was the threat that caused reduced consumption earlier.

248. United States General Accounting Office: *Improving and Maintaining Federal Roads—Department of Transportation Action Needed,* February 1977.

249. Meyers, 1987.

250. Ibid.

251. Ibid.

252. "Group says taking highway trust fund 'off budget' would spur road investment." *Traffic World.* Journal of Commerce, Inc.: March 13, 1995.

253. Ibid.

254. "Transport interests, lawmakers say trust funds must go off-budget, or new ISTEA will be needed." *Traffic World.* Journal of Commerce: January 2, 1995.

255. Melton, 1966.

256. Jeff Nesbit. "Billions in Highway Trust Fund must not be off-budget." *Washington Times,* June 9, 1995.

CHAPTER 8

257. Joseph E. Stiglitz, *Economics of the Public Sector* (W.W. Norton & Company, New York: 1986), p. 307.

258. U.S. Department of Education, *Getting America's Students Ready for the 21st Century,* 1996.

259. E-mail response from Andy Rogers, LAUSD.

260. Nasser, 1997.

261. U.S. Department of Education, *Getting America's Students Ready for the 21st Century* (1996), p.64

262. Nebraska Department of Education (verbal confirmation)

263. West Virginia Department of Education (verbal confirmation)

264. *USA Today*, February 18, 1997.

265. "Georgia, it's full speed ahead on the information superhighway." *Marketing Computers Magazine.*

CHAPTER 9

266. Kavita Varma. "Internet brings high school home." *USA Today*, February 21, 1996.

267. U. S. Department of Education, *Getting America's Students Ready for the 21st Century*, 1996.

268. Zeiger, 1994.

269. Ibid.

270. Baker, 1996.

271. Ibid.

272. Means and Olson, 1995.

273. West, 1995.

274. Zeiger, 1994.

275. Kowsky, 1995.

276. Wagner, 1995.

277. Paul, 1996.

278. U.S. Department of Commerce, 1996.

279. Tejada, 1995.

CHAPTER 10

280. Milken Family Foundation, National Education Technology Poll, General Public. June 1997.

281. Ibid.

282. Comments made at 1997 Milken Educator Awards Conference in Los Angeles.

283. Sipchen and Lindsay, 1996.

284. Repp, 1983, p. 11; Zigler, et al., 1990, p. 2; Kirk, 1993, p. 29.

285. Zigler et al., 1990, p. 2; Winzer, 1993, pp. 3-4.

286. Winzer, 1993, pp. 309-10.

287. Zigler et al., 1990, p. 3.

288. Tyor and Bell, 1984, p. 123; Kirk, 1993, p. 25; Winzer, 1993, pp. 331-32.

289. Kirk, 1993, p. 30; Winzer, 1993, pp. 372-75; Tyor and Bell, 1984, pp.127, 139-41.

290. Kirk, 1993, pp. 23-24; Winzer, 1993, pp. 375-76; Zigler et al., 1990, p. 4; Tyor and Bell, 1984, pp. 139-40.

291. Kirk, 1978, pp. 7-8; Kirk, 1993, pp. 26-27; Winzer, 1993, pp. 333-34, 377-78; Repp, 1983, pp. 27-28.

292. Winzer, 1993, pp. 373, 375-78; Zigler et al.; 1990, p. 4.

293. Winzer, 1993, p. 376.

294. Winzer, 1993, p. 376; Kirk, 1993, p. 24.

295. Kirk, 1993, p. 24.

296. Winzer, 1993, p. 376; Kirk, 1993, p. 24; Zigler, et al., 1990, p. 5.

297. Tyor and Bell, 1984, p. 144.

298. Tyor and Bell, 1984, p. 146; Kirk, 1978, pp. 8-11; Winzer, 1993, pp. 377-78.

299. Kirk, 1993, p. 30; Winzer, 1993, p. 379.

300. Winzer, 1993, p. 380.

301. Cited in Scheerenberger, 1987, p.156.

302. Winzer, 1993, pp. 379-80.

303. Cited in Scheerenberger, 1987, p. 156.

304. Weiner and Hume, 1987, pp.27-28; Scheerenberger, 1987, pp. 156-57.

305. Winzer, 1993, p. 380.

306. Winzer, 1993, pp. 372-73; Kirk, 1993, p. 284.

307. Kirk, 1993, p. 284.

308. Dunn, 1968.

309. Zigler, 1990, p. 5, Winzer, 1993, p. 381; Scheerenberger, 1987, pp. 153-54.

310. Winzer, 1993, p. 382; Weiner, 1987, pp. 16-18; Scheerenberger, 1987, pp. 160-61.

311. Scheerenberger, 1987, p. 162; Winzer, 1993, p. 382.

312. Funding for special education has risen significantly since the passage of the Education for All Handicapped Children Act in 1975 which "provided that all handicapped children have available to them a free appropriate education designed to meet their unique needs." Except for the several years in which data was collected from the states on their spending for special education, there is no hard data on state/local spending. As we see in Table 10-1, we estimate spending on special education to be over 75 billion in 1996. We estimated this figure by multiplying special education enrollment by the current expenditures per pupil based upon fall enrollments. This would give us the amount of money spent on special education based upon regular per pupil expenditures. Earlier studies, however, indicate that approximately 128 percent more is spent on special education students than on regular-needs students (Moore, Strang, Schwartz, and Braddock, 1988). As a result, we increased the amount calculated above by 128 percent. The Dept. of Education budget office uses the following formula to figure the total cost of educating disabled children:

Number of disabled students x average per pupil expenditures x 2.28.

Estimates calculated by the NCES Education Finance Statistical Center (FAQs sheet) suggest that $30.9 billion to about $34.8 billion are currently being spent on special education services in the U.S. However, these estimates *do not adjust per-pupil expenditures for inflation.* Moore et al., 1988. Available: NCES:http://nces.ed.gov/edfin/faqs/speced.html.

APPENDIX

313. Katz and Murphy, "Changes in Relative Wages, 1963-1987," *Quarterly Journal of Economics,* February 1992.

about the authors

LEWIS C. SOLMON

Lewis C. Solmon is senior vice president of the Milken Family Foundation and a member of its board of directors. From 1991-97 he was founding president of the Milken Institute for Job & Capital Formation, which he built into a nationally recognized economics think tank. Recently, he has been studying school reform and the role of education technology in improving our nation's public schools, and he has completed a book on funding technology in America's public schools. He is advising the governor of the state of Nevada and the superintendents of education in California, Nevada and Arizona in the areas of funding school technology and school finance. In 1996 he participated in the Governor's National Education Summit.

Dr. Solmon has published two dozen books and monographs and more than 60 articles in scholarly and professional journals. His books include *Labor Markets, Employment Policy & Job Creation* (1994), *From the Campus: Perspectives on the School Reform Movement* (1989), *The Costs of Evaluation* (1983), *Underemployed Ph.D.'s* (1981), and three editions of *Economics,* a basic text. He has written on teacher-testing programs, foreign students, demographics of higher education, education and economic growth, the effects of educational quality, the links between education and work, national service, and job creation; and he appears regularly on the opinion editorial pages of national news dailies.

He is currently an associate editor of the *Economics of Education Review.* He has been an adviser to the World Bank, UNESCO, various government agencies, and many universities. He frequently provides litigation support and expert witness services to attorneys on economic issues. Dr. Solmon has served on the board of trustees of three independent schools in the Los Angeles area.

He received his bachelor's degree in economics from the University of Toronto and his Ph.D. from the University of Chicago in 1968. He has served on the faculties of UCLA, CUNY, and Purdue, and currently is a professor emeritus at UCLA. Prior to joining the Milken Institute in July 1991, he was dean of UCLA's Graduate School of Education for six years.

KALYANI R. CHIRRA

Kalyani R. Chirra is a former research analyst of the Milken Institute. She holds a bachelor of science degree in cognitive science from the University of California, Los Angeles. While in school, Chirra explored various aspects of education and education policy by interning at the Capital Children's Museum and Senator Dianne Feinstein's office in Washington, D.C. Chirra's research topics at the Institute included the effectiveness of technology in the classroom and the impact of educational resource allocations on student outcomes, and cost estimates for state technology programs. She is currently a student at NYU School of Law.

Printed in the United States
113283LV00001B/43/A